NICE GIRLS FINISH FIRST

Mark Bradfel

12-22-01

Mark Bradly
12-22-01

NICE GIRLS FINISH FIRST

THE REMARKABLE STORY OF NOTRE DAME'S RISE TO THE TOP OF WOMEN'S COLLEGE BASKETBALL

By Mark Bradford

Foreword by Coach Muffet McGraw

Diamond Communications,
an imprint of the Rowman and Littlefield Publishing Group
Lanham, Maryland

NICE GIRLS FINISH FIRST
THE REMARKABLE STORY OF NOTRE DAME'S RISE TO THE TOP OF WOMEN'S COLLEGE BASKETBALL

Copyright © 2001 by Mark Bradford

10 9 8 7 6 5 4 3 2 1

Manufactured in the United States of America

Diamond Communications,
an imprint of the Rowman and Littlefield Publishing Group
4720 Boston Way
Lanham, Maryland 20706
Distributed by NATIONAL BOOK NETWORK
800-462-6420

Library of Congress Cataloging-in-Publication Data

Bradford, Mark, 1953-
    Nice girls finish first : the remarkable story of Notre Dame's
rise to the top of women's college basketball / by Mark Bradford.
        p. cm.
    ISBN 1-888698-47-0
    1. University of Notre Dame--Basketball. 2. Lady Irish
(Basketball team)   I. Title: Remarkable story of Notre Dame's
rise to the top of women's college basketball. II. Title.
GV885.43.U55 B73 2001
796.323'63'0977289--dc21
                                                    2001047687

TABLE OF CONTENTS

ACKNOWLEDGMENTS

At first, writing a book is a labor of love. Halfway through it, it becomes more like labor. The love returns when you finish. There were many people who helped me immensely and I would like to thank the following:

The Notre Dame Sports Information Office, in particular Eric Wachter who gave me access to nearly anything I wanted at a moment's notice.

The Notre Dame Women's basketball office, including Muffet and her staff (Jeri Lucas in particular) who were always more than helpful and all of whom earned my respect with their honesty.

The players and families of the players, who opened their lives to me for a tiny peek.

Sean Stires and his crew at WHLY for giving me the tapes of their broadcasts as well as an enthusiastic endorsement of the idea.

Bill Bilinski and the *South Bend Tribune* Sports staff who did a great job of writing throughout the season and on whom I relied heavily for the season's facts and flavor. Charlie Adams at WSBT-TV also gave me advice and support.

I thank my parents for giving me my skill to write.

I thank my wife, Wendy, and my three children — Glen, Julie, and Madeline — for giving me up for three months while I wrote.

I thank my brother Ken, the best writer who never wrote a book, for editing and vastly improving this one.

I thank Barry Sarchett, my English 102 teacher at Purdue University who, in 1972, first told me I was a lousy writer and then proceeded to make me a good one. May he somehow see the fruits of his labor if by some twist of fate, he ever reads this.

And, I thank Ethel Pratt, a little older lady in my church, who kept telling me that she loved everything I wrote and that I should write a book.

Well, Ethel, I did.

This book is dedicated to all the youth sports coaches who are able to keep some sort of perspective while others around them are losing theirs.

FOREWORD

When I first started coaching, I don't think I ever imagined what it would be like to win a national championship. I've loved coaching since my first practice at Archbishop Caroll High School in Radnor, Pennsylvania. I didn't know where it would take me or how long it would last, but I knew there wasn't anything else I'd rather be doing.

I was fortunate to be married to a man who was very supportive of my career choice even though neither one of us could have predicted what the future would hold. But I do know that I couldn't have accomplished anything without Matt. He did anything I needed him to do, from driving the team van, filming the games, keeping the parents and fans involved with what was happening with the team.

When Murphy was born, it was the happiest moment of our lives. After 13 years of wondering and waiting we finally got our wish. Murphy is why I believe in miracles. As excited as I was to become a mom I never considered giving up coaching. I love my job and couldn't imagine my life without basketball. I also thought that if I were happy, I'd be a much better mom. Murphy grew up in the Joyce Center. I used to put him down at one end of the floor and we would go to the other end. Occasionally the players would lose focus by watching him slowly crawl towards us, but he never disrupted our practice and the team felt like they had a little brother to spoil. As he got older we would play games of duck-duck-goose while we were stretching. The players didn't like it nearly as much as Murphy did, so I used it as a motivational tool by saying, "If we don't make all of our layups in this next drill you have to play duck duck goose!" He loved bus rides with the team, staying in hotels, and exploring each new arena with Dad. As he got older he eventually moved from the front of the bus (where the coaches always sit) to the back where he unfortunately acquired his taste for rap music.

Since Murphy only travels with the team during vacation periods and for the post-season, he was as excited as anyone for the team to make the Final Four. After all, missing school for an 11-year-old is about as good as it gets.

This year was an incredible experience. In all my years of coaching I have never seen a group of women who were so unselfish, who were willing to sacrifice their individual goals for the team, and who played with a sense of wonderment and joy. They loved being together and our chemistry was the best I have ever experienced.

Our seniors were determined, motivated, and willing to do whatever it took to get to St. Louis. Part of that motivation came from watching Niele Ivey suffer through two season-ending knee injuries and the long rehabilitation she had to endure. Everyone played a vital role in our success, but it was the leadership of these five seniors that made the difference.

Ruth was a dominant force at both ends of the floor, and she gladly assumed the role of "go to" player. There is a lot of pressure when you are the focus of every team's defense, and you are still expected to have a double-double (points and rebounds) every game. Ruth performed magnificently in every game, and it was so fitting that the final game was decided by her clutch free throws. She was without a doubt the best player in college basketball. Fortunately for us, we could surround her with plenty of talent.

The point guard position is the most important one on the floor. I'm always toughest on the point guards because they are responsible for everything that happens on the floor. It is the point guard's job to run the show. She has to get the ball to the right person in the right spot at exactly the right moment with intense pressure from our opponent's best defense. She has to handle the press, read the defense, control the tempo of the game, lead the team in assists, free throw percentage, and floor burns.

Niele Ivey was all of that and more. She was at her best when she was getting a steal and leading the break. Her work ethic and desire to improve helped her earn her first All-America honor. Niele was the coach on the floor. She directed the team, executed the defense, got the players together for free throw huddles and did all the talking. Of course, doing the talking comes easy for Niele. She kept the team loose with her wonderful impersonations of all of us. You have to have a good sense of humor to get along on our team — nothing is sacred. So if you even say or do anything in front of Niele, be prepared for her humorous interpretation of your most embarrassing moment!

She is the most delightful person to be around and her smile lights up the Joyce Center. She came through a lot with her injuries and I am so thankful that we accomplished our goal of winning a national championship in her hometown.

Kelley Siemon contributed a sense of spirituality and a positive outlook to our team. She was always upbeat and had an amazing mental toughness. She battled through so many injuries, but played with a broken hand was the most memorable. She wore an Adidas glove over a great taping job by our trainer, Mike Miller. I think we'll put that glove in our trophy case. It's now more famous to Irish fans then the one Michael Jackson wore.

Kelley was the perfect complement to Ruth. She was athletic and quick, ran the floor better than any post player in the country, led the team in charges taken, and was a adept at finding a lane to the basket when her man would double team Ruth.

Meaghan Leahy and Imani Dunbar were as important to our success as Ruth, Niele, and Kelly. In order for a team to be successful, you need to have talent, but you also need great chemistry. Meaghan and Imani were tremendous role models for all of our players because they were the most unselfish people on our team. It's hard to be a senior and watch your career unfold a little differently than you planned. Meaghan had a lot of options for scholarships coming out of high school and I am thankful that she chose Notre Dame. Meaghan is a warm and caring person who was the subject of many of Niele's comedy routines. She was good natured about it and often kept us laughing with her own accounts of things that happened to her.

Imani Dunbar will eventually be running a Fortune 500 company. She is intelligent, poised, and loves video games! She was Murphy's favorite player to hang out with — especially in the airport arcades.

Imani contributed to our team in a lot of ways both on and off the court. Early in the year when Niele had to leave the Purdue game because of cramps in her leg, Imani came in and led us to victory. She had a great attitude about her role on the team and was the honorary captain for the gold team.

The mix of personalities on our team kept things interesting. They were like 12 talented musicians who at any time could perform a solo act on center stage, but who preformed the symphony that they made together.

Our fans fell in love with this team and our team felt the same way about them. I remember often our last game at home, and how everyone stayed in their seats and I didn't want to leave the court. It was such a touching moment for me and the team and one of the many memorable moments from the season.

The city celebration was a lot of fun and we would all like to thank everyone in the community for their loyal support throughout the years.

You can't be successful without the support of the administration and we have enjoyed great support throughout the years from Father Malloy, Father Beauchamp, Gene Corrigan, Dick Rosenthal, Mike Wadsworth, and our current athletic director, Kevin White.

Muffet McGraw
June 2001

INTRODUCTION

Leo Durocher, that grouchy old baseball coach, never claimed he was misquoted. He just says the period was put in the wrong place.

"Nice guys finish last" is the way the quote appears in *Bartlett's Book of Familiar Quotations.*

"Nice guys. Finish last," is the way he claims to have said it, as part of his tribute to his favorite player, Eddie Stanky.

In conversations about baseball's meanest-spirited players, some names always come up.

First there's Ty Cobb. He's said to have sharpened his cleats so he could carve into the shortstop's leg when stealing second base. Leo Durocher followed in those footsteps, and so did Eddie Stanky, and even later there was Pete Rose. These guys would chew their arms off to beat you. They would never quit and wouldn't let you quit either.

During batting practice one day at the old Polo Grounds in New York City, Durocher was chatting with Frank Graham, a writer with the old *Journal-American* newspaper. The conversation had turned to why Durocher, manager of the Brooklyn Dodgers at the time, liked Stanky so much. Everyone else seemed to hate him.

Durocher borrowed a statement from Dodger owner Branch Rickey, who was known to praise a player with, "Well, he can't hit, he can't run, he can't field, he can't throw. All he can do is beat you. He might not have as much ability as other players, but every day you get 100 percent from him, and he was trying to give you 125 percent."

Just then, Durocher saw the opposing New York Giants team come out of the dugout, led by Mel Ott. Ott was a living legend, an immensely talented player, a true gentleman, a person well-respected throughout America. Durocher then ticked off the names of each player and said, "All these guys are really nice guys."

"Nice guys. Finish last," he said.

"They lose a ballgame, they go home, they have a nice dinner, they put their heads down on the pillow and go to sleep. Poor Mel Ott, he can't sleep at night.

"He wants to win ...You surround yourself with these kinds of players, though, and you're going to finish in the cellar with them. Because they think they are giving 100 percent and they are not.

Give me some scratching, diving, hungry ballplayers who come to kill you.

"Now, Stanky's the nicest gentleman who ever drew a breath, but when the bell rings, you're his mortal enemy. That's the kind of guy I want playing for me."

That whole quote isn't in *Bartlett's*. Instead, Durocher is remembered for one of the most cynical statements in sports history.

"That was the context," Durocher said, before his death in 1981, "and Frank Graham wrote it up that way. But the other writers who picked it up ran the sentences together to make it sound as if I were saying that you couldn't be a decent person and succeed."

"But, do you know, I don't think it would have been picked up like that if it hadn't struck a chord. Because as a general proposition it's true. Or are you going to tell me that you've never said to yourself, 'The trouble with me is I'm too nice. Well, never again'?"

So, what was it? An off-hand comment about a bunch of guys walking out of a dugout for batting practice? Or a sweeping social comment on American life in general?

"Nice guys. Finish last," or "Nice guys finish last."

Put the period where you want.

(Reference: *Nice Guys Finish Last*, Leo Durocher with Ed Linn Copyright, 1975 by Leo Durocher; Published by Simon and Schuster)

CHAPTER 1

THREE INCHES
TO A CHAMPIONSHIP

Hero *(hir'o; also he'ro) n., pl -roes*. 2. Anyone regarded as having displayed great courage or exceptionally noble qualities.

That's how *Funk & Wagnalls* defines a hero.

Neither Funk nor Wagnalls mentioned anything about winning or losing basketball games.

But you can't talk about the 2000-2001 championship season of the Notre Dame women's basketball team without talking about heroes. And in years to come, it might be hard for Notre Dame fans to think of heroes without remembering this incredible team.

Last-minute heroics on April 1, 2001, in the Savvis Center in downtown St. Louis gave Notre Dame its first ever national championship in women's basketball. It was as thrilling a game as most fans had ever seen.

Like most big games, Notre Dame's 68-66 nail-biting win over Purdue in the NCAA final game came down to a matter of inches, probably three inches total at most.

Three inches at the end of a long, 84 feet of basketball hardwood determined which team went home a champion and which team just went home. At one end of the hardwood, clearly in the eye of the storm, in front of millions of TV viewers on ESPN, stood Notre Dame's Ruth Riley. She was a small-town Indiana girl living out what was in decades past just every small-town Indiana boy's dream.

There she stood, alone at the free-throw line with a mere 5.8 seconds remaining on the clock in the final game of the Final Four of the NCAA Women's basketball championship. The score was tied at 66.

If she hits her free throws, her team will probably win the game. If she misses, who knows what would happen?

It was, in fact, a scene right out of a made-for-TV movie.

But the scene was nothing new for the 6-foot-5 All-Everything

Irish center. She had played that same situation over in her head countless times on playgrounds, in pickup games, and on sultry summer nights in the tiny town of Macy, Indiana.

"Actually, it was like the scene from the movie *Hoosiers*," Riley would say later, recalling one of her favorite movies. "Only Ollie shot the ball underhanded in the movie. I didn't have to do that." Instead, with her long brown hair held out of her face by her signature white headband and with teammates looking anxiously on, the senior star pushed her shot barely over the front of the rim, where the ball flirted twice with the iron before falling through the net to give her team the edge.

Good by an inch. 67-66.

Purdue called a timeout designed to ice her. Finally, Riley was given her second foul shot. Again, it narrowly cleared the rim, bounced off the iron, and settled through the net.

Good by an inch again. 68-66.

Riley barely watched as the second shot dropped through the hoop. Instead, she pushed her worn-out legs for one last time, down the 84 feet toward the Purdue bucket where she had to go to defend the fragile lead.

She arrived too late, gasping helplessly for air as Purdue's All-American Katie Douglas took her turn at history. Douglas, a senior forward, had played her heart out and practically wore Notre Dame out with her outside shooting and stellar defensive play. She took a quick pass from another All-American, Camille Cooper, and launched a hurried 17-footer with just over a second remaining.

It looked like a tie-maker.

But only one hero could win this game. The inch Douglas needed just wasn't there. Her shot mercilessly hit the front of the rim. Instead of rolling over the lip as Riley's had, it bounded hard off the backboard and caromed high into the air as the horn sounded ending the game.

It was an incredible moment. Most heroic moments are.

The significance of that moment would settle on the players and on the university they represented over a period of weeks and months following the exciting finale.

Notre Dame, for most of its history, has been a man's school.

In fact, women weren't admitted to the exclusive private Catholic school in South Bend, Indiana, until 1972.

And it has always been a football school. The seven-story mural on the Hesburgh Library is nicknamed Touchdown Jesus, not Jump Shot Jesus. Even during mediocre football years, the men's basketball program — with stars such as Austin Carr, Adrian Dantley, and Troy Murphy — has stayed in the shadow of that mural.

This is a school that has produced seven Heisman Trophy winners — Leon Hart, John Lattner, Johnny Lujack, Angelo Bertelli, Paul Hornung, John Huarte, and Tim Brown. Its football coaches — from Knute Rockne through Ara Parseghian through Lou Holtz — have stood among the best of all time.

Is there room on that list of Notre Dame's finest for Ruth Riley, two-time All-American and winner of the Naismith Trophy, the basketball equivalent of the Heisman? And what about women's coach Muffet McGraw, who has won every coaching award available to her, including National Coach of the Year.

This season's women's basketball team fit well with Notre Dame's tradition of winning something the right way, without shortcuts. The recent past of college sports, one in which major institutions vie for alumni dollars through get-rich-quick athletic departments, had made it tougher for Notre Dame to maintain its championship heritage.

The alumni want winners, even at Notre Dame. And the recent past had produced few. The university needed a hero.

Then, along came Muffet and her team. The players had worked hard to earn their moment in the spotlight on their own. That moment is normally reserved for the very few and the very fortunate.

It is, in fact, a moment reserved for heroes.

If this were just about basketball, you would get all the information you need from the box scores and the postgame write-ups in the local papers.

But there is a story behind the championship that is much more interesting than the game itself.

That story has heroes too. But the heroes are not the athletes who hit the free throws or drew up the key plays on a sideline chalkboard.

Each player on this once-in-a-lifetime team was inspired by

everyday heroes, people whose names will not engraved on cups, or written in record books, or splashed across the bottom of a TV screen. Their everyday heroes get up for work, figure out how to pay the electric bills and still get their children to practices, or piano lessons, or to summer school.

They take off a day of work to hold up a giant foam finger, proclaiming the Lady Irish are No. 1. They hold up the placards that say "You Can't Handle the Ruth." They look at this group of dedicated athletes and decide it's time to fill all the seats at the Joyce Athletic & Convocation Center.

Heroism can be measured by free throws scored, with 5.8 seconds left in a championship game. But there are real-life heroes outside the gym every day, struggling to feed someone too weak and feeble to feed themselves, adjusting the wheelchair as they push their son down the street on a bright and sunny day, painting the walls of a rehab community building.

You see, heroes are all over if you look for them, though very few everyday heroes get much recognition. Be it good or bad, sports have become an outlet for hero-recognition in our society. And, for an amazing few months in the winter and spring of the year 2000-01 in South Bend, Indiana, the definition found in the *Funk & Wagnalls* dictionary came to life on a basketball court in Notre Dame, Indiana.

CHAPTER 2

RUTH RILEY —
A STAR IN MANY SKIES

Ten-year-old Ruth Riley was confused.

Why, she wondered, was she so much taller than all her friends?

Why was she so much taller than all the boys?

Why was she taller than some of the teachers?

Was she some kind of freak?

Tough questions for anyone, let alone a 10-year-old girl.

Even tougher questions for her mom, Sharon, who had a high school diploma, not a master's degree in psychology.

But she was a mom. And a dedicated mom, at that.

She couldn't tell Ruth why she was almost so tall. Sharon knew that being tall was a family trait, but certainly not that tall.

She couldn't shield Ruth from the cruel taunts of fifth-grade boys, for whom making fun of anyone's physical differences is daily pastime.

Or worse yet, the fifth-grade girls with their own daily pastime of deciding who was cool and who wasn't. Being almost six feet tall was decidedly uncool.

But Sharon herself had been through her share of uncool stuff. She had married Ruth's dad out of high school. They moved to Kansas, had three kids and then he left.

She was left alone to scramble and scrimp, and raise the kids. "It wasn't easy," Sharon said, "But we did it."

So if you try to talk to Ruth Riley about what it is like being a hero, she will say she's just emulating her mom. Scraping up money for a security deposit on a rental house is much tougher than defending the post position.

So Ruth, at age 10, turned to her mom with questions that had no answers. And night after night, Ruth would cuddle with her mom, trying to be little but eager to be big.

A typical 10-year-old...with a decidedly untypical problem.

So, Sharon, like any other mom, let her instincts take over. At night, she would sit on the floor so Ruth could curl up in her lap. And Sharon would talk about boys, and school, and family and where she was heading. Things that only moms and daughters can talk about.

Sharon began to call Ruth her princess, for such little girls dream of being princesses, and this little girl was no different. The talks would soothe this scared little girl until the time that she accepted who she was.

These days, Ruth says that she understands everyone has something that is a little bit different about them, and that she no longer feels weird about being tall. And now, when the little kids shyly ask for autographs, she gives them.

She is simply, in her own way, returning her mom's favor from years past, when Ruth was 10, sitting on the floor those many evenings, talking about things that neither fully understood.

Ruth Riley, future Naismith Award Winner as the best basketball player in women's basketball, did not make the first string of the junior high team in seventh grade.
She didn't do it in eighth grade either.

Ruth was born on August 29, 1979, in Kansas, the middle of three children. "Ruth came into the world setting records," Sharon said. "She was the longest baby ever born in the state of Kansas."

The marriage fell apart when Ruth was four and Sharon moved the family — including Ruth's older sister Rachel and younger brother Jake — back to her hometown area of Macy, in Miami County, Indiana. A few years later, she married Mike Riley, who adopted all three of the children who took his name as their own.

Sharon believes in honesty and respect. "I pretty much raised the kids alone," Sharon said. "I demanded their respect and I demanded their obedience.

"I took my kids with me wherever I went. I didn't get all dolled up and leave them with a babysitter. When we had extra, we did things together. It is my personal feeling with regard to raising kids is that you are either there or you are not. I was going to be there.

"I drew a very solid line," Sharon continued. "If you crossed that line, that was disobedience and it came with a price and sometimes we would talk it out and sometimes there would be discipline, but it was because I loved them. I always had high expectations and I was relentless with that.

"When the kids were five," Sharon said, "they all started playing piano and they kept it up into high school. Ruth was always very strong in wanting to be able to do as well as her sister Rachel did, so getting them to practice was not a problem."

But sports would be Ruth's real forte, and Sharon made sure she got the opportunity to play. Sharon moved her family again, when Ruth was 12, to Grove City, a suburb of Columbus, Ohio, to be with Mike. "I was a very active kid and sports became my outlet," Ruth said.

All junior high girls and boys go through teasing, but that doesn't make it any easier. "Being the tallest person in the room has its disadvantages, especially when you are a girl," Ruth said.

"But the way I look at it now, we are all born with advantages and disadvantages. I do think, however, that I became more and more shy because of my height."

Rather than strike back at her tormentors, Riley turned to sports, where she could practice on her own, get better on her own, and discover her own, specific destiny. Sports fit Riley well and became her refuge. All she needed was someone to get her places to play.

The problem was getting playing time in seventh grade. "In junior high, I was tall, skinny, and uncoordinated," Ruth said. "I just wasn't any good."

"Bah," said Sharon. "There was a lot of politics."

Therein lies the strength of the mother-daughter relationship. As humble as Ruth is, Sharon is just as proud. Not obnoxious, just proud.

"Ruth was not the coach's favorite," Sharon said. "So she sat the bench a lot. I think the most she ever played straight was 55 seconds.

"And that is something I've never forgotten. At that age, every kid puts in the same amount of work so I think coaches should play the kids as equally as possible. But it was in the eighth grade that she learned rebounding, because she figured that she could get the basketball for easier shots and put them in. And she wanted to win, so she did it."

She also learned humility. "In seventh grade when she was sitting on the bench, she found out she could either sit and stew and worry and complain while she was on the bench or she could cheer for her teammates and keep her head in the game and know what was going on," Sharon said. "She found out that if you sit and stew, when you get in to the game, you will screw things up.

If your head is in the game even when you aren't, when you do get in, you do better."

Even at her young age, Ruth had a sense of fair play. "There were times when the bullies in the class in junior high would make fun of the smaller kids," Sharon said. "Ruth wouldn't stand for it. She would step right in."

After two years in Ohio, Mike got a job near Peru, Indiana, and the family moved back to Macy before Ruth entered North Miami High School. Sharon Riley started an in-home beauty parlor to help support the family of four.

Macy is about two miles east of U.S. 31, a four-lane highway that snakes its way from South Bend to Indianapolis and points south. It is a heavily traveled road. Most people do not notice the small green sign that points the way to Macy when it sneaks up on them as they round a bend at 65 MPH or more.

Heading east on Miami County Road 1350 brings you into Macy, (pop. 200), which strikes the visitor as a little town that progress forgot.

You'd be hard-pressed to find a house built later than 1985. The town cemetery is in someone's backyard. It is a town with three churches and no bars. As a matter of fact, there isn't even a gas station, nor a restaurant.

Every thing in the town is old. There is even a store called Oldies. At least, there was. It's closed.

The sign on one end of town says, "Welcome to Macy, founded 1836 by J&D Wilkerson." The sign on the other end says, "Welcome to Macy, home of 1936 Miss Indiana-M Ewer Wilson."

It is the kind of place where family is everything and no one's in a hurry. Dogs can nap on Main Street on a warm summer day.

Ruth Riley is a Macy-type girl at heart — a small-town girl at age 15 with big-time potential.

In the country school of North Miami High School, Ruth towered above her peers, boys and girls alike. When she stepped into North Miami as a freshman, the obvious question arose. "Do you play basketball?"

Ruth knew she had to say yes. Her answer came in two parts though...one public and one private. "I knew I was tall and therefore expected to play basketball," Riley sighed. That was the public response.

But it was the private response that made her the first Notre

Dame woman icon. She states it this way: "Because I wasn't good, that drove me to get better."

It was to be a long trip.

That trip began at 6:45 in the morning, every morning, a full hour before her high school chums poured out of their yellow buses and headed for their homerooms and their English classes. Either Rachel or Sharon would drop Ruth off at school and Ruth headed immediately to the gym, where she worked through a set routine which she had designed on her own.

There, in the predawn darkness in the gym, the uncoordinated, gangly 15-year-old worked on pivot moves, worked on free throws, worked on jump shots, worked on footwork.

Three days a week, she would go to the weight room, where school athletic director Tim DuBois would help her with her strength. "I wasn't very strong at first," Riley said.

But strength is not a gift, anyway. Strength is something you purchase with time. Time spent lifting weights until your biceps burn, until your hamstrings ache, past the point where you want to give up.

But perfectionists never give up. and Riley is a perfectionist. She figured out after taking a hard look at her self as a teenager that she didn't have the body for a ballet dancer, nor the coordination of a tennis player, nor the brains of a physicist.

But she was tall, by golly. And she could post up better than anyone she knew. And she had something that separates the real players from the ones who show up at the basketball camps to appease their parents. She had the love of the game.

So Ruth chose to make basketball her everyday job. Sure, there was fun involved, but for her, the sport had to come first.

In many ways, sacrifice came naturally. Her family, by now put through two broken marriages, sacrificed with her. That's the way Sharon ran the Riley family.

"I had kids because I wanted kids," Sharon said. "I wasn't planning on getting dumped on my butt with them, but I wasn't planning on hiding in a hole with them either.

"We went camping, we went kite flying. Little things, but we did things and nobody minded seeing us coming. I told them that if they didn't go to college, their life would be like mine and they would be struggling to raise kids.

"We always had to do without something. If we ever had extra, we enjoyed it together," Sharon continued, "When we didn't, we toughed it out together."

Sharon also put her kids into 4-H, a directed activity for youth that began in rural communities and has since made inroads into the smaller cities.

"The real value to 4-H was that it taught goal-setting," Sharon said. "You were given a project, some standards, and a goal in which to complete that project. You had to complete the project within the guidelines, but the more creative you were, the more original you were, the greater the reward was. It was just such a terrific thing for the kids to learn. Heck, Jake even learned to sew."

Ruth added volleyball to her repertoire as something fun to do. Obviously, with her size, she was very good at that. She was the only one who could almost see over the net. It was in her sophomore year that Riley had to make a decision about which sport she wanted to seriously pursue.

"In a small high school, if you are an athlete, you were an athlete all year long because the school needed your help," Sharon said. "And during her sophomore year, Ruth spent a lot of time figuring out what it would cost her in real terms to pursue basketball and what it would cost her to pursue volleyball.

"She was ready by the end of her sophomore year basketball season to commit. We called a local AAU coach, Tom Jacoby [his daughter Jennifer had played basketball at Purdue], and he was just thrilled. I don't think he was expecting us to call, but we really liked him. He's just good country people. Real compassionate, kind-hearted, and a great role model for Ruth, as far as a male figure."

During the summer between her sophomore and junior years, she played in a national AAU tournament in Indianapolis with a high-powered team from Fort Wayne, Indiana, called Lady Legit.

"Tom even got her an invitation to the Olympic Trials, which were held at Mackey Arena on the Purdue campus that year," Sharon said. "That was when I first noticed there was something special about her. To me, it was like a neon light or something, even though she physically immature as she was playing against college players there. She just shone."

She didn't make the team that year, but the secret about the youngster from Macy was out. A week later, letters started pouring in from all over the country, inquiring about her interest in college ball.

Ruth knew she was on the right track.

But that wasn't good enough. Being on the right track doesn't mean you are going to get to the end of the road. Being on the right track simply means you have the potential to get there.

Potential wasn't enough for Ruth. Reality is all that would suffice. So she went into the higher level of AAU ball. She wanted to play stiffer competition. She wanted to improve herself.

"I'm not sure what drove me," Riley said. "I didn't really set a goal to play professional basketball. I did set small goals, however, and in that way I am very goal-oriented. I do know it is fun in the strength training to see how far I could go on a daily basis."

Small goals for a big girl.

"Ruth was blessed with a love of life," Sharon said. "She loves to play and she loves to win."

Sharon practiced what she preached, which gave Ruth her first up-close role model. "I tried to instill my values into Ruth," Sharon said. "That you don't take advantage of people in order to gain for your own personal self. Everybody is in this thing together, whether it's sports, and then the basic Do Unto Others As You Would Have Them Do Unto You.

"Our house had strong Christian values," Sharon continued. "But I believe you have to live them, not just preach them. The whole point is to live it. We always tried to do that. There were always people in worse need than we were."

Sharon, like so many other divorced moms, relied on family to help out. "My sister helped me a lot," Sharon said. "My mom and dad lived close by, also. But for the most part, I did not really use a lot of people. I just did not leave my kids off all that much.

"We had a chore chart," Sharon continued. "And there were four names on it, including mine. Everyone was expected to carry their own weight. The chore chart thing gave everyone an appreciation of all the jobs.

"Laundry is never done, and the only way to teach someone not to roll their socks up and just toss them into the laundry is to make them do the laundry and see what a mess it can be. Having them see for themselves saved me 10,000 words."

Finally, Ruth was to learn respect and honesty.

"Honesty really is the best policy," Sharon said. "I don't think

Ruth ever lied to me. One time there was a busted-down old schoolhouse close to us that I prohibited the kids to go in because the floors were rotting and it was a real hazard. Of course, the three kids couldn't stand it. They had to explore it.

"So I'm outside, calling and calling for them to come home, and pretty soon here they come, all three of them. They knew that I knew where they had been. They didn't lie, they knew they were going to get a whipping. They stood in line, they knew what was coming."

Ruth kept working in the early-morning lights of the North Miami gym and in the hot summer practices of her AAU team. The more she played, the more letters she got. The mailman would deliver letters from interested coaches almost daily. "We got boxes and boxes and boxes of letters," Sharon said.

The more letters Ruth got, the more confused she became. Big names were after her. Teams with national championship banners hanging in their rafters were after her. Connecticut was in the running, Purdue was in the running, Butler was in the running. And Notre Dame was in the running.

For the recruiters, finding the Riley house was a problem. At the time, Sharon and her family lived in a rented farmhouse close to Macy and Muffet McGraw and Carol Owens set out at sunset and ended up cruising the county roads in the middle of the night. "There were no lights, no one to stop and ask for directions ... nothing," Muffet laughed. "Finally we see some lights off in the distance and thought 'Holy Cow, we made it.'"

Ruth, while dominant on the hardwood, was painfully quiet.

"I remember trying to talk to Ruth on the phone during the process and holding a very short chat before asking to speak to Sharon," Muffet laughed. "Sharon was great. She was always straight-forward and really helpful through the whole process."

There was a reason she was recruited so hard. As a senior at North Miami, she had averaged 26 points, 14.7 rebounds, and 5.2 blocks per game. Her team went 20-1 and Riley set 17 school records. USA Today selected her Honorable Mention All-American.

Notre Dame had the inside edge, however. Older sister Rachel had ranked No. 2 academically in her North Miami High School class ("just missed by .0001 point," laughed Sharon) and was accepted at Notre Dame. Rachel and Ruth had played on the same varsity basketball team, which won a sectional title in 1996. "As soon as Rachel got accepted, I knew that's where Ruth was going also," Sharon said.

"I really wasn't that big on sports in high school," Sharon said. "I mean I pay my taxes and I send my kids to school to get an education, not to play sports. But Ruth knew a scholarship would play her way through college, and I wanted all of my kids to go to college. That was part of Ruth's convincing me to go play basketball, to pay her way through college."

On July 1 between her junior and senior year, the recruiting began in earnest. That was the day the coaches could make physical contact with the recruit. "Our phone rang off the hook for days," Sharon said. "Finally, I told Ruth to give me the top 10 schools that still had a shot so I could tell some of the rest to stop calling."

The offers for scholarships on her official visits came just as quickly. As a matter of fact, she had them in hand before she left every campus she visited. "I thought everyone always got offers immediately," Riley said. "I later found out I was wrong."

Her idol was none other than Larry Bird, another state of Indiana legend, if not THE Indiana basketball legend. The Hick from French Lick. And French Lick looks like a metropolis compared to Macy.

In the end, proximity of family, academics, and the strength of the Irish program would win the day in the recruiting of Riley. In choosing a college, Riley chose Notre Dame in large part due to its nearby location. Sharon, her biggest fan, would be able to attend the games. Homesickness could be solved by a 75-minute drive, if necessary, or a visit to her sister.

For all her on-court prowess, Ruth was painfully shy as a teenager.

"I think it was because I was so tall that I was getting a lot of attention and I really wasn't comfortable with it," she said. "I think I just didn't want to draw any more attention to myself that I was already getting."

She had met future best friend and teammate Meaghan Leahy at a WCBA camp after her junior year at North Miami. That fall, by sheer coincidence, they would be on the same recruiting weekend in South Bend.

"Ruth may have said 10 words the whole weekend," Leahy laughed.

The one word she didn't say was "yes" to the scholarship invitation, and it was driving Irish coach Muffet McGraw nuts.

Assistant Coach Carol Owens had called Riley a must-have for the future of the Irish program, and McGraw had been assured by Sharon that Ruth was, indeed, Notre Dame-bound. Still, the deal wasn't closed.

"I think she told everyone except us that she was coming," McGraw said.

"Muffet was a nervous wreck," Sharon laughed. "But I told her that Ruth would go where Rachel went because besides being sisters, they are best friends. I liked the idea because it was only an hour away and we have lots of family in Miami County and a lot of them went to Ruth's games over the years. It was like a family reunion sometimes at the ballgames."

But it was a little more complicated than that. "I was nervous about making the decision," Ruth said. "I wanted to be sure. The closeness of the campus, the academics, and the fact I felt comfortable with a team eventually led me to the decision. When I was on campus for my visits, it just felt right."

A phone call on October 5, 1996, made McGraw feel right. Notre Dame had its unfinished aircraft carrier in the middle. Now it was a question of setting the course and building around her.

For all her ability and practice, Ruth's body was still growing when she hit campus that fall. The practices would show that her adjustment time would be at a lesser pace than a player with natural ability, such as Kelley Siemon or Niele Ivey.

In addition, Riley's talents were as different from Katryna Gaither, the previous year's post player, as hot is different from cold. Gaither was thin, quick, and ran the floor well. Riley was slow, unsure of herself, and unfamiliar with the system.

In addition, McGraw had to reorient her thinking and design plays for her new style of team. The fast break run-up-and-down-the-floor offense embraced by the Beth Morgan-Gaither unit would not work with Riley, at least not as a freshman.

Riley also had a mortal flaw as a freshman that would have to be corrected if the team was to get too far. Ruth was foul-prone, more likely foul-unhappy. She committed a foul every four minutes her first six games as Notre Dame stumbled out to a 3-4 start.

McGraw, not used to "rebuilding seasons," saw the campaign reeling out of control, and she did everything except hit the panic button. Finally, after a less than stellar performance by the team in a home loss to Wisconsin, McGraw faced the decision. Knowing that she had come into the season with the idea that it indeed was a rebuilding year, McGraw decided to do just that.

Riley would be the cornerstone. She had fouled out in just 21 minutes during that disappointing 89-77 home loss to Wisconsin. McGraw told her young center it was time to grow up and take charge.

Notre Dame's fortunes would be set on the shoulders of the 6-foot-5 freshman, and they would not be taken off. It was to be Ruth's team.

"I was a little shocked," Riley said. "Mostly because I had not played much. However, it gave me the confidence I needed."

Confidence didn't translate to restraint. Riley started and promptly fouled out of after 21 minutes of playing time the next game against eventual national champion Purdue, a game which Notre Dame surprisingly won, 77-71.

McGraw, though disappointed with the Purdue performance, started Riley in the next game against South Florida. She also began a mental assault into Riley's defensive psyche. "You don't have to block every shot," McGraw would say. "You don't have to get every rebound."

Riley took the instruction to heart, but she had to undo some bad habits. In high school, she could block every shot and she could get every rebound. Her ability to do so almost without jumping had burrowed into her psyche. The quickness and positioning of the college players, however, were resulting in slap fouls and over-the back fouls, let alone the natural fouls and bad calls.

Old habits are the worst habits. In the heat of the game, habits take over. The fouling problem would be the one that Riley was to battle her entire college career.

But left to her own devices and assured that she would start, the lanky freshman began to work on her weaknesses. She knew plenty about weaknesses. She had been working on them all of her teenage years. Now, with the simple goal of getting better firmly in mind, she stayed late, practice after practice, as Assistant Coach Owens showed her how to play the post, how to take the drop step, how to keep from fouling.

Practice, as always, paid off. Ruth finally burst onto the scene that January, running off double-doubles in five straight Big East games. Opposing coaches were learning that the Irish had a new player, a new look, and were creating a big new problem. That five-game streak helped her earn a place on the All Big East All-Rookie team as well as the *Basketball Times* All-Freshman team.

More importantly it settled McGraw's mind. She had made the right decision. She would now begin saying "Get the ball to Ruth" more times than she would order hamburgers and fries over the course of the next four years. Riley thought her major break-through as a freshman came in an upset over Texas Tech in the NCAA tournament. "I was playing against an All-American player," Riley said. " And I played well [23 points, eight rebounds]. I was intimidated at first but very excited. It was one of the highlights of my four years."

Not so coincidentally, it marked the first time the Irish had beaten a top-seeded NCAA team . . . ever.

The season ended with a loss to eventual national champion Purdue.

Off the court, Riley was adjusting to college life. Leahy had become her best friend and the two spent time exploring college life.

"Meaghan is much more outgoing than I am," Riley laughed. "We actually complement each other. She's the funny one and I tend to be much more serious. As a freshman at Walsh Hall, I wasn't known as a basketball star because I wasn't a basketball star at the time. My section would come out to the games, though, and cheer me on, and that was really neat. My best friends at college and probably beyond came from that dorm in many ways."

Ruth was chosen to be part of the USA Under-19 Traveling National Team. It took her to places far away from Macy, to play national teams in Puerto Rico, Poland, and Spain. The next year, after an improved sophomore year with the Irish, she played in the World Games off the coast of Spain.

But all was not well with the Notre Dame team. During that

sophomore season, the Irish made it to the NCAA's Sweet 16. And hopes were high for the 1999-2000 squad.

However, the 1999-2000 team, which was Riley's junior year, was beset with internal leadership problems. The season, though highly successful on paper at 27-5, went down in flames twice. The first was a 81-72 overtime loss in the Big East semifinal to Rutgers. Ruth played only 20 minutes before fouling out with 20 points.

The second, and most bitter, was the NCAA Mideast Regional semifinal game against Texas Tech. Notre Dame bolted out to a 17-0 edge 10 minutes into the first half. The mortal flaw again was exposed, with Riley fouling out after playing just 27 minutes and scoring 19 points. Tech took advantage of the Ruth-less Irish and won 69-65.

The point was made. You can only use an aircraft carrier as long as it is in the water. Notre Dame couldn't use its Pass The Ball To Ruth strategy if Ruth was out of bounds, on the bench.

To say that Muffet McGraw was bitterly disappointed with her team in March 2000 is an understatement. And a disappointed McGraw is not a happy McGraw.

The annual post-season team meeting was to be a calm one, or so Riley thought as she headed across campus that day. "Usually, we would just talk about how we felt about the season just ending, what our plans were to get better, and the usual team togetherness stuff," Riley said.

Her expectations were off, way off.

That meeting became a blistering, soul-baring session in which McGraw released every frustration she had pent up during the year. McGraw thought that the team had suffered from a lack of senior leadership and had become fragmented with personal goals and objectives replacing the team concept.

As McGraw railed against her squad, Riley burned inside. "I got quite emotional," Ruth said. "I knew that I had only one chance left and I was very upset with the way the season had ended. That meeting got our attention."

The team now in pieces, it would be the five seniors' job to put it back together. The trick wasn't to glue the same pieces together in the same way, but to create a new team, with a new attitude, using most of the old pieces.

McGraw had thrown down the challenge. She was releasing some of her control. It would be the five seniors' responsibility to take it on.

Riley did her part. She declined another invitation to play on the national team and decided to stay on campus that summer, another small decision which would have a large impact.

"Staying here served two purposes," Riley says. "For one, I took summer classes which would get me to my goal of graduating on time with my class. For the other, it allowed me to play pickup games with my teammates and work on my individual weaknesses versus playing with the national team and trying to learn their new systems. I wanted to focus 100 percent on the Notre Dame team."

Riley knew the talent was there, even if the bench was somewhat thin. The starters complemented each others' weaknesses with their own strong points. But she also knew she had to stay on the court during the games if the team was to succeed.

She did.

As a freshman, she had committed a foul every four minutes she was on the floor. As a senior, she would reduce that to a foul every 12 minutes. She fouled out only twice that year and increased her average time played per game to a personal best of almost 29 minutes. In Ruth's senior year, it was finally McGraw's option to rest Riley, not having to yank her out for fear of fouling out.

In addition, the hours in the gym were paid off in other areas. Her shooting percentage stayed above 60 percent, she averaged 18.4 points per game, her free throw percentage stayed near 80 percent, she set a team record for rebounds at 261. Most importantly, her assists went up over 70 percent, to 69.

"I love seeing my teammates do well," Riley said. "Coach McGraw designed a new offense which had Kelley breaking down the lane for layups, versus getting open at the elbow of the free-throw lane."

The second game of the Coaches versus Cancer tournament in Madison, Wisconsin, would become a big confidence builder for the already-confident Irish. The 75-73 victory over the sixth-ranked Georgia Bulldogs told the team they were on the right track. The Irish were confident, winning, and loving it.

It would take the UConn game, however, was to make Riley a nationwide superstar.

Two days before the UConn showdown, in the same Saturday afternoon game against Virginia Tech in which Siemon broke her hand, Riley suffered an ankle sprain with 12 minutes remaining. She was not allowed to even practice during the light workout McGraw had scheduled for Sunday. Riley, like Siemon, would play the game of her life at 85 percent capacity.

Riley, twisted ankle and all, scored 29 points, including an incredible 13-for-13 from the foul line. She played all 40 minutes, pulled down 12 rebounds, blocked five shots, and dished out four assists. She didn't commit a single foul in the first half.

"I had to stay on the court and do my job," Riley said after the game. "I had to give up a couple of shots rather than try for blocks, but it was a good feeling not to have the fouls."

The mortal flaw, discovered first as a freshman, then worked on for four years, was gone. The Old Bad Habit had been defeated.

The Irish defeated UConn 92-76, shocking the collegiate basketball world and putting notice out that the hotels in St. Louis should be expecting a large contingent from South Bend for the NCAA Final Four. As the crowd rushed the floor, Riley knew that what had been accomplished on that floor had been special, and she also knew there was more to come.

"Ruth was more than a Bill Walton today," McGraw would tell Bill Jauss of the *Chicago Tribune*, comparing her to the legendary UCLA star. "I've never seen a player dominate a game from start to finish as she did. She was the best player in the country today."

UConn head coach Geno Auriemma agreed. "Ruth's presence made us a jump-shooting team," he said.

The klieg lights of the publicity machine, thanks to the NCAA and ESPN, now focused squarely on Ruth. And no one could help her.

"I felt sorry for Ruth," McGraw said. "If she was getting 200 letters a week from people, she wanted to send 200 replies. That's just how she is. But after the UConn game, it seemed like everyone in the world wanted to talk to her.

"We discussed it several times and began trying to limit her interviews to certain days, but that was proving difficult. You can't hide a 6-5 girl behind sunglasses and a hat the way you can a 5-6 girl."

The shy tall girl from small-town Indiana was now center stage. She would simply have to adjust. For a person who had always adjusted her way of thinking to address things beyond her control, it was just another challenge.

"Now it didn't matter where I went, grocery store, gas stations, everywhere," Ruth said. "People were coming up to me and telling me how proud they were of our team and how much we meant to them. Meaghan would start having fun with it, because everywhere we went, people recognized us."

Fortunately, her four years out of high school had changed her approach to life, also. "I'm not as shy as I used to be," Riley said. "Losing my privacy was just something I had to accept. I had no control over it."

The No. 1 ranking which followed the next week left Riley happy but unimpressed. "I was thrilled for Coach McGraw because she had worked 14 years to get a team there. But it was something I thought we could do and something I really expected to do," Riley said.

The top ranking also became an open invitation for the Big East teams to take their best shot at Notre Dame with really little to lose. Riley led her team to six more easy wins, averaging 23 points and 10 rebounds. The Irish record was 23-0.

But the Irish were ripening for a loss. And the Rutgers Scarlet Knights were more than happy to oblige.

The formula for defeating the Irish in 2001 always began with getting Riley into foul trouble and then defending the guards. The athletic Scarlet Knights did just that.

Ruth played only 25 minutes. With her on the bench, Rutgers had no trouble with her replacements, limiting Barksdale and Leahy to no points and two rebounds in her stead.

Needless to say, the Irish undefeated streak ended amid the raucous Louis Brown Athletic Center. "I played poorly," Ruth said. "I shot poorly and got into foul trouble. I was very upset with myself. Afterward, Coach pulled me aside and told me not to worry about it, that I was still the best player in the Big East and to just let this performance go."

Riley doesn't let anything go. She just concentrates harder. The next game against Miami, Notre Dame blew out the Hurricanes, 81-43, with Ruth scoring 20 points in 25 minutes on an 8-for-11 shooting effort from the field.

A 21-point, nine-rebound performance during a 65-53 win over Georgetown on Senior Night before another sold-out house concluded Riley's regular-season career in the Joyce. As the streamers rained from the ceiling, Ruth and her teammates gathered on the floor to receive the well-earned thunderous applause from thousands of newly converted women's basketball fans.

The return to UConn in the Big East final was another Riley classic. Ruth scored 23 points while playing 33 minutes. But the Irish lost to the Huskies when Sue Bird dribbled the length of the floor and hit a 12-footer for a 78-76 UConn win.

"Connecticut has a lot of pride in their program, as they rightly should," Riley said. "But our goal was to go in there and win the Big East Tournament. We had confidence in our ability to do it. Somehow Sue Bird got open at the end of the first half for that 3-pointer and then she did it again as the game ended.

"I was so close to blocking her last shot, though, and that will always stay with me. You put so much energy and effort, and it all comes down to whether a last shot like that will go in or stay out."

But it was on to the tournament. Ruth and her teammates wasted little time adjusting to the second season. Notre Dame hosted the first and second rounds of the NCAA and swept their opponents like so many gnats off a farmer's shoulder. Riley barely broke a sweat in her 20 minutes of play in first round 98-49 win over Alcorn State. Two days later, Michigan felt the brunt of the Irish determination and confidence. Ruth scored 21 points in 26 minutes in her last-ever appearance in the JACC before almost 9,600 fans. The Irish walked away with an 88-54 win.

Notre Dame then went to Denver, where Riley was named MVP of the NCAA East Regional. She scored 24 points and pulled down 14 rebounds as the Irish overcame Utah, 69-54, and then scored 32 in the 72-64 win over Vanderbilt. The Final Four, a dream for so many little kids in their driveways on summer afternoons, had become a reality for Riley.

The week between the Regional Final and the Final Four was thankfully short.

"We got back to South Bend at 3:30 AM Tuesday morning and then I had to fly to Minneapolis on Thursday to accept the ESPN award," Ruth said. "I know I tried to go to some classes that week, but it was obviously very difficult. When I am in class, I usually sit with my friends. But by now, even some students were coming up and asking for autographs for their nieces and nephews or friends."

The awards given to Riley were getting almost to the ridiculous point. She was named the Naismith Award Winner (similar to the Heisman award in college football) and was the first Notre Dame player to win the award. Other awards soon followed.

She was a unanimous pick to the Associated Press All-America team, she was named Player of the Year by *Sports Illustrated, Sports Illustrated for Women*, and *Women's Basketball Journal*. She was named to the Verizon Women's Basketball Academic All-America team for the second year. She was the Big East Player of the Year, and on and on.

"I really like getting the awards," Riley said. "It is nice to be noticed for all the hard work. But to try to get all of it done in the middle of the NCAA tournament was a bit much. All I wanted to do was focus on the games coming up. At the same time, I understand the awards are important."

Sharon was also getting her share of attention. "People were coming up to me and congratulating me," Sharon said. "I couldn't go too many places where that wouldn't happen. It is always a pat on the back. My cup runneth over. I really can't take it to heart, though. I just have to let it go over me and trickle down on somebody else.

Ruth flew to Minneapolis with Irish men's basketball star Troy Murphy.

"Troy and I are friends," Riley said. "But the men's and women's basketball players are all friends. I wouldn't say that we are extremely close or anything, but he is very funny. He jokes around a lot, and he and I will ask each other for autographs. It's really fun."

Ruth arrived in St. Louis after the team had gotten there. "The practices that week had been intense, but they were fun too," Riley said. "Everyone was really excited to be in to the Final Four. Of course, Niele suffered the brunt of the publicity and she had all kinds of people calling her and asking for tickets."

That Sunday night against Purdue, Riley assumed the mantle of superstar. In a moment lived by many in their minds but only a special few in real life, Riley calmly sank the two free throws that would assure her of a special place in the history of Notre Dame and in the hearts of the common people in South Bend.

If Ruth Riley isn't just common people, then just who is? The day before she won the Naismith Award, Riley and Leahy were out at Walt Disney School on Day Road in nearby Mishawaka taking part in a reading program for fifth-grade students. It was only one of the many community service projects to which Riley has lent her support.

"Her love of kids is naturally her," Sharon said. "She has always been good for kids. She is a natural ambassador. Kids just naturally come up to her."

Humility is also a trait associated with Ruth. "She can slam dunk a ball easily," Sharon said. "But she figures why make a big show of it when it's easier to make a little layup? Why slam your wrist against the rim? Maybe in the pros they will want her to do that. She hates showing off. She despises arrogance. She doesn't believe that belongs in sports."

"My mom has helped me stay real," Riley says. "So have my sister and Meaghan. With all this stuff happening to me, it has sometimes been difficult to stay real and not lose sight of who I really am."

To young girls whom idolize her, Riley has a few words of advice. "In junior high, I was made fun of because I was so tall," she says. "Everyone has something at that age that other kids make fun of. To be honest with you, going through that helped me become stronger as a person. It made me seek out real friends, the real people who will help you and who care about you."

If she wasn't a basketball player, Riley admits to having no idea what she would do with her life. "I have never considered a life without basketball or sports," she laughed. "I suppose I would like to be a coach or a teacher or an announcer if I couldn't play, but...

"I think my most favorite thing to do is to go out where the little kids are," Riley said. "One thing I remember is one day I was out at a school and I just walked up to a little girl, stuck out my hand to say hi, and she just burst out crying because she was so happy I was there.

"Sometimes I don't think athletes realize just how much impact they have on people," Riley continued. "I have always been a people person and the most fulfilling part of what I do is talking to the kids. The awards are really nice and all that, but I'm most proud that I have been a positive role model to so many kids."

"Ruth is one of the greatest people I have ever met in my life," Muffet said after Riley graduated. "And I've met some really great people. She is special, she really is. One in a million. She even wrote a letter to the city of St. Louis after we won, which was in the newspaper, thanking them for being so nice. I was thinking to myself, 'Gee, I should have done that.'"

Praise like that can't help but make a mother proud.

"Ruth is almost a spitting image of what I looked like when I was that age," Sharon concluded. "She is a lot like me, and she accomplished our goal for her of graduating from college. It's that degree from Notre Dame, That's what the whole thing was about. It is that degree that will lift her level of living.

"Honestly, I am more proud of her for her attitude and outlook on mankind after she had achieved such fame this year, moreso than the fame and success itself."

Sharon no longer cuddles with Ruth on the floor of her home in Macy, Indiana. As a matter of fact, Sharon no longer lives in Macy. She's moved north, closer to South Bend.

Ruth is continuing her basketball career with the Miami Sol in the Women's National Basketball Association.

For Ruth, the journey to Miami, Florida, still includes that county road that leads to North Miami High School.

North Miami is at the intersection of four cornfields about seven miles outside Macy. To get there, you go east off of U.S. 31 on County Road 1000 North and drive until you have just about given up hope of ever being found alive again.

It's a narrow road, full of potholes. A small green direction sign points to the south and you follow Meridian Road until another little green sign points east. You wait for the farm tractors to pass from the other direction before you turn left onto County Road 900 North. On the left is the high school, cut from some of the richest cornfields of the Indiana plains.

The school is justifiably proud of the greatest athlete ever to walk its halls. A picture of Riley hangs on the wall outside the main entrance of the gymnasium, as does an enclosed case with her retired jersey, No. 25.

Her jersey number was retired in the fall of 2000, in a ceremony as part of a game against rival high school Whitko. Coach McGraw was there, teammate Niele Ivey was there, Kelley Siemon was there, and so were about 1,500 of Ruth's closest friends and fans. As the ceremony was concluded, the crowd rose as one and gave the embarrassed Riley a long standing ovation.

Big things don't happen often in small towns. When they do, it is a uniting feeling. Pride swells in the chests of those around the school as it can only in a small community.

Because of small towns like these, things between mothers and daughters don't change. "Ruth and I go for walks when we can," Sharon said. "And we talk about all kinds of things, not just basketball...but about guys, and memories, and family and where she is heading."

And, probably, other things that only mothers and daughters can talk about.

CHAPTER 3

NIELE IVEY — DREAMS REALLY CAN COME TRUE

The rookie point guard was wearing a big 33 on the back of her brand new yellow and red jersey of the Indiana Fever.

It was only her second game as a professional player in the WNBA (Women's National Basketball Association), and this was an exhibition game against the Detroit Shock.

She had played poorly in her first game less than a week earlier. She hadn't scored and had played only six minutes before sitting on the bench with nothing to show for her efforts except two personal fouls.

Tonight, however, she had been given a starting position so her coach could see what she could do. With 18:20 remaining on the first-half clock, the ball came to her and she faded quickly to her left. She eyed the basket and launched a shot from just beyond the 3-point line.

Shooting the ball was as natural as breathing for her by now. She had shot thousands of times before in school yards, in small gymnasiums, in giant coliseums. So this shot was somehow the same and at the same time somehow different. The ball reached its apogee, then descended and fell through the net with a soft swish.

The 5,000 fans in attendance that evening of May 22, 2001 murmured in appreciation. The young woman allowed herself a quick pump of her right hand and an even quicker smile before hustling back to play defense.

Niele Ivey had just made some personal history. She had also made history for her family. The small commemoration was allowable and just. "It is only an exhibition game," she reminded herself as she headed upcourt.

Still, your first points as a professional basketball player only come once.

And, besides that, Niele Ivey had just achieved her dream.

Niele Ivey was in street clothes at her first Final Four in Cincinnati on March 28, 1997.

She had become accustomed to it, like a poodle might become accustomed to wearing the silly little housecoat its owner may decide to make it wear. Accepting, yes. Comfortable, no.

She watched as a team manager Christy Grady took warm-up layins. She watched, sitting next to teammates Kristina Ervin, Adrienne Jordan, and Diana Braendly.

They all had one thing in common. They were all injured. And they would not play in Notre Dame's historic first-ever visit to the NCAA Final Four.

There was nothing they could do except watch as the women's college basketball Goliath known as the Tennessee Volunteers swamped the upstart Irish that Friday night, 80-66, to knock Notre Dame out of the tournament.

That Niele was even sitting on the bench was just part of an incredible journey. She's a rags-to-riches story in many senses. From the working-class streets of St. Louis to the ivy-covered walls at Notre Dame and eventually the condominiums of Indianapolis.

Niele's a true example of working hard to get opportunities, taking advantage of those opportunities, and then overcoming tremendous odds to maximize them.

She is proof of the power of the human spirit, of the value of determination and commitment, and the fact that in the final analysis, whatever race or gender you are doesn't matter. It only matters what type of person you are.

Niele Ivey is a winner.

Like many other young women in the WNBA, Niele began life on the wrong end of the economic court. Her parents were poor, but they were strong, committed to the success of their family. Niele was the youngest of five children and had to share a single bedroom with her four older brothers.

"It wasn't the best neighborhood, for sure," Niele said. "It was an inner-city neighborhood. But it wasn't any Cabrini Green [a notorious housing project in Chicago] either."

Her house is about four miles north of downtown St. Louis, a long city block from the park where she would begin the long process of becoming a star. The house itself is not impressive, but it's folly to measure the worth of a family by the house they live in.

Niele's mother, Theresa, is a striking, outgoing woman who has a fierce pride in her family. While Niele may be the most immediately successful of her five children, Theresa carries the feeling of pride for all.

Niele's father, Tom, is much quieter, preferring to let Theresa run the family issues. His job, it seemed, was to make sure the food was on the table when the time came.

They basically double-teamed their young family through the difficult times of growing up with all the temptations of life surrounding them. "My parents kept us busy," Niele's older brother Cedric said. "That kept us out of a lot of trouble."

Unfortunately, keeping them busy cost money. The boys played on travel soccer teams, where parents had to kick in for expenses, as well as played basketball in high school. The Iveys put their money where their heart is. The investment was to be in the real people, not in the real estate.

But God had bestowed upon their only daughter a gift. Niele was incredibly fast, athletic, and an intelligent young person to boot. Theresa and Tom recognized it.

As a young girl, Niele would hang out at the local basketball courts just down the street. There, she would watch her brothers, Cedric, Nicholas, Emilio, and Philippe play ball. Sometimes she played too. Sometimes she just hung out. The basketball courts were the social scene.

"We had a lot of friends from the surrounding neighborhoods," Niele said. "It was really a lot of fun."

"She was just like one of the boys," Cedric said. "She tagged along with us to the park and after a while just started getting into games. When I played for our high school team, she was always on the courts shooting during halftime. She was the only girl playing ball in the park. She would go up against whoever was on the court. She just loved it."

"Back then, one court were just plain dirt and a couple were pavement but they had chains for nets," Theresa said. "When the nets disappeared, they played without nets. I think some kids these days would look at that and say, 'I would never play on that.' "

On those courts, Niele would hone her skills, playing street ball for hours against anyone who would pick up with her. She attended Immacolata Grade School, and her teams won the city-county championship in both seventh and eighth grade, a feat which Ivey still points to with pride.

"I started playing organized ball the year round after that," she said. "Basketball was something I knew I was good at and I wanted to get better. At the time, I was a very good shooter and had real good ball-handling skills. I was the go-to person, I guess."

Theresa agreed that winning the city-county championship was no small feat. "Those girls may have been small, but they were out for your hide," Theresa laughed. "They would take you to the wall.

"At that time, there was a school named Holy Redeemer, which was the Connecticut of the grade schools. Each time they played, it was bloody war. One time one team would win, and the next time the other might."

Ivey's mom decided to send her to a Catholic girls school. All four of her boys had gone to a Catholic boys high school.

"I guess she wanted a 'safe' school for me," Niele said. "She wanted me to have a strong background education-wise, and we had heard about Cor Jesu. We went to an open house there and she eventually chose that school for me. It was a 40-minute drive and every day she would drive me up there and either her or my dad would pick me up."

For Niele, the school represented her first great opportunity to fulfill a lifetime goal of going to college. "No one else in my family had ever gone to college," she said. "But my mom had planted the idea in my brain from a very early age, and I knew that if I did well there that I could get a college scholarship. At Cor Jesu they constantly stressed the value of college."

Equally as important to Theresa was Cor Jesu's value system. "I had grown up with nuns as teachers," she said. "And Cor Jesu had a value system similar to what we were trying to teach at home. We wanted somewhere where Niele would learn how to become a young lady and how to conduct herself once she left home. The nuns were right on it."

Niele was not recruited to play basketball for Cor Jesu. As a matter of fact, Cor Jesu was not a basketball powerhouse before Niele enrolled.

"Basketball had nothing to do with our decision to send her to Cor Jesu," Theresa emphasized. "The academics and the values are what we made our decision on. Niele had to pass a bunch of exams just to get admitted."

Niele learned a lot at Cor Jesu, including basketball. "Gary

Glasscock was my coach there and he is so dedicated to the sport," she said. "He has been there for a very long time and really he is the reason I am where I'm at today. He was always building me up, building my confidence.

"I really learned how to play the game from him. He knew I had the raw talent and he showed me what I needed to work on and some practice methods to achieve my goals."

"Niele always had talent," Theresa said. "But she needed to develop form and Gary had great form on his shots."

Niele, who would later become a team favorite at Notre Dame because of her continual impersonations of nearly everyone she knew, would watch Glasscock and imitate him. The method worked. Ivey's shooting improved dramatically.

Glasscock called Niele the most natural athlete he had ever seen. He would also end up calling her "friend." She would only half-kiddingly call him her "white father," for it was Glasscock with whom Ivey would occasionally catch rides home with an occasional strawberry milkshake along the way. It was also Glasscock who made Niele decide to pursue basketball as her sport of choice.

Niele had been a great volleyball player. And coaches in both sports wanted her to play for them. "We had been all over the Midwest as part of a traveling volleyball team," Tom Ivey said quietly. "I thought volleyball was going to be her sport."

Glasscock knew that Niele, just a freshman at the time, needed to decide early between the two sports, if she were to become a Division I player in either.

"We had to basically make a rule that the girls either played basketball or volleyball, and the volleyball coach also wanted her for the weekend tournaments. I knew Niele was playing, and one Monday she came in to practice and was really sluggish. I sat her down and told her that the time had come for her to make a decision between basketball and volleyball. She spent the whole practice crying, but the next day she was committed to basketball."

That commitment meant a huge financial outlay for the cash-strapped Ivey family, but there really was no other decision to be made. "We paid our own way to each of the AAU tournaments," Theresa said. "We even went to Albuquerque once. There were no sponsors and we paid the whole thing. It was all for Niele."

Given the opportunity, Niele did not disappoint. She was the type of player who could turn a game, a team, and a season around, according to Glasscock.

"Niele was amazingly fast in high school," he said. "The knee injuries took some of her speed away in college. But she took our program, which was average or a little better, and took us to the only state championship in school history as a junior and back to the Final Four as a senior."

Ivey's final game also provided Glasscock with a one-minute highlight film to cap four years of memories. "I think she scored 10 points in less than a minute, stealing passes, hitting 3-pointers, everything," Glasscock said. "She just took over the game."

Glasscock also said Niele was a hidden jewel.

"I couldn't get Niele to the bigger Nike camps and things because our AAU team just wasn't one of the powerhouses," he said. But he was Ivey's biggest supporter. "I wrote a long letter to Coach McGraw during the recruiting process and told Muffet if Niele ever got out of line, to pull out the letter and make her read it."

"Every word of his letter was true," Muffet said later. "You don't get that from a lot of high school coaches."

Ivey became a legend at the all-girl school of about 500 students. She averaged 24 points and eight rebounds a game her senior year and was named *USA Today* Missouri Player of the Year, Miss Show-Me Basketball, *St. Louis Post-Dispatch* co-player of the year, and *Street and Smith's* honorable mention All-American, among others.

She was a four-year starter for Glasscock's team and set school records for points (1,977), rebounds (813), assists (600), steals (603), and blocked shots (95). She had led her team to a perfect 31-0 record and the state championship as a junior. As importantly, she maintained a 3.7 GPA.

Not surprisingly, when she left, they retired her jersey.

Ivey's life was on a roll. As a junior at Cor Jesu, she began receiving letters from schools, including Notre Dame. Molly Peirick, at the time a sophomore at Notre Dame, told McGraw about Niele, and her mom accompanied Muffet to a pickup game at the YMCA. Niele and Peirick had actually guarded each other in high school games, so Mrs. Peirick was well acquainted with Niele.

"All it was was noon-ball," Ivey said. "It was something we just did every day and I was impressed with the fact that Coach McGraw was there and I figured that she was probably pretty interested."

She was.

"Notre Dame was beyond my wildest dreams," Theresa said. "We were being visited by all kinds of different schools and it was making the decision very hard to make. Notre Dame was just one of those schools we listened to."

After a home visit, McGraw and her crew invited Ivey to South Bend for a campus visit. Theresa, who worked in a gourmet food factory and is an acknowledged good cook, had served the coaches some pound cake during the home visit, much to the delight of Muffet and her staff.

"When Niele got off the plane in South Bend, she had with her another pound cake and was wearing this little skirt, looking like a little Catholic school girl. She hands us the cake and says, 'My mom wants you to have this cake,'" Muffet recalled.

"I think my mom was buttering them up," Niele laughed.

If Niele had grown up on the streets of urban St. Louis, she must have grown up on Nice Street. Manners like these hadn't been seen much, even at Notre Dame.

It wasn't the first time Niele had been to South Bend, however. In fact, at age four, Niele suffered her very first knee injury while swimming at a Roseland hotel.

"Our boys were in a Junior Irish Memorial Day soccer tournament in South Bend one year," Theresa said. "And we ended up taking Niele to Memorial Hospital that night because she scraped her knee in the pool of the Holiday Inn and we had to have her knee stitched up. Every time we pass that place now, we laugh about that. After that we had to carry her around to all the different soccer fields."

The knee problems, of course, would revisit her in South Bend years later.

"I thought the idea of going to Notre Dame was beyond me," Niele said of her recruiting trip to Notre Dame. "I thought it was like Yale or Harvard. I really never expected a letter from them, and my trip to South Bend was the first time I had ever been exposed to the 'feel' of Notre Dame.

"But I felt like it was an extension of my high school, being a Catholic university and all. That's what I was looking for when I went there, but coming on campus was like going into a whole new world. I knew that if I could get an education there, that I could compete in life, not just in sports but also in real life.

"Molly Peirick was very honest about the pros and cons of coming to Notre Dame," Ivey continued. "She told me the truth about everything. The alumni base was another large factor in my choosing Notre Dame; they really are all over the world. The education was a given, but I also felt very comfortable with the team.

"Molly told me that if I chose Notre Dame that in the long run it would be the best choice I would ever make. Besides that, after you graduate it will be something you cherish the rest of your life. You are not just a graduate. You are something special."

Notre Dame extended an offer immediately, and Ivey went home to think about it. She didn't wait long.

"She was the sweetest kid," Muffet said. "She called us back after the visit and said, 'If you would still like to have me, I would be happy to come.' I just loved her."

Once accepted, Ivey began to show some of the personality that would make her a champion. "She came back to watch one of our games," Muffet said. "And rather than the Catholic uniform, she's wearing her hat backwards and blue jeans and she's sitting behind our bench screaming at the officials.

"My husband, Matt, asks me later who that girl was and I told him it was Niele. He did a double take and said 'No way.'"

To say that the transition from the streets of East St. Louis to the ivy-covered walls of Notre Dame was a bit of a culture shock that first fall would be an understatement. Her competitive nature kept her head above water in the classroom and when practice opened, it was apparent she would make some quick contributions to the team. Her natural speed and ability to read the floor gave her some immediate playing time. She averaged over 17 minutes a game during the first five games.

But life was about to change dramatically.

In the first minute of the sixth game versus Bowling Green, Ivey made a sudden cut and heard her knee pop. It was a torn ACL — sometimes a career-ender, always an injury that requires an intense rehabilitation effort.

"I had never had an injury before that," Ivey said. "I was just getting started in my career and I was just devastated and scared. I had heard of the injury, but I wasn't very well-informed of it at all. I had heard it had happened to a soccer player, but I was really scared and confused, not knowing what was going to happen to me."

The torn ACL sentenced Ivey to a year off the court. She spent game days sitting on the bench and cheering her teammates on. "Niele that year did the best she could trying to motivate us from the bench," said Katryna Gaither, a senior on the 1997 team. "Even as a freshman, she was trying to lead."

The trainers and team doctor could take care of the physical part of the rehabilitation, but it would be Ivey's biggest challenge to overcome the mental and emotional scars of the injury.

"I had to really push myself," Ivey said. "But I lost a lot of confidence that year. I had never been on a team that I could not contribute to from the floor. It really was a struggle that year.

"I was just so frustrated because I knew that besides going to school, I was supposed to be playing basketball, but there I was sitting on the bench," Ivey continued. "I didn't understand why it had happened. I worked hard, I stayed in shape, I got to wondering why it had happened to me…What did I do to deserve it?"

As the frustration settled in, so did her desire to get back on the court. Ivey made it her business to meet or exceed the trainer's goals. By her sophomore year, she was ready to go.

But now it was a totally different team. Five seniors had departed. Gone was Beth Morgan. Gone was Gaither. Gone were Roseanne Bohman, Jeannine Augustin, and Adrienne Jordan. Ivey would reconstruct her now cracked psyche at the same time McGraw would reconstruct her whole team.

Ivey got off to a slow start in her second freshman season. "I still didn't feel like I was 100 percent," Ivey said. "But I was playing through it, even though I had no confidence in my game."

She worked into a four-guard rotation that included Peirick, Sheila McMillen, and Danielle Green. McGraw shifted lineups to determine the best combination. After the slow (3-4) start, McGraw made Ruth Riley the starting center, replacing Julie Henderson.

"That change didn't affect us much, " Ivey said. "We kind of expected it. We knew Ruth would eventually be our center, but at that point she was pretty soft and needed a lot of work. She had height, it was just a question of when her talent was going to kick in for her."

Ivey's breakthrough performance, ironically, was the same Wisconsin game that made McGraw give the center position to Riley. Niele scored 16 points and added seven rebounds and four assists in that 89-77 loss at Madison. The team had committed 28 turnovers, adding to McGraw's consternation and motivation to make the change. For the season, Ivey averaged over eight points and three assists in 26 minutes of playing time per game. She had started 19 of the 31 games that year. However, she committed 97 turnovers against only 90 assists, far below standard for a point guard.

The next season, her third on campus, became the year she established herself as the solid starter Muffet had envisioned on the day she sat in that hot YMCA gym watching Ivey play against men five and 10 years older than she.

Her assist-to-turnover ratio improved dramatically as she recorded 181 assists against only 85 turnovers. She was now playing over 31 minutes a game, scoring 13.2 points a game, and shooting at over a 50 percent clip. What could possibly go wrong?

Fate entered Ivey's life again. This time she was playing in a Big East tournament contest at Rutgers when she felt a familiar pop, this time in her left knee. Again she went down, again she missed the balance of the season.

She was replaced on the floor by Sherisha Hills, and the numbers coming from the point guard position declined dramatically. It was simply too late in the season to be replacing such a key player.

With Ivey's leadership missing, her team got whacked by UConn in the Big East final, 96-75. The NCAA, aware of Ivey's value to Notre Dame, decided not to award the Irish a home seed for the tournament, despite the team's 25-4 record and No. 8 ranking in the final AP poll.

The Irish struggled past St. Mary's in the opening round and then suffered through a disappointing 74-64 loss to LSU, who had been awarded the host site over the Irish.

This knee injury was not as bad as the first. She was back and ready to play for her junior year, her fourth year in school. She established herself as the team's defensive leader, setting a team record for 95 steals as the team went 27-5 despite growing internal problems.

Ivey's offensive output dropped to 11.2 points per game despite playing over 32 minutes a contest. But the disappointing 81-72 overtime loss to Rutgers in the Big East semifinal was an indicator of things to come. The Irish advanced to the Sweet 16 after hosting the first and second rounds of the NCAA. Ivey suffered through one of her worst games of the year against Texas Tech, shooting only 1-for-9 from the field and scoring only seven points. The result was a disappointing 69-65 loss.

Not a way to end a dream.

After the season, Ivey committed to and was approved for her return to the team as a fifth-year senior. She received her undergraduate degree, but knowing the NCAA Finals would be in her hometown the next year and that four of the five starters were returning (Kelley Siemon would be the fifth starter), Ivey chose to spend another year taking graduate courses in South Bend.

The emotional year-end meeting held by McGraw proved a uniting force for the returning members of the team. As Muffet raised the roof, the returning players raised their expectations.

The road to St. Louis started immediately. Any players on campus at the time would gather to play pickups and work out as a group. "We definitely worked extremely hard during the summer," Ivey said. "The seniors knew it would be the last go-round and the bonding that occurred that summer improved the team chemistry. It became a 'whatever it takes' attitude and the freshmen stayed right with us."

The preseason workouts paid immediate results. Muffet herself, did her share of soul-searching and came back in a less confrontational manner.

"She wasn't as strict from Day One," Ivey said. "She was much more relaxed in practices. Sometimes in prior years, she would leave practice in a bad mood and that put pressure on everyone. But coming back, she was different. Part of it, though, was because she let the seniors take more of a leadership role.

"I really think the reason that she didn't get so mad in practices was because we didn't give her a reason to get mad. We were a mature team, and we were focused."

The personality of the team turned from a look of determination and fear to more of an intense smile. One of Ivey's personal strengths is her quick smile and friendly demeanor. She began to loosen up her teammates.

"Niele is a master of imitation," Muffet said. "She will imitate just about anyone."

In particular, she imitated Muffet. On the now less-frequent instances where the coach would storm out of practice, Ivey would at times loosen up the atmosphere by imitating her.

"One time Coach stormed out of practice and had trouble

getting a door open," teammate Ericka Haney said. "Niele had a lot of fun with that one. She also imitated her doing a pep-rally speech about waking up the echoes. I still laugh about that one."

It wasn't Niele forcing her personality on the team. It was more a case of, with the pressure of a perfectionist coach now lessened, the team loosened up and Ivey's natural sense of humor took over.

"I think it was my job to make the team loose," Ivey said. "I never really acquired that role, it just happened. We had such a wide variety of personalities, from Ruth who is so quiet, to Kelley who is much more like me, it was easy for me do what just came naturally."

In addition, Niele started keeping a diary, which was published periodically in the South Bend Tribune as the season progressed. There was no doubt as to the goals for the team.

Here's one of her articles she wrote on October 14 when practice opened:

> Some of the goals that I am setting for myself and my team would be to win the national title in my hometown of St. Louis. I want to make First Team Big East, win the Big East tournament and beat some of the teams that made it to last year's Big Dance.
>
> Everyone is catching onto the new offense very well and working hard. Personally I am putting it all on the line this year. They always say "Save your best for last" and that is what I am trying to do.
>
> After today's practice I thought about those sad and lonesome nights in the infirmary with my knee injuries, when I prayed I would be happy and healthy again. I used to just look out the window and pray I would be healthy and confident enough to be one of the best point guards in the country. I finally feel like I am strong, confident, and healthy enough to make some of those wishes come true.

A strong Ivey combined with a focused Riley to get Notre Dame off to an impressive start in the fall of 2000. The Irish stormed through their first three games, rolling up huge winning margins over good teams.

The Georgia game played as part of the Coaches versus Cancer Tournament proved to be the true indicator of the potential of the team.

"No doubt about it," Ivey said, "The Georgia game was a huge one for us. Actually, so was the Wisconsin game. I was named MVP of that tournament and I think we saw how good we could be. It became a building block, a confidence builder.

"Especially the way we won it. We had a big lead, they came back, we made some mistakes late in the game, yet we stayed poised and won 75-73. We had never been a good team when the game was close in the last few seconds. We won that way. It was a very important win."

A building-block win is not any good unless it serves as a cornerstone. "Whenever we would play poorly later in the season, we would always bring up the Georgia game and remind ourselves just how well we were able to play as a team," Ivey said.

The January 15th win over UConn was a high-water mark for Ivey's career. She scored 14 points and dished out 10 assists as the Irish vaulted over the Huskies to take the top spot in the national rankings for the first time in Irish history. As she left the floor with 19.6 seconds to go to a thunderous ovation of new believers, she knew her dream of playing in St. Louis was within her grasp. In the middle of the 11,416-person group hug which occurred after the game, Ivey found her father and one of her brothers.

It was, of course, a perfect moment.

"What an awesome feeling," she said. "To have the crowd rush the floor for a women's basketball game at the JACC had never happened before. The real impact of what we had accomplished did not hit me until later."

"One of the most memorable experiences in my life was the victory over Connecticut in front of a sellout crowd at the Joyce Center," she wrote in her *Tribune* diary. "During that game, I felt the team chemistry combined with great effort and determination helped us beat UConn and earn our highest ranking in the history of Notre Dame basketball.

"However, while our heads were in the clouds for a couple of days, we eventually settled down and focused on our task at hand. Our goal as seniors was to maintain our focus and make sure we didn't become complacent. I feel as though the only team that can beat our team is ourselves."

Focus is hard to maintain when you're suddenly in the celebrity spotlight.

"All of the sudden, we were being noticed," Ivey said. "Everywhere we went, people would point us out. The student body was great, and when the No. 1 sign went up on Grace Hall, that was really fun.

"Everywhere we went, we were signing autographs. We realized pretty early on that we had become role models and we had responsibilities in that area."

Ivey wasn't even in the same state with her teammates on March 11 when the pairings were announced. ""I didn't get to share in the excitement Sunday with my teammates," she wrote in her *Tribune* diary. "I had planned to go to Coach McGraw's house to watch the pairings, but my dad took a look at my roommate's car and decided he needed to work on it.

"I shouldn't have let him near it, but he was just trying to help. I didn't get back to campus until late Sunday night."

It was the second time Ivey had missed the team meeting the night of the pairings. Ironically, when she was a freshman, she was stranded in St. Louis by a huge snowstorm that night. Tom would eventually drive 12 hours one way on Tuesday just to get her back on campus.

The Irish the stormed through the four tournament games and suddenly were on their way to the Final Four.

Ivey's gamble had worked. She was returning to St. Louis with a chance to become a champion in her hometown.

It would be a hectic, almost frantic week for Ivey. Up until now, the media herds had focused on Riley and McGraw. But the allure of the hometown hero returning in triumph proved to be fresh and real enough to warrant attention.

Almost fortunately, the week would be a short one. The team returned to South Bend at 3:30 AM Tuesday morning and flew out Thursday afternoon. In between that, the spotlight widened now to include Ivey.

Not only did she have to deal with reporters' questions and the media demands, her phone was ringing with people looking for tickets. Still, Ivey took to the attention like a duck to water, her natural smile and self-confidence coming through on the national stage.

Returning to St. Louis brought Ivey full circle. In fact, she had played on Savvis Center court once before as senior in high school, when it was known as the Kiel Center, in an all-day Gateway Classic which invites top girls teams from all over the country to play. The NCAA championship game would be played less than five miles from where she grew up.

The Irish plane landed at the airport in St. Louis and Ivey looked out her window and wondered who all the people that were standing around were waiting for.

They were waiting for her. Old friends, family, old classmates, teachers, coaches, and nuns. It was an impromptu greeting. It was a simple thank you expressed by those whom Ivey had affected over her years at Cor Jesu. It was something nice that nice people did for one of their own.

"I had no idea there would be anyone waiting for me at the airport, certainly not as large a crowd as there was. I was so happy to see everyone, but I was overwhelmed at the same time. Some of the faces were people I hadn't seen since I left for Notre Dame."

If this was a feel-good season for the Irish, this was one of the most feel-good moments as far as Ivey was concerned. "The overall sense I had was that it was really nice to be appreciated so much," she said. "I was just so proud to be associated with something that was just so good."

Once they had battled their way through the welcoming scene, Ivey treated her teammates to a quick tour of the town they were about to take over. Then it was time to focus on basketball.

First up was the third matchup with UConn. "We went into the game with a lot of confidence," Niele said. "It was weird, but the game in the NCAA tournament didn't seem as big as the one in January. Even when we were down at halftime, I still expected to win."

UConn, however, wasn't convinced. Ivey was one of the speakers at an inspiring halftime session. The goal was to turn the UConn bus, which was 12 points ahead and headed for the championship game for the second straight year, around.

"We decided at halftime to come together for 20 more minutes and it was 0-0 in the second half," Ivey told the assembled media after the game. "When we came back out there, our leadership and chemistry took over. We just decided we were going to take advantage of every second."

With just under six minutes to go, Ivey made a cut and her ankle gave way. As she rolled around the hardwood, those who knew Ivey's knee's medical history held their breath. Could fate be that cruel, to pull the hometown hero off center stage after she had been so instrumental in getting the Irish there in the first place?

Ivey knew right away she was OK. It was only an ankle sprain. Her teammates, though initially concerned, also recognized the difference and gathered around McGraw for some instruction.

"I didn't want to be off the floor, especially at that time," Ivey said. "I wasn't worried at all about my ankle; I just wanted back in the game."

Ivey sat out for about a minute and returned to a thunderous reception.

Her return again raised the emotional level of her team, and UConn was busted. Ivey scored a game-high 21 points, including a 3-for-5 effort from the 3-point area.

On to the Purdue finale.

Ivey would also play a pivotal role in the final countdown to a championship. When Notre Dame rebounded a missed Purdue shot and called timeout with just over 29 seconds remaining, it was Ivey who McGraw designated to make the entry pass.

The plan was to wait until there were about 10 seconds to go. At that point, Siemon and Riley were to post high on the elbows of the free throw lane. It was Ivey's job to pick the better target, and pass the ball to her. The other player would then cut to the basket.

Ideally, Riley was to take the last shot, no matter what.

"Kelley had the better angle for the entry pass," Ivey said. "It was the same play we had run all year."

The entry pass was perfect, the pass to Ruth efficient, and the foul on Purdue's Sharika Wright called. "I knew Ruth would make the free throws," Ivey said. "Then we had to keep another Sue Bird thing from happening. We had changed the defense since the UConn game."

Seconds later, as the last-gasp Purdue shot rolled away and out of bounds, Ivey finally lost control. "I didn't know what to do," she said. "I found Coach K [Kevin McGuff] and jumped on him and then I started jumping on everyone else."

Ivey is proud of the legacy her team will leave at Notre Dame.

"We took a good program and made it great," she said. "I think it was a storybook season. It took a lot of hard work, determination, and perseverance on the parts of lots of people. But it paid off."

Ivey also knows she is a role model to a lot of young girls, on and off the court.

"I know I have to set a good example, staying in school and let them know that I am more than just an athlete," Niele said. "Actually, Ruth is a prime example. She was the one everyone wanted to see and touch. I'm so proud of the way she handled herself through it all."

Ivey also ascribes color blindness as part of the reason the team had the chemistry to win.

"I think that in prior seasons, all the black kids kind of hung together and all the white kids hung together off the court. We, of course, were all friends, but there was that separation. And I think that held us back. This year, it just wasn't an issue. Color wasn't really an issue. It just sort of disappeared."

Do not be surprised if Niele returns to her St. Louis roots after her WNBA career is over. After all, it used to be called the Matthews-Dickey Boys Club that Niele and Gary Glasscock would hang around at. Somehow, that got renamed to Matthews-Dickey Boys and Girls Club.

"She's there all the time anyway," her brother Cedric said. "She comes home, talks a little, and then she's off to the club. She officiates, coaches, runs the clocks, whatever it takes. Out of everything that I am proud of my sister for, I think that is the thing I'm most proud of."

Cedric also predicts big things for the Indiana Fever. "Think about it," he said. "She goes to Cor Jesu and an average team wins the state championship. She goes to Notre Dame and they win the national championship. I don't see why it would be any different in the WNBA."

Winners do what winners do, that's one thing Cedric knows. And his little sister is a winner.

So, don't look for Niele in the boardrooms of a major corporation any time soon. And don't expect her to get all hung up about money and fame.

The only hanging up she is likely to do is hanging up a net at a local youth club, giving someone else the same opportunity her family and friends gave her.

CHAPTER 4

KELLEY SIEMON —
IT'S ALL ONE COURT, ANYWAY

Kelley Siemon needed to know the play.

But with 29 seconds left in the national championship game, with the score tied, it appeared to her that Coach Muffet McGraw just wasn't communicating well.

"What's the play?" Kelley kept asking Coach McGraw. In the back of her mind, she knew she had not played well in the last five minutes, committing three key turnovers and keeping the game a tossup.

But now it was crunch time. "What's the play?" Kelley asked again.

Finally, McGraw whirled and said, "High."

"Oh, my gosh," Kelley thought. "That means I have to make sure to get a good pass to Ruth or else we might lose the game."

Many high school and college students would love to be a sports heroes.

Kelley Siemon is a sports hero who just wanted to be a college student.

Siemon credits Notre Dame with allowing her to play ball with the women she now calls her sisters while at the same time experiencing the personal side of college with those she now calls her friends.

Her time spent in the locker room and on the practice floor was balanced by the Notre Dame housing theory which places athletes in the same dorms as the regular students.

It was in the dorm where Kelley would sometimes spend the wee morning hours in the dimly lit hallway, chatting with best friend Ellen Quinn. The time Kelly spent talking about X's and O's with her teammates was balanced out by time spent with Quinn talking about boyfriends and bridesmaid dresses.

The Notre Dame experience was, for Kelley Siemon, the best of both worlds.

But it came with a price.

Being a student-athlete is hard enough, but Siemon did not discover her niche on the basketball floor until midway through her senior year. "I'm not a real good go-to player," Siemon said. "I'm much more a role player."

Her self-discovery was to become the final piece of the national championship puzzle.

Fortunately for Siemon, classmate Ruth Riley was handed the task of learning to become a superstar. So Kelley became the consummate role-player.

Often called a dirty-work player, the role player toils in relative anonymity, scraping knees diving for balls, blocking out under the boards, and passing the ball to the superstar.

Without the role player, the superstar is limited to being simply human.

Without the role player, the superstar doesn't get open for shots, doesn't have someone to pass to when she is trapped, doesn't have help rebounding.

Kelley Siemon is a role player. Always has been.

It's in her blood. After all, her father, Jeff, was an all-pro linebacker for the Minnesota Vikings in the 1970s and '80s. Three Super Bowls, four Pro Bowls. The dirty-work doesn't get much dirtier than that. It is a classic role player position.

In fact, on January 15, 2001, the very day that Siemon would perfect her position as role player against undefeated and top ranked Connecticut, arguably the biggest game in Notre Dame history to that point, Kelley ironically wore a football lineman's pad to protect a left hand she had broken just two days earlier against Virginia Tech.

"I really don't know how I broke it," Siemon said. "It was some kind of impact injury."

After swallowing some pain pills and then some more pills to calm a queasy stomach caused by the pain pills, Kelley took the floor feeling more like a M*A*S*H patient than a 21-year-old woman about to play against the perennial best team in the nation.

But it was to be the day that Siemon stepped forward for good. It was the day she changed her role from support player to a secondary star. She scored 15 points and almost as importantly provided a chilling emotional lift when she appeared on the floor after two days of doctors' visits and indecision.

"I had told the newspapers that I wasn't sure I was going to play, just in case Connecticut was reading the paper," Kelley said. "But there was no way I was going to miss this game."

The day that would define Kelley as the "S" in what *Chicago Tribune* writer Bill Jauss would later call the "IRS," standing for Ivey, Riley, and Siemon.

And it was the addition of the "S" to the Irish senior "s-two" (of Riley and Ivey) that would make the team complete in the month of March.

Siemon came to Notre Dame as part of a highly touted recruiting class. At Edina (MN) High School, she was named honorable mention *USA Today* All-American and as a senior averaged 21 points and 11 rebounds a game. She was the school's all-time scoring leader (of both boys and girls) with more than 1,418 points and also set the school record for rebounding.

Her AAU team won two national championships (1995 and 1997) and Kelley was eventually selected as one of 10 finalists for the honor of Miss Basketball in Minnesota.

Siemon was equally impressive in volleyball, setting a school record for blocks in a game (22) and being named three-time all-conference.

"Athletics was always a big family thing for us," Kelley said. "I can remember playing basketball in the front yard and throwing the football around. It wasn't until late in junior high where I realized that I was pretty good. Up until then, it didn't matter if I was the star of the team or whatever, I just had fun playing.

"My parents never pushed me to play, nor did they ever coach a team I was on, although my dad did coach a flag football team I was on once and all my friends thought it was a big deal to be coached by a real football player."

Success followed her into high school as well. "I think I'm one of those players who underestimates herself," Siemon said. "I think I'm good, but I don't think I'm great. In our school, you could try out for the varsity as a freshman, but if you didn't make it, you would be put on the freshman team, not the JV team.

"I was not going to try out for the varsity, but I had some friends who were juniors on the team tell me that I would make the team. I was so nervous when I tried out, but I made the team, started as a freshman and played every game for four years. I had a great coach named Jenny Johnson, who helped me out tremendously. She really focused on the positives and the things you did well but at the same time she would recognize the negatives and help you correct them.

"I was and still am very athletic," Kelley continued. "I can run the floor and I shoot pretty well. I've always been a role player and not necessarily a standout. When I was a senior, Coach Johnson told me to shoot the ball 20 times a game. Prior to that, I think I was taking about eight. I did it, but I just didn't feel it was my place."

Siemon played volleyball simply because she loved the sport. Volleyball and singing in the school choir are among her fondest memories of those years.

"We had such a great choir," Kelley said, her eyes now dancing. "It wasn't like that 'nerdy choir' thing at all. It was something really special for me."

Siemon also enjoyed playing on the AAU team that won two national championships. "Actually, that is where I first saw Ruth Riley play," Kelley said. "She was a great player then, too."

It was also where McGraw got her first view of Siemon.

"I was actually at the tournament to look at another player," McGraw said. "But I noticed Kelley right away and thought she was the better player. I liked everything about her. I thought she had a lot of positive energy, she ran the floor well, and she rebounded well.

"She wasn't afraid to bang around and mix it up. She was obviously a tough kid. She even took charges. I loved it."

McGraw told recruiting coordinator Carol Owens to check Kelley out.

Kelley was ready for the recruiting onslaught. Her father helped her design a strategy to keep the confusion to a minimum.

"I prepared about 50 to 60 form letters which I mailed out to schools that I was pretty sure would be trying to recruit me but which I knew I had no interest in attending. On those letters, I thanked them for their interest but told them not to bother.

"As it was, I narrowed my choices down to five schools — Notre Dame, Duke, Wisconsin, Iowa, and Iowa State. I made visits to all except Duke, which canceled mine after they had signed another player. Notre Dame was my last visit and I remember trying to sort out the pros and the cons of the other three schools before my visit to South Bend.

"Each school had its own positives and negatives," she continued, "and I remember asking my mom how I would know when the right school came along. She just told me that I would know."

Kelley had spiritual help in her decision. By that time, her father had begun a group called "Search Ministries," a non-denominational ministry designed to help both Christians and non-Christians deal with the tougher questions in life. Which school to attend was, for Kelley, one of the toughest decisions she had ever had to make.

"My whole family had been praying about it. I am a very strong Christian and I had been praying about my decision for a long time. I really didn't know anything at all about the basketball program before I got here. But I had talked to Coach Owens on the phone and she is a Christian and that was very important because there would be someone on the staff I could relate to spiritually, and that was a real positive.

"My parents and I visited Notre Dame on a beautiful fall football weekend," Kelley continued, "and Notre Dame was playing one of the service academies. Notre Dame ended up losing, and we walked around a lot on campus. My mom remembers me leaning over to her while we were strolling the quad and saying, 'Mom, I think this is it.'"

Her mom just smiled and kept her mouth shut.

"My parents had always tried to keep from saying too much to influence my decision, and so she told me to wait until the weekend was over," Kelley said. "We went to Coach McGraw's for dinner and afterwards we played some games like Charades and stuff, which is so much like what my family does. That evening, Coach pulled me aside at the house and offered me a spot. I didn't say yes immediately because I wanted to make sure."

McGraw unintentionally got some help from Jeff Siemon's football connections that weekend, too. Jeff knew Lou Holtz, the Irish football head coach at the time, from his own playing days and arranged a chat with Holtz on the Friday.

"That was Lou's last year at Notre Dame," Kelley recalled, "but he could have sold Notre Dame to anybody. Everything he said was so positive. What stuck with me was when he said he had never seen an institution that is actually better on the inside than it looks from the outside.

"Notre Dame has such prestige and such an aura about it and here he was saying it was even better on the inside. Everyone I talked to that weekend felt the same way.

"I could have told them Sunday night that I had accepted, but I waited until Tuesday," Kelley said. "It was a very happy day for everyone."

So, Kelley hit campus in the fall of 1997. A little dazed, a little scared, a little homesick. Just like every other freshman at Notre Dame.

It was at her first calculus class where she met the person who was to become her best friend off the court. Ellen Quinn and Kelley would find out they had a lot in common, including living just down the hall from each other.

It would be Quinn to whom Siemon would talk about boyfriends, and God, and family, and classes. It would be Quinn who would type a letter to Coach McGraw explaining how frustrated Kelley was in her junior year — and then not send it.

It would also be Quinn who would go to every single home game that Kelley played in, except two.

"My seats were in the yellow section, right across from the team," Quinn said. "Kelley always knew where to find me. For the first three years, I could arrive anytime I wanted to and my seat would be open. My senior year, I had to get there early sometimes just to get a bleacher seat."

"Good for the team," Quinn concluded, "but what about my seat?"

Siemon started her first practice the way all freshmen do under McGraw. "I was so nervous at the first practice," she said. "The upperclassmen had told me that Coach McGraw is a perfectionist and she has a bit of a temper when things go wrong. I sure didn't want to be the one she yelled at. I had never played for a coach that got mad when things went wrong. It was hard to get used to it at first, but I got used to it."

Then history repeated itself in Kelley's life. She was named to the starting lineup for the first game of the season.

"Kelley started the first game because she rebounded better and ran the floor better than anyone else to that time," McGraw said. "She had a great freshman season, including 20 points in overtime at UCLA when she went 12-of-12 from the free-throw line."

"Starting that first game was not something I expected at all," Siemon said. "I remember coming into practice thinking that I wouldn't play at all until I was a junior. I figured I would be that girl sitting at the end of the bench. Really I think that being on that great AAU team helped me prepare for college ball. Our AAU team played a very fast game and everyone on the team was a great player.

"At Notre Dame, I don't know if my skills were as good as other people's and it was hard to play over some of the upper-classmen, but they were all very good about it. Another reason I think I started is because we had just graduated Katryna Gaither and Roseanne Bohman and there were some holes to fill there."

She exceeded expectations, scoring 11 points in her first game in a 71-65 win over Butler. She followed that up with a 10-point performance while her team got stomped at Duke.

Her best game of the year soon followed, that 20-point performance in a 93-91 double-overtime gut-check win at Pauley Pavilion against UCLA. She went on to start 30 of the 32 games that year and averaged eight points and five rebounds while playing over 23 minutes a game for the 22-10 team.

Her tournament play was impressive and included 10 points and seven rebounds in the 74-59 upset over sixth-ranked and top-seeded Texas Tech in Lubbock.

But all was not well in Siemon's life.

"I think I fell into the idea that athletes are not supposed to do well in school. I had maintained an A-minus average all through high school, but when I got here I decided to do just enough to get by. My whole goal in life was and still is to get married and be a great mom and wife and so my thought was I didn't need good grades. My future husband wasn't going to look at my résumé."

In addition, Kelley chose to test her wings in the college social scene.

"I was out quite a bit my freshman year. I wasn't doing anything terrible or bad, but I wasn't adhering to my Christian upbringing. So that summer I went home and began thinking about my freshman year and how I had done some stuff that I really considered wrong. It was definitely a low point for me."

Having a best friend like Quinn really helped.

"I met Ellen early in my freshman year and we just sort of

became instant friends. She was a person I identified with very well because we both have similar backgrounds and are very family-oriented as well as strong Christians.

"There were many nights that Ellen and I would get kicked out of our rooms because our roommates wanted to sleep, so we would just sit on the floor in the hall and talk about families and practices [Ellen played field hockey] and who we were going to invite to our weddings. I really needed her for that outlet and as a friend not on the basketball team."

She came back to her sophomore year with a new perspective and her motivation crystallized in the form of a campus group called ISI (Iron Sharpens Iron).

"A friend of mine took me to the meeting and I heard a couple of speeches and that is when it all happened for me," Kelley said. "I knew I had an empty feeling in my heart and I asked myself if I wanted to spend my four years of college living that way. God told me it was time to come back to what I believe and do those things."

Her sophomore year, though easier socially, proved more frustrating on the court. "I was the epitome of the sophomore slump," she said. "To be honest with you, I put a lot of expectations on myself and the coaches had their own of me. As a freshman, you have no expectations. You put them on the floor and if they do well, that's great. But now I was a sophomore and I could not use the freshman excuse. So it was tough.

"I did not have that peaceful feeling in practice that I had done this before and I now knew what to expect. I felt just the opposite. I felt like I had all this pressure on me."

The McGraw coaching style that year added to the pressure. "Coach McGraw that year was a coach who would pull you out when you made a mistake," Siemon said. "That was very difficult for me to adjust to because no other coach had done that.

"For some players, it doesn't bother them, but my confidence went downhill. I was in there thinking that I could not mess up a play or do certain things because I would get pulled out. It upset my game and made me very nervous. It was definitely something I wasn't used to."

Still, Siemon started every game except Senior Day. However, her offensive output began to decline as the team began to use the inside power of Riley and balance that with the outside sharp-shooting of senior Sheila McMillen.

Siemon averaged 5.8 points, playing 20 minutes a game, splitting time with junior Julie Henderson as a sophomore.

Siemon lost her starting position in her junior year, as Henderson joined Riley, Danielle Green, Niele Ivey, and freshman Alicia Ratay as the starting unit. However, Siemon adjusted to her role of coming off the bench remarkably well, placing second on the team in rebounding despite playing less than half the game. She recorded a career-high 23-point game on February 1 in a 90-60 romp at Providence and the next game recorded a career-high 14 rebounds at home in a 72-59 win over Boston College. She would tie that rebound mark in a second-round NCAA 95-60 win over George Washington.

Siemon recovered her starting position as a senior, solidifying it with a season-high 21-point performance in a 83-56 pasting of Wisconsin in Notre Dame's third game of the season. As the season rolled on, the opponents began to double and triple-team Riley, leaving Siemon open.

McGraw had changed the offense from the Chicago Bulls' triangle offense to more of a motion offense that allowed Siemon to drive to the bucket more. Though she will be forever remembered for her inspiring 15-point, eight-rebound performance versus UConn on January 15, she gave her best performance of the year in the 54-53 loss at Rutgers, scoring 19 points and pulling down 15 rebounds.

Her gutsy performance against UConn on January 15 solidified her position as the ultimate role player. Playing with a cast on her broken hand, Siemon inspired the Irish to their first win in history over UConn in front of their first ever sellout at the JACC, and eventually their first No.1 ranking.

"Ruth was on fire that day," Siemon said, "so she was really the star. But the press coverage I got astounded me. I think any player in that position would have done the same thing I did. I was just doing the best I could."

The press coverage changed Kelley's off-court life also.

"A couple of days later, I was on a date and we went to a local movie theater. The lights were still up and as we walked to our seats, a lady recognized me and called out, "Hey, Kelley...Great job." Other people recognized me and starting saying things like that too. Suddenly someone stood up in their seat and started clapping for me. It's a good thing the lights went down because my face was really red."

Mall trips also became more difficult. The girl with the friendly personality, cover-girl looks, and God-given athletic abilities proved irresistible to the general populace of South Bend, who now rushed to embrace their new heroes.

Kelley spent more time taking pictures and signing autographs in the University Park Mall food court than she did eating there. "Being a celebrity was really neat, I think," Kelley said. "I didn't care that a ton of people were asking for my autograph. I really enjoyed it.

"The neatest part was seeing the little kids and the impact we made on them. I had little girls almost crying talking to me and they were saying, 'You are my favorite player.' I would never want to be someone like Michael Jordan. I can't imagine being in that spot. It is a scary spot to be in because you cannot slip up, even once."

After the UConn game, Siemon sat out three straight games but returned to the lineup with her new role as a secondary star firmly in her mind. She scored in double figures in 10 of her last 11 games wearing the Irish uniform, a streak normally reserved for the Rileys and the Ratays.

The S in the IRS had arrived late, but she had definitely arrived. Teams now had to be concerned with Siemon as well as Riley and Ratay. It was a not-so-subtle change in the Irish offense, but it was to be the change which would propel them to the White House as National Champs.

The emergence of the more aggressive play of Kelley down the stretch was the final piece to the Irish puzzle. It would be what carried her through those final few frantic seconds in St. Louis.

The role player had become a star.

Kelley doesn't allow many conversations to go very long anymore without letting the listener know that she is a strong Christian. And her actions speak louder than words. She feels she is following God's wishes by turning down an offer to play for the LA Sparks in the WNBA.

"I really didn't think I was WNBA material until late in my

senior year," she said. "I was invited to the combine [a league tryout of sorts] and a group of coaches from the Sparks took an interest in me and sat down with me to talk about my play.

"The focus was on some of the more negative aspects of my game and it just wasn't a good feeling when I left the room. Just about the same time, I heard about an Athletes in Action [AIA] tour which was going to Prague. Believe it or not, Prague is one place I have always wanted to go. I had heard so many unbelievable things about it and I knew I wanted to play with that team.

"But I had no idea what God wanted me to do. I prayed about it so much. I didn't want to close any doors.

"When I was drafted by the Sparks on the third round, out of all the teams that could have drafted me, I felt it was God speaking directly to me. It was the one team I didn't feel comfortable about and yet it was the one team I was drafted by. I felt that it was such an answer to prayer, but being human I needed a little more assurance."

She would get that assurance a few days later. "A friend of mine and I were discussing the urgency of being a Christian one day in his car. And about spreading the Word to people who don't know the Word, and all of the sudden it hit me. Prague was where I belonged, spreading the Word as well as playing basketball.

"That was what I wanted to do. I was just getting out of his car when all of the sudden a very peaceful feeling came over me. I broke into a huge smile and I felt like a big weight had been lifted off me. God had spoken, and I was going to Prague."

So, maybe it is Kelley Siemon's time to be the role player again, just not on the basketball court. Maybe the role playing she did on the courts in Edina and South Bend was just preparation for something much larger in the overall scheme of things.

Maybe the national championship was just the way the personal path has been prepared for the daughter of a football-playing preacher. Maybe her next role will be played in a much larger arena than she has ever played.

Maybe, she thinks, God needs a good role player.

CHAPTER 5

ALSO STARRING...

MEAGHAN LEAHY

Fourteen-year-old Meaghan Leahy had been tossed out of her eighth-grade classroom again.

Banished to the hallway for the umpteenth time, Meaghan sat in the dimly lit passage with her mind racing.

Why can't I concentrate?" she wondered. "Why do all the other kids laugh at me? Why do the teachers not want me in their class?"

It seemed to her that her world was always moving. Like an older person with Parkinson's disease is not able to control their limbs, Meaghan knew she could not control her thoughts.

Simple paragraphs escaped her. Trying to concentrate in class was like trying to pick up marbles spilling out of a bag. Just about the time she grabbed one, another fell out.

Meaghan, at age 14, was frustrated, alone, and wondering if she was a loser.

She would soon find out that, in life, there really are no excuses. At least none that anyone wants to hear about.

"I have ADD," Meaghan Leahy said one sunny Saturday afternoon in May 2001. It was finals week, and not only was she going to graduate with her senior class, but she was going to graduate with honors — and was going to do it wearing an NCAA national championship ring.

"My mom and I talk about if we went back to my junior high school, they never would believe that I graduated from Notre Dame," Meaghan laughed. It is a winner's laugh. This battle won. On to the next battle.

No excuses.

ADD is Attention Deficit Disorder. It is a brain disorder that keeps people from concentrating in what many consider a normal manner. Not only does Leahy have ADD, but she also has ADHD, which is Attention Deficit Hyperactive Disorder. Not only was she unable to concentrate as a youngster, she simply couldn't sit still.

ADHD is perhaps one of the cruelest of disorders for young people. The only symptom is a constant need for movement. Youngsters with the disorder are in trouble in school, excluded from parties, and are subjected to ridicule at the worst of all possible times, early youth and puberty.

Meaghan Leahy's biggest accomplishment in life has been overcoming herself.

"I view ADD as simply an obstacle I was given," she said. "Everyone has some obstacle or another. But I was getting kicked off the school bus pretty often in junior high school as well as being tossed out of class. I was a mess."

Leahy left the public school system after a horrendous eighth-grade year. Her parents enrolled her at the nearby Suffield Academy (Connecticut) as a day student. "Suffield Academy and Notre Dame are the two best things that ever happened to me," she said.

At Suffield, basketball head coach Dennis Kinne and assistant coach Lisa Tenerowicz became teachers, mentors, and eventually friends of the now-towering youngster.

It was at Suffield where teachers, who knew Leahy's SAT scores were high, would recommend that Meaghan go to a psychologist, and it was the psychologist who diagnosed the ADHD. "It was embarrassing to go through it, but it turns out my dad has it also. I really didn't know much about it," Meaghan recalls.

It was also at Suffield that Meaghan would meet her best friend in high school, a young man named Brian Hetzel. He also had ADD and spent one long July afternoon with her the day after she had been diagnosed. It was a long discussion, it was a hard discussion, and it was a unifying discussion.

Hetzel and Leahy would become great friends — friends understand what others don't know.

It was her mother, Molly, who impressed in Meaghan that it was her responsibility to deal with the affliction. "My mom, once we had it figured out, told me that I could use ADD as an explanation, not an excuse," Meaghan said.

No excuses.

It has been Leahy's approach to life ever since. The 6-foot-3 post player was one of the most sought after players in the country in 1997 after leading her Suffield (CT) Academy to two straight Prep Class A state championships.

In her four years as a starter, Leahy's teams were an amazing 85-2 and Meaghan averaged 24.3 points per game, 11 rebounds, and four blocked shots. Three times she was named New England Prep Player of the Year and she was named honorable mention on the USA Today All-America Team.

Pretty heady stuff for a teenager. She was invited at the last minute to the WBCA camp, a camp where top players from across the nation play in front of Division I coaches. Connecticut had invited her, and it was the camp where she met her future best friend, Ruth Riley.

"Ruth and I and another girl went out for lunch, and I was telling Ruth that I really liked UConn and Ruth was telling me that she really liked Notre Dame, " Leahy recalled.

After a telephone number mix-up, McGraw was finally able to contact Leahy two weeks later and invited her out to South Bend for a visit. This was the weekend of the Ohio State football game and when she arrived, Leahy thought she recognized one of the other players there for her official visit. It was Riley.

"We were both real quiet that weekend," Leahy said. "But I don't think Ruth said 10 words. Coach McGraw really tried to get to know me as a person and that was quite a difference.

"I had originally decided that it was between Boston College and UConn, but I canceled those visits and committed shortly after the visit to South Bend. The whole recruiting process wasn't that stressful for me, although it was for some of my friends. My parents were actually pretty laid back about it."

Leahy and Riley would become friends off the court and combatants on.

"Freshman year, I was very nervous. We all were. But the whole freshman group really stuck together, especially me and Ruth at the post. Sometimes we would look at each other and our eyes would be welling up with frustration. Now we joke about it.

"I used to come off the bench to play before she did. People think Ruth had everything handed to her, but she really had to work her butt off for everything. Imani Dunbar and I started to bond toward the end of the year because we were coming in at cleanup time."

"I remember meeting with Coach at the end of the season for my review and saying, 'I'm so sorry, I didn't play well and I let you down," Leahy said. "Coach looked at me and said, 'Whoa, wait a minute, this was only your freshman year.'"

At the end of that freshman year, Leahy was confused and disappointed. "I was questioning my purpose and what I was adding to the team," Leahy said. "I did a lot of soul searching during the summer. I knew I would never be an all-star, but at the end of the summer I understood my role better."

Her role, as it turned out, was to make the first team better.

"Imani and I almost took over the second team and we created pride in it," Leahy said. "During practice, we wanted to beat them 4-on-4 or 5-on-5 and a lot of times we did. We were trying to get under their skin and it was always great to see us score and then have Coach pull the first team over into a huddle. We knew we could play."

Leahy accepted her role so well that she wrote a letter back to her old high school team, addressed to all the girls who didn't play that much. "I explained that I had forgotten sometimes where they were coming from when I played there," Leahy said. "That, because I was a starter, I didn't even know where they were coming from."

"It was very important for Meaghan and Imani to keep their attitudes up despite their playing time," Assistant Coach Kevin McGuff said. "Everyone on the team had a different role, and if Ruth kept hearing Meaghan complaining about her playing time, it would have affected Ruth's play. Meaghan and Imani accepting their roles was absolutely critical. That demonstrated how good our team chemistry was."

Leahy was smart enough to understand that.

"The great thing about the championship team," Leahy said. "was that we all understood our roles. Usually I know I'm not going to play a lot and I accept that, but this year everyone knew that we were going for something bigger and people put their personal stuff aside."

Getting through Notre Dame wasn't easy for Leahy. Since being diagnosed, Leahy has settled on a drug regimen that allows her to concentrate better.

"I had to write a paper about what it was like having ADD," she said. "And it is kind of like a kaleidoscope. Without ADD, the kaleidoscope either never turns, or it turns slowly. With ADD, it is turning faster and faster. For instance, if I'm reading a paragraph, I lose concentration halfway through.

"I mostly have trouble in classes and in long basketball practices," she continued. "I really struggled learning the defenses. One small change and it will have an entirely different name and I always wondered how am I ever going to remember. So I had to make up ways to remember it."

Leahy graduated with a 2.9 GPA (essentially a B average). "I treat ADD like a learning disability," she said. "I take extended-time exams in most classes, where they allow me extra time. I did not take the SAT with extended time, although I could have. I didn't want that notation with the implication on my application."

Like most players on the Notre Dame team, the UConn win in January was the one of the bigger events in Leahy's life.

"Just coming out of the locker room and hearing the crowd, it was hard for me to run out because I had chills so bad," Leahy said. "It was exactly what I dreamed of when I signed to come to Notre Dame — to play before a soldout home crowd against UConn and beat them. In my area, we call it UConn Mania. People were asking me when I chose to come to Notre Dame, how I could choose not to go to UConn. My parents and best friend had flown out for the game and I came out of the locker room after the game and couldn't handle my emotions. I just had to sit down and cry."

Leahy has plans to follow her mom into the field of educational psychology. "First, I'm going backpacking in Europe," she said. "Then I have some connections for grad school. I want to help younger kids with ADD. I still have the disorder and I know I'm going to do what I can with it. Everyone has to overcome something."

Without excuses.

IMANI DUNBAR

Imani Dunbar knows about divine intervention.

No, she doesn't believe that the hand of God swatted away the last gasp Purdue shot that allowed the Irish to win the national crown. God didn't make Notre Dame No. 1.

Instead, she can point to three instances of divine intervention that brought her to Notre Dame, kept her there, and then gave her the greatest moment in her life.

Dunbar grew up in California but moved to San Angelo, Texas, as she headed into her sophomore year in high school. She thought she had the talent to play Division I basketball, but she knew big-time coaches rarely visit San Angelo.

During her senior year, she averaged almost 15 points a game while leading her team to a 26-7 record and its first-ever appearance in the top 10 in the state rankings.

She made the all-West Texas Super Team. Still, the coaches weren't calling. So she used her growing interest in media and technology to put together her own highlight film. She shipped the film to 20 different schools. Notre Dame wasn't even close to being on the list.

Enter the Divine.

One of the highlight films landed on the desk of Vanderbilt coach Jim Foster, who had just signed a point guard. Foster, a longtime friend and mentor of Muffet McGraw, knew the Irish had a spot open as the signing season was coming to a close. He decided to pass the Dunbar highlights along to McGraw.

Muffet liked what she saw. She invited Imani to campus.

"We were in the building where the Golden Dome is and they were reconstructing it at the time," Dunbar recalled. "It was a very rainy, gloomy day and I was supposed to meet with my academic adviser, and here I was sitting in the hall with all this mess all around me.

"But it was the sunniest gloomy day of my life. My mom and I decided that night at the Jamison Inn that this is what I wanted to do."

Imani verbally committed on the last day of her visit, two days before the signing deadline.

"I remember the scene exactly," Imani said. "I heard Coach saying, 'I would like to formally extend you the invitation to play basketball here at Notre Dame.' Instantly, I responded, 'And I would like to formally accept.' Carol Owens said, 'Welcome to the family,' and we jumped up and hugged everybody. And I thought, 'Oh my God, this just went down.'"

This isn't one of those happily-ever-after stories. Dunbar found plenty of gloom under the Golden Dome.

"It was after my freshman year and I had really struggled academically, on the basketball floor, and socially. It was the beginning of summer school and I was rooming with Meaghan and all I really wanted to do was go home. Her and her friends went out for something to eat and I just got lower and lower. Finally I just lost it."

Enter God again.

"I couldn't sleep very well that night because I was so upset. I woke up at 3 AM and I told God he had to give me a sign, just give me a sign. I tossed and turned and finally decided to go to the bathroom.

"First of all, you need to know that there is never a radio on at 3 AM and, secondly, that the station that happened to be on the radio is one we never play. But that night, in the bathroom, there is a radio on and it is on this station, and on comes this song called 'Hold on' by the Sounds of Blackness.

"The song talks about holding on because God is coming to help. I broke down right there. I was like, 'Wow, that's as close to speaking to me as God is ever going to get. I still refer to that moment when I feel the whole world is closing in on me.'"

Imani is a technology aficionado and began taping the women's off-court activities midway through the championship season. She, in short, has the goods on her teammates.

This team's success was made as much off the court as it was on the court. Dunbar toted her camera to the dinners, on the bus trips, on the plane flights, and into the locker room. The arrival of the team at the St. Louis airport was all dutifully recorded by Imani.

"It didn't really hit me that we were in the Final Four until we got off the plane in St. Louis and there was a huge crowd of people waiting to see us," she said. "I know they were all there for Niele, but there were a lot of kids wearing our jerseys and nuns screaming and everything.

"We were thinking 'Wow, this is amazing.' Niele gave us a tour of the city and I thought their arch was supposed to be a double arch, like McDonald's arches. That was when it hit me that we were in the Final Four."

Imani was on the bench for the final few frantic seconds of the championship game. Her role as a senior had been to keep the second team motivated, even though they would not see a lot of playing time.

She and Meaghan Leahy had bonded the second unit together, making the first team keep their edge during practice. Now, she stood with the rest of her teammates as Riley decided their destiny.

"Ruth hit her first free throw, and Purdue calls timeout and Ruth comes over to our bench punching her fists in the air and screaming. 'Come on you guys, we've got it now.' And I'm thinking to myself, 'Girl, you're the one with the free throw. You've got it now.' I knew she would hit the second one and so did she.'"

"We actually had a great game plan after the free throw," Dunbar continued. "We had our defense set and were ready for whatever came. But I swear, in those two seconds from the time Katie Douglas shot the ball until the time the game ended, five minutes worth of stuff happened.

"Meaghan was grabbing onto me on the bench, trying to hold me off the court. Then it looked to us like Cooper traveled before she passed to Douglas. Then it looked like Douglas was outside the 3-point line. Then it looked like she wasn't, but we couldn't tell. And then it looked like the shot was going in and then it hit the rim and didn't and then it was pandemonium."

Enter God again.

"When the shot rolled out, it was one big blur," Dunbar continued. "Meaghan took off and we stormed the court. We were hugging everybody. For that single moment in time, for the first time in my life, there was no more hunger in the world, no more violence in the world.

"For that single moment, with all of us jumping up and down and hugging each other on that court in St. Louis, everything was perfect."

"It was," Dunbar said "as close to heaven as I've ever been."

Possibly.

ALICIA RATAY

If Alicia Ratay were a guy, she would be Clint Eastwood.

The Dirty Harry version of Clint Eastwood.

The "Go ahead, make my day" Eastwood of few words and all results.

For Ratay, for all her youthful appearance, has the heart and mind of a gunslinger.

A cold-blooded poker-faced gunslinger.

They don't call her "Dead-eye Ratay" for nothing.

Her job is to fire three-pointers into the hearts of her opponents.

The 5-foot-11 six-gun for McGraw's team takes her job seriously, and she does it well.

As a matter of fact, she does it better than anyone in the country. During the championship season, she nailed 76-of-139 3-point shots, an amazing 54.7 percent.

Yet her expression on the court never changes. Even if she has just scored four straight threes, she has that Eastwood look, bored and a little angry.

If she has just missed four straight threes, she still looks bored and a little angry.

Her cold, expressionless game face belies her competitive heart. Her specialty is inspiring her team with timely threes or maybe driving stakes into the other team's hopes with the same.

Ratay is a basketball purebred. Her grandmother played basketball, her mom played basketball, her dad played basketball, her sister played basketball, her brother played basketball.

You get the idea.

She is the student most likely never to say anything during class. She is also the student most likely to answer the following essay question as follows:

Q: Discuss the results of World War II

A (According to Ratay): We won.

She started playing organized ball in the third grade. While her female friends were off doing whatever little girls do during recess, Alicia and a friend would wander over to the basketball court and take on the boys.

"I was always into sports," she said. "I used to play in our driveway and pretend I was the commentator.

"I've really worked on my shooting," Ratay said. "I used to shoot a lot when I was in high school, and my mom used to come out and help me with my form and stuff. But she would never push me. It was definitely me wanting to play the game."

Alicia is soft-spoken, her voice often straining the ears of the listener. She prefers to let her shooting percentages do the talking. Highly recruited out of college, Alicia narrowed her choice down to Duke and Notre Dame.

To get to Notre Dame, Alicia's mom would have only to drive two hours from her Lake Zurich (IL) home, around a lake. To get to Duke, it was a 12-hour trip around the lake, through the prairies, and across the Appalachians.

Notre Dame won.

"When I came on my unofficial visit, I did not know anything at all about Notre Dame," she said. "But it was a really fun football weekend and you could tell the people really push for Notre Dame. I came in knowing that we had a chance for the national championship. I knew Ruth would be great as a senior and she had Kelly and Niele around her."

She called Coach McGraw after she had decided to accept the invitation to attend Notre Dame. According to Matt McGraw, who answered the phone, the conversation went something like this:

Alicia: Hi, this is Alicia. Is Coach there?

Matt: Yes.

Alicia: Can I talk to her?

Matt: Sure. (He hands the phone to Muffet)

Alicia: Hi, Coach. I'm coming.

Muffet: Great.

Alicia: Bye.

End of conversation.

Even Ratay, however, had a case of nerves when she arrived on campus. "I was really nervous for my first practice," Ratay said. "I did not want to be the one screwing up. The college pace was a lot quicker than high school and I knew it would be a hard adjustment."

Hard, but not impossible. Ratay stepped right into the 3-spot (small forward or shooting guard) vacated the year before by her near look-alike, Sheila McMillen.

McGraw knew Ratay was good, but it was her two 3-point shots late in regulation — one of which was a buzzer-beater — in a surprising 78-74 win over Rutgers on February 19, 2000, that told her that, even as a freshman, Ratay had star potential. The Rutgers miracle, as some called it, ended with two magnificent shots by the freshman.

Notre Dame was down by six with 26 seconds left in that game. McGraw had called a timeout, and everyone in the huddle knew the ball was going to Alicia. Her first shot was a fairly open one, according to McGraw, but the second one as time ran out was made with three people guarding her.

"We still have a tape of when that second shot went in," McGraw said. "And her expression never changed. Me, I was jumping up and down, and we were all trying to hug her. But she was getting mad, telling us to get off her because we had to play overtime. Of course, I straightened myself up right away," laughed McGraw, "and I said, 'Yeah, you guys, let's go. We still have five minutes to play.' It was an incredible moment."

Ratay would provide more incredible moments. In basketball, there is nothing as exciting as when a 3-point expert gets hot and puts up a flurry of points to either bring her team back or widen the gap for good.

A shooter shoots. And Ratay is a shooter extraordinaire. "I don't think about the 'zone' she said. "I just keep shooting. If it goes in, it goes in."

Gunslingers are, of course, a lonely group, so it wasn't surprising to find Ratay alone in her Varsity Club hotel room that January day before the UConn game. Ratay likes to focus, to block everything out, and, on that day in particular, the sophomore wanted and needed to be alone.

The game face needed to be on. The gunslinger needed to concentrate. Game time could not come fast enough.

"It was amazing to arrive at the JACC," Ratay said, "and to see all those people there. We knew it was a sellout and all that, but to walk out on the court for the shoot-around an hour before the game and see the place more than half-full really pumped us. I was really excited. I couldn't wait to get started."

But the game face was clearly on. Her Eastwood expression never changed as she went through warmups, never changed as the National Anthem rang out in the JACC, never changed as the lights went out and the players named were announced.

"That's when I started getting nervous," Ratay said. That's what she says, but you couldn't tell it by her face.

UConn never saw the Irish onslaught coming.

"The crowd definitely helped us out. UConn had no one backing them and the place was really wild," Ratay said. "The crowd stormed the floor after the game as if it had won the national championship."

Ratay and her teammates were enveloped in a huge crowd of blue and gold well-wishers amid a wild celebration.

"The campus was electric that night," Ratay said. "Everyone was congratulating us."

It would be an hour before Ratay would finish with her post-game interviews, take her shower, and finally head back to her room at Lewis Hall.

Ratay had other things on her mind, however, as her Altima swung out of the parking lot and headed for her dorm room. Second-semester classes were to begin the next day.

Still, you only beat the best team in the nation once or twice in your life. You only play before the first full house in Notre Dame's women's basketball history once. You only get to put your team into the No. 1 spot in the nation for the first time in school history once.

Even gunslingers understand that.

So, as her Altima eased through the dusk of a cold January afternoon in South Bend, Dead-Eye Ratay finally did about the last thing you'd expect a poker-face gunslinger to do.

She cried.

ERICKA HANEY

Getting cut from the cheerleading squad in seventh grade almost crushed little Ericka Haney.

But it proved to be one of the best things that ever happened to her.

Haney had never played much basketball until she was 12, but when the alley that led to a cheerleading career suddenly was blocked, Haney got bored.

So she decided to play sports.

Eight years later, she's wearing a national championship ring.

Life does strange things sometimes.

Haney, as it turns out, is a natural basketball player. She wasn't supposed to be a cheerleader. She is supposed to be the one the cheerleaders cheer for.

"I started playing basketball when I was in seventh grade," the 6-foot-1 small forward said. "I guess basketball was just something that came naturally. I got picked to play on an AAU team, and that is where I got better competition. I found I loved the game."

She also found out the game loved her. She was a two-time, first-team all-state selection and in her senior year led Toledo (OH) Central Catholic to a final 25-2 record and an appearance in the state semi-finals.

That year, Ericka averaged over 16 points and 10 rebounds a game and was named Toledo Player of the Year and Metro Player of the Year. Nationally, Haney was listed among the top 40 seniors by Blue Star Basketball, as well as being chosen honorable mention for All-America Teams chosen by *USA Today* and *Street & Smith's.*

The trick was getting her out of Ohio. She was recruited heavily by Ohio State and was also considering Georgia before Notre Dame entered the picture.

"Notre Dame came late in my recruiting process," Haney said. "First, I got a letter. Then after they could invite me for a visit, they called. They seemed pretty nice and something clicked, so I decided to give them a visit.

"It seemed like a family environment as a team and the surrounding community embraced you and made sure you minded your P's and Q's. My mom kind of liked the atmosphere, so she persuaded me to come.

"Ohio State was all about keeping players from Ohio in Ohio. They had the three top players in there for a visit all at once, and so they wanted to keep us all together.

But "Three-point Jesus" was waiting at Notre Dame.

"When I walked on the campus and saw Touchdown Jesus I was impressed. It seemed like a calm, collected, traditional sort of place. It was a place I was comfortable with. I was very comfortable with the coaches and the players, so that had a major impact on my decision."

Academics are the main challenge Haney and her teammates have to face off the court. "Keeping up with the classwork is very hard," she said. "Sometimes we have to do our homework in between or on flights. Catching up this last season has been hard because it is the longest season we have ever had. I really had to learn how to manage my time well.

"I usually communicate with my professors over email. I will arrange things with them, and that is the most important part, the relationship with the professors. Most of it is individual. I mean you have to do it on your own. Some professors are great with athletes, others try not to cross the student-athlete line.

"Personally, I think athletes need some advantages because the regular students are here every day and we aren't," she said.

Niele Ivey was the on-court emotional leader, according to Haney.

"Niele has a joke for everything, and she keeps everyone on their toes. She used to imitate Coach when Coach wasn't there, and it was a riot. One practice Niele told us to scream every time Coach said a particular word. I think the word was defense and every time she said it, we would all scream. It didn't take long for Coach to catch on.

"Another time, we all hid from Coach before practice in the JACC. We were supposed to be stretching out and we all hid out behind the seats. Coach came out, got the idea, and said, 'Come out, come out wherever you are' and no one moved. A few seconds later, she threatened us with laps and we all came out in a snap."

Haney has enjoyed watching McGraw balance the demands of her job with keeping a strong family bond. "I found it amazing at the Final Four, where she was being pulled in 100 different ways. It is amazing how she can balance it all. She and Matt are really great together."

JENEKA JOYCE

The 5-foot-9 guard came into the season with high expectations. But she missed 10 games early in the season. That not only set her progress back, but it probably kept her from serious contention for a starting job.

Joyce hails from Washburn Rural High School where she averaged 21 points, 4.3 rebounds, 2.4 assists, and 1.8 steals in her senior year. That led to a *Parade* All-American (third team) selection. In addition, Joyce, was a two-time *Street & Smith's* All American honoree as well as being named to the Adidas and Nike All-American squad.

She was highly recruited in high school but chose Notre Dame because of the academics, the opportunity to play for a Top 5 basketball program, and the family atmosphere she felt in South Bend.

Unfortunately, the stress fracture she suffered in high school was re-aggravated in the fourth game of the season (November 24 vs. Georgia). It gave Joyce a chance to watch the Irish gel from the bench.

Once she healed, her talented was not to be denied. Joyce slowly but surely earned more playing time. After a 13-point performance against Miami on February 20, Joyce averaged about 20 minutes a game for the balance of the year.

"Janeka is one the smartest players on the team," McGraw said. "She is definitely one of the most poised. I think she only had 14 turnovers this season and she played the point position in some huge games.

"She is one of those players that coaches love because she recognizes her weaknesses and works on them to get better, which is a lot like Ruth."

Joyce has an excellent work ethic. "Sometimes we do some one-on-one full-court drills, and she will take the defensive position because she thinks she needs to work on her defense," McGraw continued. "She has tremendous confidence. I remember she came into her first game and her first shot was an air ball, about eight feet short. But her second shot went in. That's confidence.

"If you yell at her," McGraw added, "she looks you right in the eye and says OK. I love that about her. She is so coachable. She's pretty quiet and serious and a very good student."

Her season highlight came in the second-round NCAA tournament game against Michigan, where her inspired play earned her a second-half starting spot over Ericka Haney. She took advantage of her 22 minutes of play to notch a career-high 14 points, including a 4-of-8 performance from the 3-point line.

"She's a pressure-type player," Muffet said. "Matt calls her the UConn killer, because she does so well there and other pressure situations. She played point guard in the Finals and she's more of a natural 2-guard [shooting guard].

"She will be a leader for us. I look for her to be our next great leader. But next year, I think they will be keying on her more because Riley and Niele will be gone."

LE'TANIA SEVERE

Severe started out her freshman season exactly where she did not want to start it...on the bench in street clothes.

Sidelined due to a preseason stress fracture, the 5-foot-9 guard made her debut in mid-December and spent the rest of the year on the second team. She came into games as part of the mop-up crew.

"She had a rod put in her shin," McGraw said. "She had surgery in September and put the rod in. It was a really unusual injury. So she came back on December 18th, I think."

Severe played 26 minutes in a 64-44 win over Providence and yanked down seven rebounds, including six on defense. She scored a season-high seven points on New Year's Eve against Rice.

"She's a lot like Niele Ivey, upbeat, outgoing, big smile," said McGraw. "She's the kind of kid you just love to have around because she is emotional. She will be the emotional leader of the team. She's funny, fun to be around and she makes fun of people, just like Niele. She is also probably our best athlete. Very fast, very strong."

Severe came to Notre Dame as part of a highly touted recruiting class after averaging almost 13 points and five rebounds at Fort Lauderdale High School her senior year. Named to the third team All-State team her senior year, she scored 33 points and gathered 11 rebounds in a game against Boca Raton.

AMANDA BARKSDALE

To see how far the Irish squad has come under McGraw, look at Barksdale.

In previous campaigns, a player as talented as the 6-foot-3 forward-center would have been rushed into the lineup and undergone on-the court training. However, with Riley and Siemon playing so well, Barksdale has had the luxury of developing her skills out of the public glare while playing against All-American talent on a daily basis.

The results have been impressive.

As expected, Barksdale is a shot-blocking machine. She has been ever since high school, where she set Houston area records for blocked shots with 273 in her junior year and 281 in her senior year — an amazing eight blocks per game — at Clear Brook High School in Friendswood, Texas. She was ranked as one of the top 100 recruits as a senior and was the two-time defensive MVP in her high school conference.

She stepped right into the action for McGraw. As a freshman, Barksdale played in 28 games, including all three NCAA tournament games. She blocked a career-high seven shots against Providence as a freshman.

"Mandy is the nicest kid on the team," McGraw said. "She is our best recruiter. Every kid who comes for a visit stays with Mandy. People love her. She has an easy-going manner. She's fun and upbeat and when you walk around campus with her, she knows everybody. She really enjoys being here."

Incredibly, despite playing only an average of 8.3 minutes a game her sophomore season, Barksdale ranked second in the Big East (behind Riley) with 55 blocks (1.77 per game. She recorded her first double-double against Alcorn State in the first round 98-49 blowout win in 19 minutes of play.

"As nice as she is off the court," McGraw said, "she can push the button and get mean on the court if she has to. I think her timing of her jump has a lot to do with her blocking shots, along with her long arms. We will need her presence with Ruth gone. We will have all-new post players except for her, and I think she will take the new players under her wing and show them the ropes."

MONIQUE HERNANDEZ

Hernandez, a former New Mexico player of the year, is another of the impressive trio of second-team guards who were pushing for playing time as the championship season wore on.

She was rated as one of the top 30 guards in the nation by *Blue Star Magazine* as a senior at Cibola High School in Rio Rancho, New Mexico, where she was a four-year starter. In her senior year, Hernandez averaged almost 16 points, 10 rebounds, four assists, and four steals for her squad.

Arriving on campus, Hernandez immediately impressed McGraw with her intensity, passion, and competitive fire. However, with Ivey and Danielle Green solidly installed at the guard position, Hernandez was relegated to the cleanup crew. She played in 27 games as a freshman, scoring six points twice that season.

"She brings energy to the team," McGraw said. "Once she gets on the floor, she is like the Tasmanian Devil, very aggressive, intense, and competitive. She is the type of person who can change the momentum of the game. She has no fear, and that is her greatest asset to the team."

Hernandez is also a tough defender. "She doesn't care who you are, she's going to stop you," McGraw laughed. "Now, it may mean she's going to foul you, but she will stop you.

"She's engaged to be married," McGraw said, "So she comes from a whole different social scene than the rest of the team. She adds so much to our team because she is so different than anybody else."

She sprained her MCL in her knee as sophomore and was forced to sit out the Big East tournament. The injury interrupted a season that saw her average over 10 minutes per game. She scored a career high 10 points at Seton Hall on January 21.

KAREN SWANSON

Every team should have a Karen Swanson.

The 5-foot-7 guard is a walk-on player who had limited playing time after a winning 11 letters from Westlake (OH) High School.

Swanson is the name the crowd shouts when the game is lopsided and the second team has had its fill of floor time. She works hard in practice and is rewarded with the green light to shoot whenever she is on the floor.

She played a career-high 11 minutes in November against Fordham and scored a career-high five points in the New Year's Eve game against Rice.

"Swannie is a crowd favorite," McGraw laughed. "Get her up off the bench and the crowd goes wild. She is somebody that you want the recruits you bring to campus to meet, because she really likes Notre Dame. She is the essence of a student-athlete at Notre Dame."

Walk-ons practice just as hard as the scholarship players. "Karen comes in and works her butt off, cheerleads on the bench, and then all she gets to play is a minute or two," McGraw said. "But she is happy to be there. Bench players may not like not playing, but they sacrifice personal goals for the good of the team."

CHAPTER 6

THE *ASSISTANT* COACHING *STAFF* — AIDING THE CAUSE

KEVIN MCGUFF

It was perhaps fitting that Niele Ivey jumped into the arms of Kevin McGuff after the horn ended the national championship game.

They had both come to the Irish basketball program the same year. They had both been in Cincinnati for the Final Four in 1997, and both had an integral part in putting the team over the top in 2001.

McGuff also works with the perimeter players, of whom Ivey is a prize student. "I also do recruiting, I do our non-conference schedule and I prepare scouting reports on some teams," he said.

McGuff is a 1992 graduate from St. Joseph's (IN) College, where he captained the Pumas to a Great Lakes Valley Conference championship and a berth in the NCAA Division III tournament. He received a master's degree in sports administration a year later from Miami (OH) University and spent three years there as assistant women's coach.

Bill Finley, who used to coach with Muffet and who is now coach at Iowa State, knew McGuff and recommended him to McGraw. "The move was definitely a step up for me," McGuff said. "Notre Dame is a much higher profile program. It's a world-renowned school, and Muffet's got a great name out there in women's basketball. I'm single, so it was easy for me just to pick up and go.

"The main reason I came was because I knew Muffet was a really good coach, especially offensively," McGuff said. "She had done a lot of research with the triangle offense. I got to go with her a couple of times when she went to the Chicago Bulls' practice to talk to Tex Winter, the guy who designed it when Michael Jordan played there. We got to watch practice and then sat down with Coach Winter afterward. We even went out to LA right after he and Phil Jackson went out there for the Lakers.

"In addition," he said, "I've learned how to run a program and get good people to work for you and then keep them wanting to stay. Muffet is really good with that. What I really like is she gives me my responsibilities and then she lets me do them, using my own creative energies and thought processes.

"It really makes you feel part of the program and part of the success. A lot of people don't get that opportunity.

"On top of that, she is a very nice person and a great family person," McGuff continued. "That is something else you don't get in a lot of other programs. That's why she is such a perfect fit here."

McGuff would like to become a head coach of a program some day, but he is in no rush. "First of all, I like working for Muffet and Notre Dame is a great school, so I'm happy here. I don't want to take just any program and right now there is a bit of a push to get women to coach women's programs. I want a better opportunity which furthers my career.

"I could coach a men's program just as well, but I would have to go out and create the contacts like I have right now. It would be like being a salesman and suddenly being given a whole new territory. I know the product, I just have to meet the contacts."

Part of the contacts McGuff is talking about is in recruiting. "We spend a lot of time in July going to AAU games as well as some camps," McGuff said. "Now it is getting to the point where we are beginning to figure out who we like when they are freshman and we follow them through their careers. In addition we get lots of calls every day and we get a bunch of tapes.

"Part of that has to do with the fact that we are Notre Dame and the parents would love to see their kids come here. That's why we really either have to see them ourselves or get a recommendation from someone we trust. If we find someone we like, we will make arrangements to go see them during the high school season.

"The easy part is the picking out the players," McGuff continued. "The hard part is in keeping them interested in Notre Dame because if we like them, so does Tennessee, UConn, Stanford, etc.

"Right now, there are about 25 or so players in the nation who can impact a Top 5 program and help you win a national championship. Out of those 25, there may be only 12 or so that can meet the academic requirements of the university. In men's basketball, there is a much larger talent pool.

"Once you determine the player has the necessary talent and

can make the grades here," McGuff said, "then we look for desire first, then coachability, as requirements we are looking for."

Getting onto the team is very similar to joining a sorority, once the campus visit is made.

"Obviously, it is difficult sometimes to tell if a player is going to fit in here," McGuff said. "So we talk to her coaches, parents and we also lean on our kids a lot. After the campus visits, we will ask the team what they thought of the player and sometimes they tell us they don't think that player would be a good fit. It doesn't happen very often, but it happens."

McGuff thought it was important that the team become clique-less. "The year before, the team would hang around as groups of players, not as a team," he said. "This year was different. Kelley and Niele became close and would spend all night talking about their boyfriends — and I mean all night," McGuff laughed.

"I think that they are very proud that they could stay up and talk all night and win a national championship all in one year."

McGuff had a feeling that the 2000-2001 squad had a pretty good chance for the title. "We had beaten some pretty good teams — Georgia, Purdue, and UConn, among others — and this year when we got to St. Louis it was a totally different feeling than it was in Cincinnati," he said. "When we went in 1997, we were all pretty happy just to be there. This time it was different. Our approach was more businesslike and that permeated the team also. The team itself, though, handled it the same way."

The significance of the year is not lost on McGuff. "Really this year, we had the team, we had the coaching staff, we had the administration, we did a good job marketing, women's basketball is getting more popular, and I think it just all came together.

"This year was, in effect," he said, "the perfect storm."

CAROL OWENS

Carol Owens knew she had made a promise.

All recruiters make promises.

But this one, she had to follow up on.

She had told Sharon Riley that if her daughter came to Notre Dame, that Owens could make her into an All-American.

You don't make empty promises to people like Sharon Riley.

"Every time Sharon saw me during Ruth's freshman and sophomore years, she would ask me how I was coming along making Ruth into an All-American," Owens laughed.

Ruth made All-American in both her junior and senior years. "I hold myself accountable for the things I say when I recruit," the soft-spoken Owens said.

That's why the mission was accomplished, by two very hard-working women.

Owens believes the key to being a good post player is as much mental as it is physical. "You can't just bring in a freshman and start hammering on them about playing basketball," Owens said. "You have to understand the players are human, and in Ruth's case, she was a very tall girl, which isn't easy to be as a teenage girl.

"I remember the first few times Ruth sat in a chair in my office she kind of hunched over. I know what it's like to be tall in junior high and high school, 'cause I was just like her and the kids in my grade gave me all kinds of embarrassing names."

So Owens begins to work on the players' psyche first. "I need to make them feel better about themselves as people," she said. "Then I can work on them as basketball players."

Owens should know. She was the first athlete in history, male or female, to score 2,000 points and pull down 1,000 rebounds at Northern Illinois University after graduating from Notre Dame High School in Chicago. She then spent three years playing in Japan and Europe before returning to the States with an assistant coaching position at the University of Michigan.

She is another Jim Foster (Vanderbilt coach) link to Notre Dame. She knew Foster through the coaching circles, and it was Foster who connected McGraw and Owens. "There were some other people who had talked to her about me also, I think," she said. "And if you know Muffet very well, then you know around her things happen really quickly. Her first call was after I sent her my résumé, and six days later she offered me the job.

"Muffet and I hit it off immediately during the interview process," Owens said of the 1995 job change. "We both had the same goals, to win a national championship and become a national power, and we were thinking this at a time when we weren't thought of very seriously like that.

"My first project was to sign Niele Ivey," Owens laughed. "Muffet told me this was a girl we had to have and that I was to call her up and go see her right away. I went to an AAU tournament she was in, in a hot gym with no air conditioning, and I just sat there and watched her play the whole day.

"Muffet was very high on her. When she made her visit to campus, she was like a choir girl, almost angelic at first, but by the time the visit was through, the real Niele had come out. Her and Molly Peirick hit it off really well, also."

But Owens' in-season job was and still is to make Division I post players out of scared 18-year-old girls. Katryna Gaither had been her first assignment.

"Katryna had great hands," Owens said. "She was also very athletic. She did everything we asked her to do and she had a lot of natural ability. But she would also always outwork her opponent."

Owens added another name to the 1997 core group of seniors as being important recruiting-wise. "Roseanne Bohman did not get a lot of the publicity as Beth Morgan and Katryna, but I would use her as an example of the kind of leader I wanted Ruth and Kelley to be. She was a coach on the floor. She knew where everyone was supposed to be. All three of them were great when it came to recruiting other players, and that really helped the program."

Then came the Riley years. "I knew after her sophomore year that Ruth would be a great player," Owens said. "When I saw her as a freshman, I knew it was going to take a lot of work because she had to understand the mental toughness she had to endure. And for her, it was a hard freshman year as well as for Meaghan. They both excelled in high school, but they hadn't had to work too hard because they were taller than everyone else.

"Several practices would end up with Ruth crying because we were on her so much. But Ruth was a special player. She would get down, but she was committed to getting better and she would ask me what she had to do to get better. She toughened a lot mentally because from her sophomore year on, every team's objective was to get her out of the game any way they could.

"I told her I had to be demanding on her in order to help her keep her poise during the games, and I think she understood that.

"This season there were several big games where I would try to tell her something, but she told me she already knew and that it was taken care of," Owens said. "That told me that she really had matured as a player. It was a great sense of accomplishment for me personally because they had become what I thought they could be when we recruited them."

Owens had a big hand in Riley's mental approach to her foul problems.

"I remember going to see the movie Michael Jordan was in at the Max Theaters, and one thing he said was that every time he stepped on the court he knew there was somebody there that was watching him for the first time and he always considered how he wanted people to see him."

The transfer from screen to court didn't take long. "I asked Ruth if she thought someone wanted to see her put her head down every time a foul was called on her?" Owens said. "Especially on the road where they were out to get her? We told her that getting the first foul was OK because she needed to see how the game was going to be called. But on the second foul, she couldn't hang her head because that is what the other teams wanted and now she was a leader on our team. Accept the foul with dignity and move on."

Ruth took the advice to heart. "Then we knew she had to get stronger and learn to use her left hand. So we brought some guys into practice and their job was to push her off the blocks. Ruth appreciated all the coaching and she respected what I had to say. The final piece was her ability to pass out of the double team. She turned into a great passer."

Owens also took Siemon under her wing.

"Kelley was actually a utility player for us," Owens said. "Sometimes she would even bring the ball up the floor for us if teams would press us. And when she did, it caused another problem for the post player defending her, because if you didn't pick her up, she would dribble it up the floor. In the early part of the season, she was even getting us into the motion offense and that helped, because it put Niele and Alicia into positions where they could score. And we wanted both of them shooting, of course. Then we started running Kelley off screens and trying to get her some better looks.

"One of the things Coach McGraw had said at the end of last season was that we would be as good as...and the first person that she mentioned was...Kelley Siemon," Owens said. "And the key to her was that she was more effective driving to the basket, although she can hit the 18-footers also."

Owens is as tough in practice as she is soft-spoken outside of it. But the maturity of the team showed through several times on the team bus when some of the players would break out in humorous portrayals of the coaches' favorite sayings in practice.

"Those were fun moments this year," Owens said, "because it showed to me just how far the team had come, how they could understand and joke about how we get on them. It was a riot how they would remember certain things."

Owens also noticed there were no cliques on this year's edition of the Irish. There simply was no color of skin issue.

"The older players, such as Niele and Kelley, made it a point to hang around with different members of the team at different times, and when you have two players with great personalities like those two, it spreads out from there.

"There was a lot of crossover," Owens said. "Kelley would hang out with Niele or with Le'Tania or Janeka, and Niele would hang Kelley or the others. The other older players took the younger players under their wing and they all hung out at each other's apartments and rooms. The whole team just got along so well together."

Owens, like Siemon, wears her Christianity on her sleeve. "I think it is good for a team to have those kinds of values," she said. "Whether they adopt it or they don't, I think it is fortunate when you have kids who do.

"Kelley and I had a special relationship. With her, I knew I didn't have to be perfect, that I was a human being. Kelley has been a great leader in her Christian walk because she has a certain amount of maturity that the players can look up to."

Owens thought the best moment of the season was when the Irish beat Vanderbilt in the NCAA regional finals.

"We had talked a lot about the blood, sweat, and tears it was going to take to get us to our goal of going to the Final Four," she said, "and it was the most stressful day of my life.

"I had prepared the scouting report and I wanted everything to be just right and I wanted to convey the information to them in a way that they could understand it. Vanderbilt was very similar to us, and had a strong post player and great outside shooting."

"But if you believe that God has a plan..." Owens voice trailed off. "You know we could have been in the Final Four last year. But with everything that happened, including Niele's injuries, to get to the Final Four this year was perfect. Believe me, winning the national championship was awesome. But the Vanderbilt win was a huge relief.

"Really, the last two weeks you are just cruising," she continued. "You can't celebrate anything because there is something more to do. As assistants, we are trying to make sure that Coach doesn't have anything to deal with and the players don't either, so you are really on for 24 hours. But you work a lifetime to get to one Final Four, and I've been fortunate enough to get to two of them."

"Really," she added, "I would not trade any moment of these last four years because we grew together as a group. We were connected."

The equivalent of Graduation Awards Day for coaches is held annually in late April in New York. It's called the WNBA draft.

This year, three Notre Dame players were picked — Riley, fifth by the Miami Sol; Ivey, 19th by the Indianapolis Fever; and Siemon, 48th by the LA Sparks.

"It was an incredible feeling being there and having those three picked," Owens said. "I really thought both Coach McGraw and I were going to cry."

So, on Friday, April 20, 2001, Owens put the final touches on her promise to Sharon Riley. She had taken a small-town girl from the low hills of north-central Indiana and helped transform her not only into an All-American, but a Naismith Award winner, a national champion and now a professional basketball player.

And, in addition, she had somehow helped Ruth sustain her most important status in life...

That of a good person.

COQUESE WASHINGTON

It is always a good indication of the overall respect of a program when one of its best players comes back to prowl the sidelines with her old coach.

Such is the case with Assistant Coach Coquese Washington. For the past four springs, she's been playing in the WNBA — two years with the New York Liberty and now two with the Houston Comets.

In 2000, the Comets won their fourth straight WNBA title with Washington sharing point-guard responsibilities.

In fate is kind, Riley and Ivey will be playing against their old assistant coach for years to come in the WNBA.

During the WNBA off-season, Washington coaches the guards for the Irish, using her college and pro experience to help cut down turnovers and help with defense.

Washington played for McGraw from 1989 through1993 and was a member of the first team to go to the NCAA tournament. She held the school record for steals (307) until this year when one of her protégés, Ivey, blew past that, ending up with over 350. Washington started 89 of the 113 games in which she saw action over her career and averaged 8.4 points, 3.4 rebounds, and 4.9 assists.

She graduated with a degree in history in 1992 and returned to the university for a juries doctorate in 1997.

CHAPTER 7

COACH MUFFET MCGRAW — THE STORY BEGINS

Muffet McGraw stuck her head out of the south entrance of Gate One of the JACC, which serves as the foyer to her basketball office. "Oh geez," she said. "Would you look at that?"

It was a March 15th kind of day in South Bend, complete with that cold wet drippy rain that seems to sink into your bones and makes you yearn for hot oatmeal, even when you hate oatmeal.

Unfortunately, it wasn't March 15. The date was June 5. It was supposed to be 70 degrees and sunny. Instead it was 50 degrees, blustery and there was no relief on the Doppler Radar screens anywhere. She had 9:45 tee time at the new Warren Golf Course just north of the campus and she hated to miss any tee time, especially one with her favorite golfing partner, her husband Matt, who had been drafted to play when some of her original foursome called off because of the conditions.

She and a friend stood there for a second and the friend suggested that today was a day neither fit for fairway woods nor two-putts. McGraw sighed again, thanked the visitor, closed the door, and strolled back to her office.

As any golfer knows, any day on the golf course is better than any day at the office, especially during the slow season. So, the allure of the fairway was too strong for Muffet to take. She showed for her tee time, armed with more rain gear than a fireman in a three-alarm blaze, and started play.

Other, more sane people, of course had called off their tee times, preferring the warmth of the Regis Philbin show or maybe a warm cup of coffee at the bagel shop to wiping the rain off the cold shafts of the clubs. But off went the McGraw foursome. Rain or shine, it was time to play golf.

It would turn in to a great day, despite the rain. As Muffet stood on the tee of the fourth hole that Tuesday morning, she stood there as coach of the national championship Notre Dame women's basketball team. She stood there as a very recognizable celebrity throughout the community at large, a woman known for her accomplishments both on and off the court. She stood there as the mom of 10-year-old Murphy and wife of 47-year-old Matt.

But she also stood there as the average golfer. She had never made a hole-in-one in her life. On any golf course, anywhere. But McGraw's basketball team had just won the first national championship in Irish women's history. They had just beaten a No. 1- ranked team (Connecticut) for the first time, had just had a player named the Naismith Award winner (best player in the nation), had just been named National Coach of the Year for the first time, and had played in front of the first ever sellout crowd in the history of ND women's basketball.

Apparently, this was a season of firsts.

The hole was 101 yards and none of the other three had put one on the green. So Muffet addressed the ball as the light drizzle fell, gave it the golfer's wiggle, twisted into her backswing, and brought her eight-iron down on the ball. The ball lept off the tee and flew straight for the pin.

The ball landed on the soft green, hopped once, and then disappeared over a ridge which obscured Muffet's view of the hole.

"Must have rolled off the green," she thought to herself as she approached the green, for the ball was nowhere to be found. She quickly scanned the area behind the hole, and saw nothing. She approached the hole the way a six-year-old approaches the biggest package under the tree at Christmas, almost afraid to look and see whose name is on the package.

This time, however, Muffet's name was on the package. "She screamed, 'It's a hole-in-one!' and started dancing around like a madman," Matt laughed. Sure enough, sitting in the bottom of the cup was her ball. A hole-in-one, probably the least remarkable first in a season of firsts, but just as thrilling as the others.

Yes, it had been quite a year for Muffet McGraw.

Almost immediately on cue as they teed off on the fifth hole, the rain began in earnest and the rest of the round was washed out. It was as if the gods of destiny were saying they had had enough of this McGraw person for one year.

And it was time to move on.

Muffet McGraw epitomizes the saying that it isn't the size of the dog in the fight, but rather the size of the fight in the dog. The diminutive small-framed coach was a sports fanatic from early in her childhood. Born in Pottsville, Pennsylvania, McGraw has four brothers and four sisters and learned early to love basketball. "I was in seventh grade when the parish priest came into our classroom and announced they were going to start a girls basketball team," McGraw recalled. "My hand went up immediately when he asked if anyone was interested in playing."

She learned the basketball basics playing in the alleys by her house and on the playgrounds during school. "There were all boys in the neighborhood and I always played with boys on the playground," she said. "I didn't know that it wasn't what girls were supposed to do. I enjoyed it so much I just kind of hung around the guys all the time. Heck, they were doing all the fun stuff. I think people thought girls were supposed to be dropped off at the mall or something and I didn't like that kind of thing. I always liked what the guys were doing.

"I kind of wondered why people looked at me kind of strangely," Muffet said. "But I was certainly a tomboy and back then it had a different connotation."

The game was dramatically different back then. There were six players on the court and some players were limited to offense and others to defense. Running, at that time, wasn't encouraged for girls.

"I hated playing six-on-six," McGraw said. "But it was all we had. There were two forwards, two guards, and two rovers. Only the rovers were allowed at both ends of the court and I was a rover. I may have hated the concept, but I loved playing basketball and it was something I was good at."

Her high school coach at Bishop Shanahan High School was Jim Heatherington. "I really liked him and I enjoyed playing for him," Muffet said. "But it was entirely different. There wasn't any weight training, no pre-season practice, very few camps, and the only people who came to the games were the parents. Heck, the girls had to wear skirts."

Not that it mattered to Muffet. "The fun part was that we played for the love of the game. By today's standards we weren't any good, but we were 10-0 one season. There were no state playoffs or anything. Most of my teammates had played some basketball, but they certainly hadn't played a lot. It was all so new and fresh. There was never the idea of not wanting to play because of that newness. I don't remember anyone on those teams complaining about not playing because even if you didn't play, at least you were still on the team."

McGraw's position was point guard and her job was to pass the ball to her sister who set long-standing records for points scored in a game.

College scholarships for women's basketball were unheard of in the early 1970s but one day, Kathy Rush, who was coach of the national champion Immaculata College women's team, made it a point to visit a game in which Muffet was playing. "Everyone on the team loved the fact that she was there," Muffet said. "She was looking at me as a possible player and after the game she hung around and we chatted for a bit. She invited me to go to Immaculata."

Even then, though, McGraw knew who she was. "My dad was excited about me playing for a national champion team and he even offered to buy me a car so I could commute the 40 minutes to school every day. The thing was, Immaculata was an all-girls school and I thought, 'No Guys, No Way.' Besides, I always liked the underdog."

So she chose to go to close-by St. Joseph's, where she eventually became captain and guided her 1976-77 team to a 23-5 record and a No. 3 ranking nationally.

It was during a summer break during college when she was working at a courthouse that she met future husband Matt. Matt was supposed to go back to New York to work for the summer. "I didn't really want to go to New York," Matt said "I was going to West Chester (PA) College and at the last minute I got an offer to work in the courthouse that summer. So my superior is showing me around the courthouse and he opens the door and there stood Muffet. I noticed her right away because she was the only one under 60 years old in the room. My superior said, 'Well, there is no one in here you need to meet,' and off we went. Three days later Muffet and I ran into each other in the hall and I said, 'Hey, do you want a cheese steak for lunch and she said 'yes.'"

"I remember the exact moment I first saw Matt," Muffet recalled with a smile. "I was like 'wow' I have to get to know this guy. I knew immediately. I took one look at him and that was it. I don't know if it was love at first sight but I was definitely attracted. I don't remember if we 'accidentally' ran into each other in the hall or not. I'm sure I made a few extra trips that I didn't have to make just to see if he was around."

Attendance at women's basketball games back then was small. "The only people who came to the game were parents and close friends," Muffet said. "The joke was that my coach always recruited from large families in order to put more fans in the seats. We didn't even have stat crews back then. Across town, Immacualta would pack their place with about 1,000 people per game with all the nuns and everyone and their crowd followed that team wherever they went."

The stirrings of gender equality began taking place during Muffet's tenure at St. Joseph's. "Back then there was a varsity men's team, a JV men's team, and us," she laughed. "In our case there were no scholarships and no cuts. If you had 12 people show up for the first practice, there were 12 people on the team. We had to sit around sometimes until eight o'clock at night, waiting for the men to get through practice. We just figured that it was a man's world and that was just the way it was going to be. We were frustrated with it for sure, but we didn't get organized and do anything about it.

"It was still a lot of fun," she continued. "We would just show up for our first day of practice and I think we played about 18 regular season games or so. We wore one pair of tennis shoes for the whole season and wore different color pinnies rather than practice jerseys. We even did our own laundry. Today the girls have a different pair of shoes for just about everything, including just to walk back and forth to practice. It is hard to believe."

Muffet graduated after that successful senior year with a degree in sociology and a minor in criminology. "I had done some work with juvenile delinquents and every Friday a bunch of us would go to the gym and play basketball with these kids. I think I figured that I could do that for the rest of my life. I had never really considered coaching as a profession, but I knew basketball was really the only thing I had a passion for. I knew I wanted to hang around the game, but I didn't really have a job lined up when I graduated so I wasn't sure exactly what I could do."

Shortly thereafter, Muffet got her first coaching job. The job at

Philadelphia's Archbishop Caroll High School came open and a couple of her St. Joseph's teammates recommended she give it a try. She accepted the job. "I really knew nothing about coaching the game," she recalled.

Now a newlywed, McGraw, also worked a second job. Sometimes dressed in what she called a "cute little white and red outfit," she waitressed at an Italian eatery named the Villa. In addition to the tips, she lived off Matt's income, and coached her high school team to two highly successful seasons. making about $1,200 each year for her efforts. A rookie season of 22-3 was followed by a perfect 28-0 record the next.

"I loved coaching that team," she said. "The girls were tremendous and had a lot of spirit. They would cover their uniforms with sayings and beads and pins and things. We all just loved to play."

McGraw also learned about dealing with parents while coaching there. A blizzard was threatening to shut down Philadelphia one day, but a young and enthusiastic McGraw called for practice to go on anyway. By the time the practice ended, trains weren't running and that left five girls stranded in the coach's small apartment. "I had parents calling me that night asking where their kids were. They were all safe in my apartment, but I got into so much trouble for that. I didn't know any better then, but I sure wouldn't do it now."

The call of professional basketball lured then 24-year-old Muffet to California, where she played a two-year stint with the California Dreams in the now defunct Women's Professional league.

Then a man who Muffet now fondly calls her mentor entered her life. Jim Foster, with 10 years of college coaching behind him, took the job at St. Joseph's College and Muffet heard he was looking for an assistant. "We got together and he offered me a raise all the way up to $1,500 per year," she said as if still amazed. "I was still waitressing at the time, but pretty soon after that I got a job at the college in the business office."

Muffet will admit she wasn't a very good assistant coach. "I was terrible," she laughs. "I was young and I had just come off a perfect high school season and I was pretty sure I knew everything. Jim, on the other hand, is a very laid-back philosophical kind of coach and I just did not understand why he did things the way he did. I would be all intense and yelling at players and he would not be and I could not understand his coaching methods. Needless to say, a few years later after I had coached on my own, I wanted to call him and tell him that now I understood what he was trying to do."

But the die was cast. "I couldn't wait to get a head coaching job," Muffet said. "I applied at every college in Philadelphia, finally landing at Lehigh to begin the 1982-83 season.

"That was very exciting," Muffet said of her hiring. "I rushed home and Matt and I got more and more excited talking about it and then he asked, 'Well, how much are you getting paid?' and I said, 'I have NO idea!' I remember the conversation with Lehigh went something like, 'Do you want it?' and I said, 'I'll take it!' almost as quickly. I was flying high and besides that I could quit my second job because they were going to pay me almost $16,000, I think."

McGraw tasted success her first year. Her first team at Lehigh went 14-9 and she was named East Coast Conference Coach of the Year. After a 13-9 campaign in 1983-84, McGraws teams posted consecutive 20-plus win campaigns, going 20-8 and then 24-4 and the ECC championship in 1985-86.

But Muffet still chafed at Lehigh's inability to be taken seriously at tournament time. "I would go to the NCAA tournament games and see the crowds and all the excitement and say to myself this is what I want," she said. "In fact, one year Matt and I went to an early round tournament game at Rutgers with some friends and they commented later that they could tell by the look on my face that the tournament was where I wanted to be."

Muffet said it is in large part due to her mentor Jim Foster that she is at Notre Dame today. "Jim called me one day and told me the job was open, but I thought it was way out of my league," she says. "I just didn't think it was going to happen."

Apparently Foster thought it would. "He called Notre Dame and told then-Athletic Director Gene Corrigan that they should take a look at me," Muffet said. "I was absolutely incredulous when I get this call from Notre Dame asking for my résumé. At first I thought that it was Matt playing a joke on me. I had been at the coaches meetings that spring and a lot of names were being mentioned for the Notre Dame job, but mine certainly wasn't one of them. Actually, Jim was rumored to have a good opportunity to take the job."

But it took an interrupted backswing for Muffet to decide to apply. "I had been 'encouraging' her to apply for the job for a couple of weeks," Matt said. "We had heard that the job was open at the NCAA tournament and so was the Kentucky job and I didn't want to go to Kentucky. Plus we had seen a game on cable between Notre Dame and DePaul earlier that year and I don't think there were six people in the stands. I thought it was a great opportunity to build a program. So I would 'remind' Muffet every two or three days. We were playing golf with a couple of friends and, just as Muffet went into her backswing, I said, "So are you going to apply or not?"

Apparently, you don't interrupt Muffet in her backswing. "Everyone else backed away and I thought I was a goner," Matt said. "And then I said, 'Hey, a year from now, don't tell me you should have applied.' "

And that was it.

Matt finally got the answer he was waiting for a couple of days later. "I came home one day and asked Matt if he wanted to take a trip with me," Muffet said. "I'm sure he thought it was to somewhere in New Jersey because every time I went there I would get lost. He wanted to know where we were going and I said South Bend and he about jumped through the roof.

"Before that, I think it was a lack of confidence thing on my part," Muffet said. "Throughout the whole process Matt had been telling me to apply and I kept telling him that I wasn't going to apply because I liked it at Lehigh and I wanted to stay. But when the call came for the on-site visit to South Bend, I said, 'Do you want me out there today?' I was so excited."

The McGraw's spent two days on campus, meeting the administrators and getting their first tour of the campus.

"We were staying at the Morris Inn and I was back there kind of wandering around looking for the old bookstore while Muffet was still interviewing and who should pull up but [former Irish men's basketball star] David Rivers," Matt continued. "So I asked him where it was and after trying to explain it, David said, 'Oh heck, I'll just take you there.' He had a class, but he walked me to the bookstore first. What a nice guy."

"I don't think I ever said I wanted to coach at Notre Dame," Muffet said. "But it had all the things I wanted in a job." Part of that was her desire to start a women's basketball tradition at a smaller university with a great reputation. She also soon found out that the current Irish team had some high quality players who had just suffered a dysfunctional year.

The two McGraws flew back to Philly and, two days later, the offer came over the phone. Muffet immediately accepted. Of the two, Matt may have been the more excited. "Matt went out and mowed a big ND in our lawn," Muffet laughed.

The McGraws were South Bend-bound. No one at the time knew that history, at least Notre Dame athletic history, was going to be made.

But not until after a lot of hard work had been done.

CHAPTER 8

THE EARLY YEARS

The first thing Muffet had to do as new coach was to get people to notice that there was a woman's basketball team at Notre Dame. Despite the impressive records, attendance at the games had been poor and media coverage almost non-existent.

After she accepted the job, the Irish sports information department set up a press conference to announce the signing. At the same time, Muffet was calling the local Philadelphia newspapers to tell them she was leaving Lehigh. "One of the writers thought I was going to coach a local high school named Notre Dame and was quite surprised when I said, 'No, I'm going to the Notre Dame in South Bend.'

She flew out for what she thought was going to be a high profile press conference to find only Forrest (Woodie) Miller, beat writer for the *South Bend Tribune* and a local TV station cameraman, there to record the event.

Corrigan's words at the conference on May 18, 1987 were hopeful, if not prophetic. "If we searched for an entire year, I don't think we would find anyone better suited for our program," he said.

Now the ball was in McGraw's hands. At age 32, she was only the third head coach of the Notre Dame women's basketball program She now had the key to the office of the most visible university in America after five successful seasons at Lehigh University where she had compiled an 88-41 record over five years, including two 20-plus win seasons, one conference championship season, and one East Coast Conference Coach of the Year trophy.

The Irish team had been under the guidance of Mary DiStanislao, who had accumulated a 115-79 record over seven seasons including three 20-plus win seasons. But her final season saw a talented squad suffer through a season best described as dysfunctional and signaled a time for some new blood in the coaches office.

Muffet's job announcement appeared on the front page of the

South Bend Tribune as an inset of a professional basketball game summary between the Milwaukee Bucks and the Boston Celtics. It was a small six-inch article.

Things were about to change.

The media coverage would slowly begin to increase over the years.

The sidelines would become used to the soles of McGraw's shoes, as she settled into her coaching style. "I'm a pacer anyway," she said. "I was extremely nervous before my first game which was at Loyola [IL, on November 28, 1987] and my assistant coach told me the game would be just like coaching back in high school, but that didn't help much. I think I wore out the rug that night."

The Irish won, 67-61, and the McGraw era was underway.

Muffet's first team in South Bend went 20-8, reversing the 12-15 record from the year before and restarting a trend in 20-win seasons started DiStanislao. "That first team was actually a very good team," Muffet recalls. "We had point guard Mary Gavin who was fourth nationally in assists and still holds the Notre Dame career assist record."

Forward Heidi Bunek was 18th nationally in field-goal percentage while center Sandy Botham picked up first team all-North Star Conference honors. McGraw herself was named Northstar Conference Coach of the Year.

"My whole goal was to get into the Top 25 within the first five years," McGraw said. "I had a goal but I really didn't have a plan on how to get there. I was coach of the year mostly because we had a really good team that had just struggled the year before with internal problems."

The crowds at the JACC were small enough to allow a bored observer to count them before halftime. "I think we averaged about 200 or so people to each game," Muffet said, "and we were dwarfed by the Joyce Athletic and Convocation Center. There was never any promotion and there was never anyone who recommended that we close up some bleachers or put curtains up to make the place feel smaller and help the crowd noise. It was just a big old empty shell. And the only press that was ever there was Woodie Miller. I think press row could have been put on a picnic table."

With the first year under her belt, McGraw set her sights on her dream, a berth in the NCAA tournament. "The problem was, I didn't understand scheduling," she said. "We would usually beat most or all of the teams in our conference and then we would try to play teams like Tennessee or the real good teams and we would get whacked pretty good. In hindsight, we should have been scheduling the No. 25 team or the No. 20 team, not the top-ranked ones. We would call the NCAA committee after not getting a bid and find out that we hadn't played a tough enough schedule or that we had not beaten a good enough team to be considered. It was a very tough time for me. At that time, it was a 32-team tournament and the MCC did not have an automatic bid, so I was really frustrated."

The team went 21-11 in McGraw's second year but were shellacked by No. 2-ranked Tennessee, 108-77, and fading powerhouse Old Dominion, 82-65. The Irish won the MCC tournament, however, and were invited to the Women's NIT in Amarillo, Texas, where they finished seventh in an eight-team tournament. Karen Robinson led the team in scoring that year with over 12 points and also averaged almost six assists in her sophomore year.

Robinson would win the first of two MCC Player of the Year awards in the 1989-90 season. The 5-6 junior guard averaged over 15 points a game as Notre Dame won the MCC regular season as well as the tournament. They finished at 23-6 but again were defeated soundly by Tennessee (77-54). The team traveled to Old Dominion on January 12, 1990 and almost pulled off McGraw's first major upset before falling, 62-61.

Robinson repeated her magic her senior season (1990-91), garnering almost 17 points a game on a team which featured four players averaging double figures and a fifth, future assistant coach Coquese Washington, would become the first Irish player to play in the WNBA. Muffet earned her first win over a Top 10 team when her squad upset 10th-ranked Louisiana Tech in the Texaco-Hawk Classic on December 28, 1990.

That win was the first indication that things were cooking in South Bend. But the meal was far from done as they suffered an 88-71 thrashing at the hands of fifth-ranked Tennessee on February 9. That loss ended a 15-game Irish win streak and was a reality check for the now-experienced coach.

That loss to Tennessee shook the team's confidence and they

went 7-5 the rest of the season. That team finished 23-9, again won the MCC, again won the MCC tournament, and again was snubbed by the NCAA tournament despite a 70-58 win over Old Dominion. The snub proved prophetic as the Irish lost all three of their NWIT games.

That was also the year that Muffet was pregnant. "That was a very interesting year," Muffet recalled. "It was an easy year though. Murphy was due in May so I was about seven months pregnant at the end of the season. It was funny because my team was willing to do whatever I said because I told them that if I got upset I might just have the baby right then and there. That team listened better than any team before or since because none of the players wanted to be the reason I went into labor.

"The other thing that was funny was I had a forgetful thing happening when I was pregnant," Muffet continued. "We would get into a huddle during a time out and I would say, "OK, you guys, this is what I want you to do...and then I would forget what I wanted them to do. My mind would simply blank out. Sometimes Karen Robinson or one of the other players would try to help me remember by asking if we wanted to play full-court press or zone, or what?

"The other funny thing was that I had taken some pages from a book called *What to Expect When You are Expecting* and I would post the page and then tell the players to read it so they would know what to expect from me.

"Crankiness...ill-tempered...irritability...they were ready for it all," Muffet laughed.

That was the year, however, that McGraw snagged her first real nationally known recruit. Michelle Marciniak came to campus and raised expectations of the program in 1991-92. However, it was not a good fit for the hot-shooting freshman and she left the program that spring. In her wake, Notre Dame had suffered through an incredibly disappointing 14-17 season but just as incredibly had landed their first ever NCAA bid. That was the first year the tournament had expanded to 64 teams and the Irish upset top seeded Xavier, 59-54, to win the MCC tournament and were awarded the automatic bid to the NCAA.

McGraw had achieved her dream, but it soon turned into a nightmare. The trip to LA with a team that included senior Margaret Nowlin, junior Coquese Washington, freshman Leticia Bowen, and freshman Marciniak was short-lived. UCLA handed the Irish their heads, 92-71, in the opening round but McGraw had gotten her goal of playing in the NCAA tournament.

The Irish suffered their most uneventful year with McGraw at the helm in 1992-93, not winning the conference, the tournament, nor being invited to any end of season tournaments. The recruiting season, however, would bring in two of the most significant players in Irish history. Highly touted Bloomington,[IN] native Beth Morgan and a 6-3 project named Katryna Gaither signed letters of intent and joined Notre Dame in the 1993-94 campaign.

The addition of Morgan and Gaither would change Notre Dame's basketball fortunes. The program was about to go Big Time.

Beth was a self-proclaimed gym rat looking for a team to showcase her formidable talents. She burst on the scene at the first whistle, averaging almost 18 points a game as a freshman and leading the team in floorburns and practice time. "Beth was recruited by everybody in the nation and it came down to Stanford and us," McGraw said. "Our pitch to her was that she could be the one to take our program to the promised land, the one to take the big shots, and we would pretty much allow her to do what she wanted on the floor. Beth, fortunately was the type of person who wanted to make an impact and in the end she told us she was coming here because she was from Indiana and had some Hoosier pride. Her parents were just outstanding people, and they treated Beth the same as they treated their other kids."

Morgan said that Vanderbilt was also in the mix as well as Stanford. "But my biggest attraction to Notre Dame was Notre Dame itself," she said. "I knew I wanted to be part of something we could build and I could just see that everything was in place. Honestly, when you combine the academics and the basketball program available at Notre Dame, I can't see why a high level player would go anywhere else."

"I was very worried about how the seniors on the team would react to this new freshman," Muffet said. "But Beth is like Alicia Ratay, very humble and not selfish at all. It was truly amazing to see her impact on the team because that group of seniors she was joining had been through some rough years and saw Beth was an opportunity to end their careers on a good note."

Muffet then added. "Beth was the best player on the floor from the first moment of practice on."

Gaither, on the other hand, was still growing into her body, arriving on campus thin enough to slip through closing doors and desperately searching for confidence in the paint.

"Katryna's father had told us on our recruiting visit that his daughter would be an All-American some day and I didn't believe it," Muffet said. "But he was right. Both Katryna and Beth were what I call low-maintenance players, which fit in well with me because I am not all that chatty or complimentary as a coach, and I did not have to tell these two how good they were. Both players knew what they had to do and worked hard to get better."

McGraw brought Gaither off the bench that year and the 22-7 Irish earned their second NCAA appearance with a 72-63 win over Xavier to win the MCC tournament again. Morgan started every game and led the team in scoring, averaging almost 18 points.

The Irish then hosted Minnesota in the opening round at the JACC that year, the first time a women's NCAA game had been played in South Bend and the Golden Gophers escaped with a 81-76 win.

However, a statement had been made. The Irish were indeed coming.

"I remember the days we used to gather around the newspaper just to see if we got any votes in the polls at all, let alone being one of the Top 25," Morgan laughed. "It is hard to believe today just how far the program has come in such a short while. It is not only a tribute to Coach McGraw, but also a tribute to the other people inside the program."

Gaither, who would eventually become Notre Dame's second-leading scorer in team history (behind Morgan), caught fire her sophomore year. She began a streak in which she scored in double figures in 76 straight games as McGraw honed the inside-outside attack using her two stars.

The upgraded schedule backfired on the Irish, however, in the 1994-95 campaign, which would be their last in the MCC. They faced four Top 25 teams in their first six games and lost all four, then ran off a 15-1 streak which raised hopes of another NCAA bid. However, an 84-67 loss to Northern Illinois in the MCC tournament (after winning the conference crown for the second straight year) resulted in the Irish accepting a bid in the NWIT for the last time in their history. Notre Dame won two of their three games and finished third.

The Irish edged into the national spotlight the next year. With Gaither and Morgan being joined by Sheila McMillen, a freshman sharpshooter from nearby Rochester (IN), Notre Dame was also accepted into the Big East Conference. It was a move long-awaited by the competition-hungry McGraw. "When the kids found out [on July 13, 1994] that we had joined the Big East, they were so excited they wanted to know if they could play right away," she told the *Hartford Courant* at the time. "I think people will become more interested in us because of the name recognition of the other teams."

One of the other teams, of course, was Connecticut. "Connecticut was the league," Muffet said. "They made the league. They gave everyone else credibility. We'd come in at 17-1; they came in at 18-0. So people would think that Notre Dame must be good, also. Nationally, we got more attention."

Another goal had been accomplished. Being part of the Big East meant better recruiting. Better recruiting meant a better opportunity to play on the national stage (the NCAA tournament) more often. Now the problem was to get better support behind the team.

Morgan would be the key, and Gaither the handle. The first year in the Big East (1995-96) ended with both Morgan and Gaither averaging 20 points a game. Gaither averaged 63.3 percent shooting from the field and also pulled down nine rebounds per contest. Both players were named first-team All Big East as juniors.

There was only one problem. They were still having trouble beating ranked teams, especially UConn. The Irish lost three times to the Huskies that year, including a Big East final whacking of 71-54. But the team made Irish history, notching its first-ever NCAA win (73-60 over Purdue) before losing to ninth-ranked Texas Tech in the second round.

Notre Dame struck gold the next year [1996-97]. With Morgan and Gaither leading the way, the Irish swept through the regular season with a 27-6 record, losing only to second ranked Tennessee, Purdue, 19th ranked Wisconsin, Ohio State, and twice to top-ranked Connecticut. The Irish at the beginning of the year were a deep squad, though not as talented as the upper echelon teams.

That season will always be remembered as the year the injury bug hit the Irish team with a vengeance. Sophomore guard Danielle Green ruptured her Achilles tendon on October 15 and was finished for the year. On November 23, promising freshman Niele Ivey tore her anterior cruciate ligament (ACL) against Bowling Green on November 23 and she was out for the season.

But the injury bug was just beginning. Walk-on Adrienne Jordan went down in the Big East tournament win over Rutgers with a dislocated hip injury, ending a horrific stream of injuries which included Kara Hutchinson, Kristina Ervin, and Diana Braendly and left Muffet with only seven roster players as she headed into the second-round game against Georgetown.

But McGraw is anything if not resourceful, and she knew that junior team manager Christie Grady had been an above average athlete in Lodi, California. Grady was awakened by Muffet in her hotel room in Stoors, Connecticut at 2 AM the night before the Georgetown game and measured for a jersey. Grady, who up until that time had been a regular on the team's film crew and had never even been to a practice session, was suddenly the accidental second coming of the now famous Rudy, an average person thrust into a decidedly unusual situation.

The team responded. The Irish, seeded third, blew out second seed Georgetown 83-43 and as the margin widened, Grady sat next to senior Roseanne Bohman as Bohman hastily sketched out an Irish play for the now-nervous newcomer. Suddenly, Muffet, showing her sense of drama and timing, pointed a finger at Grady and sent her in for Gaither at the 6:02 mark.

Within a few seconds, everyone in the Gampel Pavillion knew what was going on, and the crowd began to get behind the misplaced junior manager. After a couple of minutes, Grady found herself with the ball under the basket and she made what she called an easy layup. An hour later, the previously unknown towel-and-water girl was featured on CNN's play of the day. She would finish the game with two points, three rebounds, one steal, and a lifetime of memories.

And, another page had been added to the Notre Dame "Believe-it-or-not" book.

But even Grady's inspiration was not good enough to help Notre Dame in the Big East final. The Huskies had a little inspiration of their own as legendary coach Geno Auriemma was absent from the tournament to attend his father's funeral. His replacement, assistant Chris Dailey was hoisted onto the Huskies shoulders after UConn dismantled Notre Dame, 86-77, to claim the championship.

In the first round of the NCAA tournament, the sixth-seeded Irish opened against 11th seed Memphis and broke out to a 41-22 halftime lead on the way to a 92-63 pasting. Five players scored in double figures, led by Gaither's 24-point, 12-rebound effort.

Two days later, the Irish outlasted third-seeded Texas on their home floor, 86-83 and, unexpectedly, Notre Dame was in the Sweet 16 for the first time in its history. Third-round action saw them in Columbia, South Carolina, where they dismantled second-seeded Alabama, 87-71, as Beth Morgan scored a career high 36 points (including six 3-pointers) and Gaither added 26. Two days later, the Irish earned the title as a Cinderella team when they defeated fifth-seed George Washington, 62-52, to cap an impressive run through the East Regional and land a spot in the Final Four.

Unbelievably, incredibly and astonishingly, Notre Dame was in the Final Four.

Cinderella's coach was stopping in Cincinnati.

It had been quite a ride through the tournament, and Muffet knew it. While Cinderella may have worn the glass slipper, McGraw knew she would need tennis shoes to play against future player of the year, Chamique Holdsclaw. McGraw knew that there was no royal ball in Cincinnati. And while they were at the Big Dance, the handsome prince would be won by points, not pumpkins.

Muffet also knew one other thing.

She was exactly where she wanted to be.

CHAPTER 9

THE DRIVE TO THE CHAMPIONSHIP BEGINS

The week preceding the Final Four was unlike any that anyone in the Notre Dame women's basketball program had ever experienced.

With the tag "Cinderella" now firmly attached to their team identification, the Irish were new to the onslaught of national media, the attention, and the time it required from the daily routine.

McGraw knew that the fairy-tale Cinderella had three mean stepsisters and she knew her squad was going to step on the floor with possibly the biggest and meanest.

Tennessee, the third-seed in the Midwest Regional, had already won four national championships and was making a third straight trip to the finals. The Lady Vols had defeated Notre Dame once already, 72-59, in the preseason NIT.

More importantly, the Lady Vols had sophomore Chamique Holdsclaw, who two years later would be the NCAA Player of the Year. The Vols were deep, talented, experienced and ready.

Generally speaking, McGraw's crew was just happy to be at Cincinnati's Riverfront Coliseum, except for Morgan and Gaither.

Morgan and Gaither felt differently. "I remember two instances where I got a feel for what they were thinking," McGraw said. "Katryna was involved in a pregame press conference and in response to a reporter's question came right out and said, 'Hey, we didn't come here to lose.' I thought that spoke volumes.

"Also, about three weeks before that, Carol Owens and I were sitting on the bus talking about where we as coaches were going to stay for the coaches meetings, which coincide with the Final Four. Carol and I were talking about getting rooms for just us, and Beth Morgan pops up from behind and says, 'Hey, make sure you get rooms for us because we are going to be there with you.' Those kind of things gave me an indication what they were really thinking."

The Irish, in front of 16,714 people, roughly double the size of the largest crowd they had ever played for, gave Tennessee a battle. They went into halftime down only by a single point (29-28) and Muffet, though pleased with the first-half score, knew they had been outplayed underneath the basket and would have to rely on perimeter shooting to win.

Holdsclaw was having a field day on her way to a 31-point performance.

"We felt good at halftime, though," McGraw said. "We knew we were still in it, but at the same time Katryna was having a tough first half and we could not contain them. We were playing a 'hide-your-weakness' 2-3 zone to keep us from getting into foul trouble. Eventually our defense was our downfall, but Tennessee was just a better team. We were a definite underdog."

The Irish stayed close late into the game. A Morgan 3-pointer with 10:51 brought Notre Dame to within two at 45-43. The Lady Vols responded with a 21-9 run to put the game away. Gaither came on strong during the second half and ended with a game-high 28 points. Morgan added 18, despite a 6-for-21 shooting effort from the field. Morgan was the main target of the aggressive and quick Tennessee defense, which also forced 23 turnovers from the normally sure-handed Irish.

The game, which had started about 9 PM ended with Tennessee winning, 80-66. It was a late night as the Irish loss began to sink in on Gaither and Morgan.

"We went over and acknowledged our supporters," McGraw said. "Then we went into the locker room and I think we were all very disappointed. Looking back on it, however, if we had known that we would get to the Final Four that year, I think we would have been satisfied. However, once we got to the Sweet 16 for the first time in Notre Dame history and then suddenly we are in the Final Four, I really think most of us thought that it was phenomenal. Like Holy Cow, this feels good."

Muffet and Matt left Cincinnati early the next day.

"I was exhausted," Muffet said. " Looking back on it now, I would have loved to spend more time there."

After the game, Morgan said she simply walked off the floor.

"As a competitor, all I knew was that I had lost," she said. "Obviously, the team had come a long way, but I was very disappointed. The team hung around all three days, soaking up the atmosphere and seeing what it was all about.

"The only thing I really was disappointed with was that I was chosen to be one of the two random players the NCAA drug-tested after the game. All of my friends from Indiana were outside waiting for me, but I didn't get out to be with them because the test took so long."

It would be 2 AM before Morgan's test was completed, and she returned to an empty, dimly lit coliseum. Pausing for an instant as the drone of the vacuum machines of the cleanup crew replaced the cheers of the crowd, Morgan pondered what could have been for a brief moment, and then walked silently off the floor and into the cold night air of Cincinnati.

The battle was lost, but the future for both Morgan and the Irish team appeared bright.

It wasn't long before Muffet reoriented herself toward the massive rebuilding job that was to come.

"The problem was that it was like, 'Gee, this person can't exactly replace that person,'" she said. "The reality was that we knew we were going to have to run an entirely different type of offense.

"At that point, we had recruited Kelley, Ruth, and Meaghan, and we knew we had Sheila and Niele and Molly Peirick at the guard. Kelley could run the floor like Katryna, but she wasn't a post-up player. Ruth and Meaghan were post-up players, but they couldn't run the floor like she could.

"Then we knew that we would miss the leadership of Beth. Beth was the kind of player who would say just give me the ball and I'll win the game for you. She was easily the best leader I've ever had in terms of on the court, knowing what to do, having the confidence and having the ability to do it."

Muffet knew her revamped team had a strong place to start because Ruth Riley had agreed to come to Notre Dame for college. Riley had been highly recruited.

"We were looking for big players that year and Carol said Ruth was the best one out there," Muffet said. "Ruth had made Parade All-American fourth or fifth team and I think a lot of people weren't sure how she would do in college.

"Carol basically said that we had to get Ruth, but I wasn't all that interested at first because I had seen Kara Wolters of Connecticut play and I prefer to play an up tempo game," Muffet said. "Then I saw Ruth play in an AAU tournament and she was playing against a very athletic center and played quite well and I originally thought that she would be more of a defensive presence than an offensive weapon.

"I did, think, however, that Carol was right," Muffet continued. "We really did have to have her. But we knew she needed some work, also. I wouldn't really call her a project as such, but in high school she didn't have to jump much for rebounds and there were always two players hanging on her.

"She needed a lot of work on footwork, getting up and down the floor, and movement without the ball. We knew that if we could get her that she would help us."

Notre Dame, however, had not depleted its cupboards entirely in Cincinnati. "Our returning players did have Final Four experience and that really takes your team to a whole new level," Muffet continued. "With our great trio at guard, I knew we would be guard-oriented for a while. We were running the triangle offense, which I learned from Bulls assistant coach Tex Winter on what I call a pilgrimage. He was like my hero.

"So we knew we would do some of the same stuff we had done in years past, but we didn't really know what to expect going in to practice," she said. "We were pretty sure that we were going to be a slower team and we didn't really want to have a lot of expectations for Ruth right away."

Muffet was in for a bit of a surprise when practice opened in the fall of 1997.

"When we got to practice, Kelley was the best post player in the gym from Day 1. She ran the floor, she rebounded, and she was athletic. We started Julie Henderson with her and I kept telling myself that this was going to be a rebuilding year and I had to lower my expectations and that I had to be patient."

Patience has never been one of Muffet's long suits on the coaching floor. Her plan of staying calm went out the window before the paint was dry on the new names above the stalls in the locker room.

"We beat Butler by six and I thought that, despite the fact we played very average, at least it was a win," McGraw said. "But I flew off the handle immediately after we had lost the next game to Duke — in a game that we were close until the final four minutes when we totally fell apart at the end.

"I just remember going into the locker room and saying, 'Help! Forget the rebuilding, now let's go. Let's get it together.' Then we went out west and beat two good teams (U-Cal Santa Barbara, 86-75, and UCLA, 93-91, in two overtimes), but then we lost three games in a row, which we haven't done since."

Desperate straits for a coach who hates to lose at anything. The 3-4 start after a Final Four appearance fit on McGraw the way a size 6 skirt fits on a size 10 body. It was in this desperate mode that McGraw decided to play her trump card, even though her trump card was having trouble staying in the game.

"We were having the team over for dinner for some reason," Muffet said. "I pulled Ruth aside and I said, 'Ruth, you know what? You just became our starting center. It is time for you to step up and play.'"

Previous to that moment, Riley had played 63 minutes and had accumulated 17 fouls, which meant more than a foul every four minutes.

Riley started her first game against Purdue on December 10, 1997, and promptly fouled out after playing 20 minutes and scoring 13 points in a 77-71 win. The Boilermakers that night got an 18-point, seven rebound performance from a freshman named Katie Douglas.

But McGraw was committed to the transition and Riley rewarded her with a 10-rebound, 24-minute performance at home against South Florida in which she committed only three fouls. She then played 30 minutes in a 62-47 win over San Francisco, scoring 11 and committing only three fouls.

Things were improving, or so McGraw thought.

"We had plans for Ruth when we recruited her," McGraw said. "We thought she could be a Kara Wolters type of player...to stay in the middle, block shots, and players would have to shoot over her. And really, who is going to stop her at 6-foot-5?

"But we did not really have plans for her early in the season. She couldn't get up and down the floor very well and she was foul-prone. Our original plans were to bring her along slowly and hope that by the end of her freshman year she would be ready to go."

Those plans, of course, changed.

Riley got back into her foul funk as the Big East schedule got into full swing. She played only 19 minutes and scored one point at Pittsburgh, then only 16 minutes and eight points at Georgetown. But she bounced back with her first double-double (29 minutes, 11 points, and 19 rebounds) in a 75-47 trouncing of Miami. Her second career double-double followed in the next game as the Irish defeated St. John's, 77-57. Riley played 19 minutes and counted 10 points and 10 rebounds.

Riley's watershed game came on January 14 at the JACC. In a 86-78 win over West Virginia, Riley scored 27 points on an 11-14 night from the field and stayed on the floor for 32 minutes while committing only four fouls. An 18-point, 11-rebound performance followed, but more importantly she sat out the last few minutes of a 78-76 loss to Boston College because she had fouled out.

The foul trend would not change in Riley's freshman year. She sat firmly on the bench in the two Big East contests (80-67 loss to Rutgers and 78-59 loss to UConn), playing less than five minutes in each game while a frustrated Muffet struggled with how to use her star recruit.

Her importance to the team could not have been stated more clearly. The balance of the season saw gradual and sometime impressive improvement. She was named to the Big East All-Rookie team on the basis of her team record five consecutive (nine overall) double-doubles. She ended up being the team's second leading scorer (11.5 ppg behind Sheila McMillen's 13.6) and leading rebounder (7.3 rebounds).

As usual, the team got whacked by third-ranked UConn in the Big East final, 73-53, in a game which Riley played only 23 minutes before fouling out.

Notre Dame was seeded ninth in the Midwest Region and traveled to Lubbock, Texas, to take on Southwest Missouri State, which featured a nifty freshman guard named Jackie Stiles. The "Get the Ball to Ruth" strategy was now firmly entrenched as the Irish offense of choice. The opponents defense of choice, of course, was to let Riley foul herself out of the game.

Southwest Missouri State's strategy worked. Riley scored 21 points in only 24 minutes of play. But Notre Dame won anyway, 78-64. The Irish perimeter defense forced 25 turnovers and Notre

Dame established a double-digit lead, which it held for most of the game. McMillen tossed in 13 and Mollie Peirick and Siemon scored 12 apiece, and Notre Dame moved to a second-round game against top-seed Texas Tech.

The Texas Tech game was to be a watershed game for Notre Dame. Texas Tech was the No. 1-seed and the Lady Raiders were playing on their home court. If they won, they would get their home floor again in the regionals.

But it was Riley and her crew who won the day, 74-59, much to the disappointment of the rabid crowd of over 8,000 Texas Tech fans. Ruth went 9-for-12 from the field and 5-for-5 from the free-throw line against All-American Alicia Thompson.

After a slow first-half effort by Notre Dame, mostly due to Riley picking up two fouls in the first 47 seconds of the game, the Irish went on scoring runs of 9-0 and then 12-0 in the second half to deflate and eventually toss the Raiders out of the tournament.

McMillen had 13 points and Siemon added 10 while Peirick contributed 11 assists.

Texas Tech had been ranked fifth nationally, and it marked the highest-ranked opponent Notre Dame had beaten in the 21-year history of its program.

The next week, it was back to Lubbock to play eventual national champion and fourth-ranked Purdue. The Boilers were out to avenge the 77-71 early-season loss and did so using the formula of getting Riley to foul out.

Ruth played only 17 minutes and her foul trouble allowed the Boilermakers to come back from a 56-40 deficit with 13:21 remaining in the game. Purdue went on a 22-5 run at that point and won going away. McMillen scored 22, Ivey 12, and Riley 10.

The necessity of having Ruth in the game, even as a freshman, was obvious. The foul problem had to be taken care of if this Irish team was going to reach the top.

Notre Dame finished the 1997-98 season with a 22-10 record. Ruth had fouled out of eight games during the year.

Those numbers, in this case, really told the story.

CHAPTER 10

A KNEE AWAY FROM GREATNESS — THE SOPHOMORE YEAR

It was just a little pop.

No one ever heard it except Niele Ivey.

Yet, that little noise Niele Ivey heard and felt in her left knee on March 1, 1999, would change the fortunes of a whole lot of people.

Ivey had led her team to a 24-3 mark in the 1998-99 season, averaging 13.2 points, almost six assists, and 31.4 minutes a game. If Riley was the aircraft carrier inside for Notre Dame, Ivey had become the tugboat outside, managing the offense and inspiring the defense.

Riley cut her foul frequency from once every four minutes to once every seven minutes. She fouled out of just three games, none of them losses and all three of them within the first nine games of the year.

In those three losses, she played only 25 minutes in the 106-81 shellacking by UConn on December 8 at the JACC, 35 minutes in the 77-57 loss to Rutgers on February 13, and 33 minutes in a surprising December 30th loss to Boston College.

The team, in fact, was learning to play without Riley, and Ivey was a major part of the reason. She got off to a rousing start, scoring 25 points and adding 11 assists in a season opening win over sixth-ranked UCLA on November 14, 1998, at the JACC. It was a statement that Notre Dame had achieved the second rung of the women's basketball elite. No longer was the basketball world surprised when the Irish won against a Top 10 opponent.

But the top rung is reserved for a very few, and the December 8th confrontation with top-ranked UConn in front of 5,102 at the JACC showed McGraw just how far the team had to go.

The Irish were never in the game. UConn shot 56 percent from the field and held Notre Dame to 38 percent. Riley got into foul trouble and left the middle open for the Huskies, who didn't mind a bit. McMillen scored 21 points, Ivey added 17, Danielle Green 12, and Riley 10 for Muffet's team.

The Huskies were confident, almost cocky. Notre Dame was still a distance from the quality of team that could defeat them.

Twenty-five points distant to be exact.

The 1998-99 Irish team mirrored almost exactly the team that would eventually win the national championship two years later. In fact, McMillen was a senior that year and would be replaced by look-alike, play-alike Alicia Ratay the following year. Danielle Green, a junior at the time, had very similar qualities as her eventual replacement, Ericka Haney.

However, there were two major differences in the two squads. First and foremost was an age difference. The threesome of Riley, Siemon, and Ivey were sophomores, each dealing with growing up in their own way, on and off the court.

That led to the second difference. The 1998-99 squad lacked the mental toughness to become champions.

That lack of mental toughness showed in a December 30, 1998, road loss to Boston College, a team that would eventually finish 22-8 and 12-6 in the Big East. Teams on the third rung of the competitive ladder now saw an upset of Notre Dame as a feather in their cap.

A crowd of over 4,133 roared their approval as the Eagles took a lethargic Irish team to the shed, 78-65. Riley still had a double-double, but Ivey and McMillen combined for only 14 points on 5-for-14 from the field.

The Irish, awakened to their own vulnerability, recovered and went on an 11-game win streak before visiting Rutgers on February 13. Notre Dame basketball teams, in general, male or female, bring out the crowds to Louis Brown Athletic Center. This was no exception.

Rutgers coach Vivian Stringer traditionally concentrates on defense and held Notre Dame to 33 percent from the field, forcing 23 turnovers (including eight steals). The combination of an aggressive crowd and a stingy defense showed the crack in the Irish mental toughness. The Scarlet Knights won going away, 77-57.

Still, as the season wound down, the Irish were ranked eighth nationally as they headed into the Big East tournament. On March 1, the Irish turned the tables on the Scarlet Knights, establishing a 43-28 halftime edge in the Big Eat semifinal game.

But the pop that Ivey heard for the second time in her career changed the course of this team. The anguish on her face was only matched by the incredulous look on Irish supporters who wondered just why Ivey would be visited twice by knee injuries. Notre Dame eventually won that game, 68-61, but then got drubbed by UConn in the finals, 96-75.

Ever the optimist, McGraw was figuring the eighth-ranked team in the nation should be awarded one of the eight NCAA opening-round tournament sites. However, the NCAA committee, recognizing Notre Dame without Ivey would be like the Chicago Bulls playing without star forward Scottie Pippen, awarded the site to LSU and dropped Notre Dame clear into a fifth seed.

McGraw called "foul" and let everyone within earshot know that she considered the decision unfair. But there would be no reversal and the Irish were headed for the Maravich Center.

Playing in front of smallish crowds of less than 3,000, considering the fact that it was an NCAA tournament event, Notre Dame defeated 12th-seed Saint Mary's, 61-57, but had to come from five points behind in the final two minutes to do so.

Riley was again saddled with foul trouble, playing only 29 minutes while scoring 16 points. McMillen added 15 and Green 12. Without their floor leader, the Irish committed 25 turnovers. Ivey was replaced by sophomore Sherisha Hills, who managed five points and seven assists in the game.

The fragile mentality of the 1999-2000 year Notre Dame team reared its ugly head one last time as they self-destructed in the final 8:32 of a 74-64 loss to LSU. Notre Dame led, 59-51, before the Tigers went on a 23-5 run for the victory.

The loss of Ivey, as the NCAA committee had correctly anticipated, was the difference as Notre Dame committed 27 turnovers, eight by Hills. Riley scored 20 and played nearly the entire game. Green added 19 and Siemon 10.

McMillen scored nine points in her last game. An impressive career over, the Rochester native still scored 1,439 points and in her senior year averaged 15.4 points per game and averaged 87 percent shooting from the free-throw line. Two years later, she would land an assistant coaching job at Western Michigan University in nearby Kalamazoo, Michigan.

Hills left the program under amicable conditions after this season, preferring the warmer climate of Florida over the harsh winters of South Bend.

As spring came to South Bend, McGraw knew that Ivey's knee would be well enough to play the next year. She also knew that Riley would get better and better. She also knew that between Siemon and Julie Henderson that the power forward spot would be OK. She also had Green coming back and was comfortable with Ericka Haney to back her up.

The big question mark was at shooting guard, where Alicia Ratay, a slightly built sharpshooter from nearby Lake Zurich (IL), would have to step in big time if Notre Dame was to climb into the stratosphere of the elite programs.

CHAPTER 11

STILL A MISSING PUZZLE PIECE — THE JUNIOR YEAR

McGraw needed not to have worried about Ratay.

Like Beth Morgan before her, the freshman stepped onto the floor and right into the spot left by McMillen. She scored 18 points in her first game, a 68-52 win over Toledo. While Ratay would be as inconsistent as any other freshman as the year wore on, she would also provide Notre Dame with an explosive talent, a player who could light up the team, scoreboard, and crowd with an almost-nonchalant 3-point weapon. There would be no competition for that spot. Writing her name in the starting lineup would become automatic.

However, competition would develop over the power-forward spot. Siemon, who had started and played that position as a freshman and sophomore, had suffered through what she called a "sophomore slump" and senior Julie Henderson had worked hard to break into the lineup. Her hard work paid dividends, and she was moved into the starting position early in the year and Siemon became the sixth (wo)man

Ivey's knee would be strong and Riley had played in the World Games as part of a national team over the summer. This could, McGraw felt, be the year when Notre Dame would step into the elite few.

Championship teams need a combination of talent, a little luck, avoidance of injuries, and team cohesiveness. The Irish, as it would turn out, had three out of four.

The talent was unquestioned. Riley kept her foul ratio under control, though showing little improvement over the previous year. Ivey played more minutes than anyone on the team, having lost a little speed due to the knee operations but none of the moxie that great players have. The addition of Ratay gave them the outside scoring punch the team required, and the other positions stood two-deep with quality players.

The luck born of hard work was never more in evidence than on February 9, in the Louis Brown Athletic Center, where the

Rutger's Miracle would ever define the cool collectiveness of Ratay. It would also become the thing of legends.

The eighth-ranked Scarlet Knights had again utilized their athleticism and defense to stymie the fifth-ranked Irish and the game appeared essentially lost. The Irish had the ball with 26 seconds to go facing a 65-59 deficit when the freshman gunslinger rode into town. Dead-eye Ratay was about to earn her nickname.

She sank her first with 17.3 seconds to go ("It was a fairly open look," McGraw said later) to get Notre Dame back to within three. Notre Dame immediately fouled and Tasha Pointer missed the front end of a bonus free throw with 16.1 remaining to leave the door open for a miracle.

That was all the opening Ratay needed, and all that she would get. Notre Dame had a set play and Ratay dribbled around a screen at the top of the key. Three defenders converged. Ratay was guarded closer than a Brinks truck at closing time.

"I swear we must have had fingertips on the leather," Stringer said after game. "I don't know if we could have been any closer without fouling."

Miracles often look like that, a great shot with a little impossibility thrown in. "She read the defense and she found the opening," McGraw said.

There really was no opening. But the freshman went up and made the shot anyway. The gunslinger had claimed her first big victim. On the night, she was 7-7 from the field (all 3-pointers), 26 points, 10 rebounds, and two incredible shots that players dream of making. Her final two free throws were the final go-ahead points in the 78-74 overtime win.

It was, in the vernacular, a night to die for.

At that point, Notre Dame was 23-2 and undefeated in the Big East. A win over Miami set up the Big East Conference regular season championship contest at the Hartford Civic Arena against UConn. The Huskies were ranked No. 1 and again sent the Irish to bed without their supper with a 77-59 win. Auriemma used the foul out Riley strategy, and Ruth obliged, playing only 22 minutes and scoring only four points.

Still, Notre Dame had gotten through the regular season with its starting lineup intact and relatively injury free, save some bumps and bruises. Rutgers avenged the regular season loss with an 81-72 overtime win in the Big East semifinal despite all five of the Irish starters scoring in double figures.

Notre Dame ended the season ranked fifth in the nation and hosted first- and second-round action in the NCAA tournament. They were awarded the second seed and demolished 15th seed San Diego, 87-61, as the whole team got into the game. Riley and Ivey scored 14 each. Siemon added 13 and Green 12 for the win.

Ivey scored 23 points to lead the Irish over George Washington in the second round matchup. Green added 16, Riley and Henderson 14 each, and Ratay 11. Siemon pulled down a personal high 14 rebounds as the Irish advanced to the regional.

The Regional was held at the Pyramids in Memphis, Tennessee and it was there that the Irish's season long internal issues would take its final toll. Notre Dame bounced out to a 17-0 edge over Texas Tech before losing their concentration and allowing a comeback. The game turned, in the usual fashion, on a critical Riley foul.

She started the second half with two fouls and picked up her third with just under 12 minutes to play with Notre Dame still ahead. However, Texas Tech coach Marsha Sharp instructed her squad to take it to Riley and she picked up her fourth with just under eight minutes to go. Her fifth came with about 1:30 to go and was an offensive foul, a foul which many called questionable.

Questionable or not, Tech advanced with a 69-65 win, sending Muffet and her Irish home.

The team, even at 27-5, had underachieved, McGraw felt. And besides that, the year had not been fun. While she blamed a lack of senior leadership, it was more of a combination of that and some intense coaching methods by McGraw. She would not go through another year like this, she decided.

She knew she had most of her team coming back that fall, but she also knew that things had to change and change fast, if her four-year project of a team would achieve the greatness she so strongly desired.

Muffet fretted.

Muffet burned.

Something had to be done, but what?

CHAPTER 12

BREAKING DOWN TO BUILD BACK UP

Very few national championships are actually won on the last game of the season.

The road to a championship is usually begun soon after the completion of the previous season and is fraught with chuckholes, sideroads, and roadblocks. And for Notre Dame the first major roadblock came early.

The weeks between the loss to Texas Tech and the final team meeting were not easy on a congenital worrier like McGraw. In her case, worry begat anger, which begat rage.

Her plan of a nice "how do you do" end-of-season meeting would dissolve into an accidental crystallization process. The team, though highly successful when measured against nearly every other program on the continent the previous season, was in disarray and would have to be righted quickly if it was to reach what many thought was to be its destiny.

At any rate, Muffet scheduled her meeting.

And it, indeed, started out as a nice "how do you do" meeting.

Then she showed the tape of the Texas Tech debacle, the one where Notre Dame jumped out to a 17-0 lead and then disappeared like the wicked witch in the *Wizard of Oz* did after Dorothy threw the water on her. Melted away, goo in a puddle.

Then all hell broke loose.

Among friends, of course.

The now-acrimonious meeting was a gamble, but the cards had been already dealt.

It was either a stroke of genius or a really bad idea and there was no guarantee what would happen afterward.

"I made them realize how much we relied on Ruth," Muffet said. "And how unfair it was to Ruth and how it wasn't good for the team because when she went out of the game, we never knew what to do."

That's when the meeting got "real ugly."

"Everyone said what they had on their mind," McGraw said.

"The coaches told them that even though the players said they wanted to get better, they would have to make some sacrifices to get the job done. I wanted them to take a long hard look at their performance. They had to mature.

"I think there was a mental issue, some leadership issues, some chemistry issues. We just did not have much chemistry in the previous year's senior class, although I thought Julie Henderson had had a wonderful year. She was the lone bright spot."

"I remember that meeting very well," Niele Ivey said. "Julie Henderson and Danielle Green were leaving, and it was a tough decision for me to come back. It was a major commitment for me, I mean it was a whole year. I didn't know what to expect when that meeting started, but we had known during the year that the team leadership was suspect."

The higher Muffet's voice rose, the deeper Ivey and her teammates had to look for answers within themselves. And it wasn't just McGraw doing the talking.

"Everyone was honest," Ivey said. "We let it hurt some feelings. We knew that every year we had the talent to win the big games and every year we lost them. We knew we had to take a look at ourselves as individuals and see what we could do to make the team better. What could we do to make us as individuals better? It was a meeting in which players let their frustrations out there."

There were no answer immediately available after the bloodletting. Each player, and in particular the seniors, left the locker room with a new weight placed firmly on their shoulders.

"Leadership was a real problem," McGraw continued. "The team had to be more important than the individual, and it didn't have to be the Ruth Riley Show to be successful. But if the rest of the team was just going to stand around and do nothing, they left us no choice.

"I really think there was some resentment about how the offense ran the previous year and it just wasn't a fun year. I wanted them to be mad going into the summer."

They were. The seniors immediately set about refocusing their energies on the following season. Meanwhile, McGraw knew she had some of her own demons with which to deal.

"That meeting left a bad taste in my mouth," McGraw said. "I'm not the kind of coach who worries about an individual's hurt

The coaching staff at the Final Four: (l-r) Kevin McGuff, Coquese Washington, Muffet McGraw, and Carol Owens. (Photo credit: Michael and Susan Bennett)

McGraw hands out instructions to her squad in the national semifinal against UConn. (Photo credit: Michael and Susan Bennett)

Junior Ericka Haney finds an opening against Purdue's Shinika Parks in the finale.
(Photo credit: Michael and Susan Bennett)

Sophomore Alicia Ratay quickly became an Irish favorite with her impressive skills. (Photo credit: Michael and Susan Bennett)

Senior Kelley Siemon inspired the team and the university with her heroics against UConn on Martin Luther King, Jr., Day. (Photo credit: Michael and Susan Bennett)

Niele Ivey returned to her hometown, St. Louis, and played a key role in the national championship win. (Photo credit: Michael and Susan Bennett)

Ivey's grimace turned out to be a mild ankle sprain in the semifinals against the Huskies. (Photo credit: Michael and Susan Bennett)

Ten years ago, who would have dared dream this up? Irish fans go nuts for women's basketball. (Photo credit: Michael and Susan Bennett)

The deciding play. Riley is fouled (or not fouled depending on your point of view) by Sherecka Wright with 5.8 seconds to go. (Photo credit: Michael and Susan Bennett)

Riely hits the first free throw for the lead in the final seconds. (Photo credit: Michael and Susan Bennett)

Let the celebration begin. The first-ever national championship for the Irish. (Photo credit: Michael and Susan Bennett)

The spoils belong to the winners. (Photo credit: Michael and Susan Bennett)

Ruth Riley gets her first-ever championship strand. (Photo credit: Michael and Susan Bennett)

University president Rev. Edmund A. Malloy congratulates the happy team. (Photo credit: Michael and Susan Bennett)

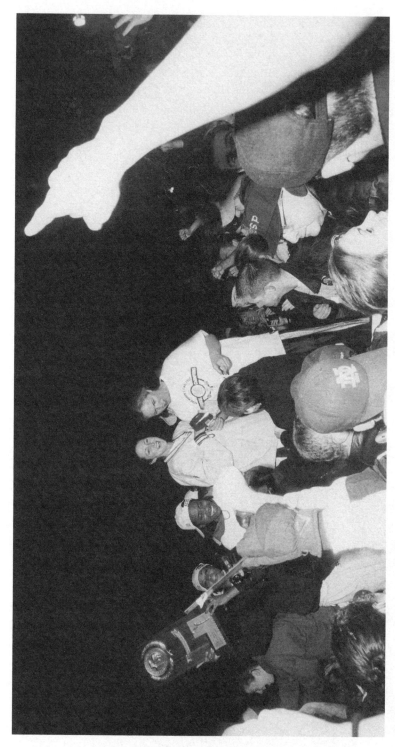

The university celebrates its new champions at 2 AM on the circle. (Photo credit: Michael and Susan Bennett)

President George W. Bush with Muffet and Murphy McGraw. Ruth Riley and Kelley Siemon in the background.

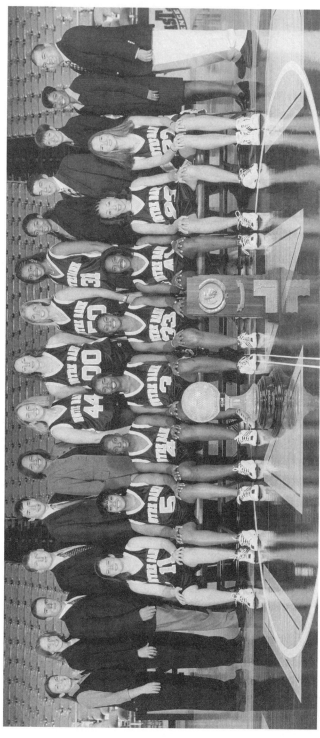

Official team photo. Front row (left to right): Karen Swanson, Jeneka Joyce, Le'Tania Severe, Ericka Haney, Niele Ivey, Imani Dunbar, Monique Hernandez, Alicia Ratay. Second row (left to right): senior manager Gretchen Schumer, marketing and promotions assistant Heather Maxwell, strength and conditioning coach Tony Rolinski, athletic trainer Mike Miller, assistant coach Kevin McGuff, assistant coach Carol Owens, Meaghan Leahy, Ruth Riley, Kelley Siemon, Amanda Barksdale, director of basketball operations Letitia Bowen, manager Ryan Baker, head coach Muffet McGraw, assistant coach Coquese Washington, senior manager Jaime Morales. (Photo credit: Michael and Susan Bennett)

feelings and so as I was watching someone make a mistake on the floor and if I thought someone else could do a better job, I sent them in. For the individual player, it was tough, but it wasn't really anything personal.

"I spent a lot of time re-evaluating my coaching methods over the summer," McGraw said. "I knew I just didn't have any fun coaching the year before and I wasn't going to go through that again."

Re-evaluation meant a call to mentor and current Vanderbilt coach Jim Foster.

It would not be out of the realm of thinking to suggest that Foster had been a godfather of sorts for Notre Dame's championship season. It was he, after all, who introduced the administration at Notre Dame to the idea of hiring McGraw in the first place. It was Foster who sent Carol Owens to South Bend, who directed Imani Dunbar to play on the team, and it was Foster who traded coaching ideas with McGraw in long intense phone calls as well as combined staff meetings during the off-season.

The combined staff meetings were of immense help to Muffet.

"It is a highly unusual setup," McGraw said. "I don't think women's coaches share as much as the men's coaches do. There is a certain point in your coaching career where you stop going to clinics and you just start calling people and say I love your defense, can we talk about it.

"Jim has been at it so long now that he gets together with people at a place called the Paris Patch, which is a bed-and-breakfast way out in the country in Tennessee, outside of Nashville. One year I went by myself, one year I took Carol, and last year I took my whole staff. It really has been helpful.

"Philosophically, Jim and I have a lot in common. We both like 2-3 zones, we both like motion offenses, but the best part is we talk and we talk about everything, from basketball to leadership and all kinds of other things about the team."

So, McGraw decided she would drop her personal level of intensity and let the seniors take more ownership of the team. She knew that the captains, Riley and Ivey, were ready for it and she also sensed the chemistry of the team in general was better. "It was a maturing process for the team," McGraw said.

It was also a maturing process for the former Lehigh coach.

Asking a nervous, pacing, controlling personality like McGraw to step back and let things flow a little more is like asking a banker to work on Sundays. OK in theory, but not really comfortable for the banker.

As fall practice started, McGraw knew it was her responsibility to set up the systems that would allow the strengths of her team to be optimized. Her first goal was to establish defense as a top priority.

"There had to be more pride and intensity in our defense," McGraw said. "Our defense had to become important to us. The goal was to limit the other team to under 50 points. If we didn't, the team had to run wind sprints."

Hold powerful UConn to 50? High-scoring Georgia to 50?

"Well, OK," McGraw said. "There was some discussion about those teams and we relaxed the rule in certain games, but for the large majority of the games, the goal was to hold them to 50. The result was that we led the entire nation in field-goal defense so the idea must have worked. We had discussed defense as being important in past years, but this year the team bought into it."

Score one for Muffet Management 101. Let the team own the idea. They were the ones playing the game anyway.

Fortunately, the starting five provided good ingredients with which to work. Riley, assuming she could stay out of foul trouble, was the quintessential shot blocker. The natural defensive leader was a now totally healthy and confident Ivey.

"Ericka Haney was our stopper," McGraw said. "The return of Kelley to our lineup added someone who was normally a good defender but who played much better in our zone defense, and then there was Alicia, who was a good rebounder as well as a very smart defender."

The second design McGraw had to come up with was an offense that would help Riley out. The problem was obvious: The whole world knew that Riley was going to get the ball at some point in the offensive pattern nearly every time out. With the higher-percentage shots always being taken from the paint, teams just had to manhandle Riley and hope the Irish outside shooting that day would be under par.

At issue was the triangle offense, which McGraw had borrowed from the Bulls. The patterns were leaving the power forward at the elbow with a wide-open shot. Scottie Pippen could hit those shots with regularity, Kelley Siemon et al couldn't.

In crucial situations, the ball still needed to be in Ruth's hands. In order to make it work, however, she needed some options.

"We sort of changed our offense at the beginning of the year," Riley said. "We went to more of a motion offense."

The idea would make Notre Dame a national champion. While Siemon may not have been a great shooter from 10 feet and out, her layup skills were unquestioned. She was one of those players who exploited openings by wriggling through them and just about the time a turnover was imminent, the ball would kiss the glass and fall through the net.

It would be a while before Siemon would truly realize her place in the offense. In fact, it would be January 15, 2001.

The team had a new radio broadcast contract also. For the last few years, WHME-FM had been working with the Irish. The FM signal carried for nearly a 40-mile radius in most cases and it was combined with a TV contract to broadcast a few number of games each year.

In 2000-01, however, broadcast rights were purchased by a new radio conglomerate that had bought a powerful FM channel (U93) and three AM frequencies, WNDU-AM (1490), WAMJ (1580), and WHLY (1620).

The management of the new station made the decision to broadcast the ND women's games on the 1620 frequency but to offer a pregame radio show featuring Muffet on its powerful FM station.

The problem was certain car radios could not even access the 1620 frequency and the AM signal barely reached the south part of St. Joseph county, let alone allow for much regional exposure. To solve that problem, the broadcast was also sent out over the Internet.

The station hired Sean Stires from KVAY in Lama, Colorado, as sports director and also to do play-by-play for the women's games. Stires, an energetic and outgoing graduate of Kansas University, had set his sights on doing sports at Notre Dame as a life goal.

"I was going through some industry websites on the Internet, looking to see what was available, and all of the sudden I see this ad," he said. "It was one of those once-in-a-lifetime things. I called and everything worked out.

"I came out here in October, leaving my wife and two kids in Colorado trying to sell our house. I had looked at the Notre Dame website and I had seen that this team was going to be a very good team. I was really excited, not only to be doing Notre Dame basketball, but also to be doing it during a season where they could be a Final Four team."

Leaving the family was not easy for Stires, but he threw himself into the job. He quickly became enamored with the players. "I met Muffet when I came out and interviewed with the team and then I attended a few practices," he said.

He didn't have an inkling of the ride he was about to take.

The season started with a November 17th contest at Valparaiso, and it seemed as if the Irish couldn't wait to destroy someone. Riley scored only 13 points as the outside shooting ruled the day in a 71-46 pasting of the Crusaders. Ratay showed there would be no sophomore slump for her as she nailed 6-of-9 three-pointers and led the team with 20 points.

Ivey became the 17th member of the 1,000 point club early in the game as she hit one of her two 3-pointers on her way to a 12-point, five-steal, 10-assist performance. Siemon scored all six of her points in a 53-second explosion in the first half as the Irish blew out to a 47-17 half-time edge.

"I remember Alicia was just outstanding that game, but it was Valparaiso and they were obviously outmatched," Stires said. "But you could tell they would do well in their conference."

There would be no wind sprints. And on top of that, Riley had not committed a single foul in 29 minutes of play. The Irish had, in fact, played a perfect game their first game into the season.

Ratay continued her early-season barrage when the Arizona Wildcats visited the JACC for the Irish home opener on November 20. She scored 26 on an amazing 5-for-6 effort from beyond the 3-point arc. In fact the shot she missed, she rebounded on her own, scored the rebound shot, and was fouled for the old-fashioned 3-point play. All that in only 28 minutes of play.

Notre Dame had blitzed out to a 57-29 half-time lead en route to a 95-65 win. Ivey recorded her second straight double-double with 14 points and 11 assists in front of a respectable 3,087 fans.

Gone were the days with crowds of only 300 people, and immediately after the game Riley emerged from the dressing room and postgame interview sessions to sign autographs. Showing an incredible touch with both the parents and the kids, Riley simply signed autographs until the last little admirer was gone. The best part was, the gentle Riley looked each little (and some big) person in the eye and smiled. Such moments make legends, such moments make memories.

South Bend didn't know it just yet, but it was about to have a love affair with this 6-foot-5 formerly shy, gangly kid from Macy, Indiana. Little blue-painted faces were about to show up at the JACC, a few at first, then many more as the season progressed.

Little boys too would soon be wearing headbands and jerseys with the number 00 on them and challenge others to beat them one-on-one.

It wasn't just Riley, of course. The whole team did it, and did it willingly. The Meaghan Leahys and the Jeneka Joyces, even the Muffet McGraws followed Riley's lead. The kids loved it, the parents loved it. The secret that was hidden in the bowels of the JACC was about to be exposed. Like a volcano about to explode, it was only a matter of time.

McGraw also established a postgame habit of going to a local restaurant called Between the Buns. The restaurant, the second of a small franchise, had opened in October and is almost adjacent to the university in a small strip mall and next to a popular bagel place co-owned by McGraw.

It is what many call a parents' restaurant. That is, it is a restaurant where the students take their parents to show them what college life is all about. The food is good and mid-priced, the beer cold and the service fast. Pictures of Notre Dame heroes, present and past, adorn the stained wooden walls — just the kind of place students tell Mom and Dad they hang out.

McGraw and her crew's first visit was a surprise, though accommodations were made immediately. As the season wore on, it became a habit, and McGraw would bring along an entourage of friends and colleagues. She would tour the restaurant, shaking hands and greeting well-wishers.

As the season rolled on and the popularity of the team increased, Buns co-owner Phil Schreiber could almost guarantee a sold-out house after the games.

Schreiber understood the growth of the sport as well as any.

His first restaurant opened about 12 years earlier in Osceola, a small town just east of South Bend. It was established as a legitimate place for the over-30 crowd to have a beer, talk sports, and enjoy good food.

"Up until this year," Schreiber said. "There really was no discussion about women's basketball. In our first location, we would fill the place up when a men's game was on and we still do. But there was nothing like that when the women played. A lot of the time, there wasn't even any television coverage anyway."

McGraw's team traveled to Madison, Wisconsin, two days later to play in the Coaches Versus Cancer tournament, where the Irish would meet stiffer competition. Wisconsin was ranked 19th at the time and the fifth-ranked Irish had no trouble disposing of the Badgers, emerging with a 83-56 win.

The Badger defensive emphasis was two-fold, shut down Ratay and Riley and see what happened. Ratay was shut down, suffering through a 1-for-6, eight-point effort. Riley was held to nine points.

But that opened up Siemon, who responded with a layup-heavy 21 points. Ivey had her third straight outstanding game, combining a 22-point, nine-rebound, and seven-assist effort. "In no way did we think Notre Dame was good enough to beat us on our home floor like they did," Wisconsin coach Jane Albright said in surprise.

That brought the Irish face-to-face with the No. 6-ranked Bulldogs. This game was as close as people thought it would be. The quality of the opponent forced McGraw to show the world that bench strength was going to be a problem, as Notre Dame received no points from its reserves. But Riley had by now slain the foul monster, and her presence in the game would enable the Irish to win a close game at the end.

Georgia had the ball and a chance to either tie or win in the closing seconds, but McGraw had the luxury of having only three fouls called on her team. She told her team to foul the player with the ball to waste away the final few ticks.

"That's something we haven't practiced on much in practice," McGraw said after the game. "When we told them to foul, they said, 'But, Coach, we are AHEAD, not behind.'"

The strategy worked, and Notre Dame had its first win of the year over a Top 10 opponent. Four players scored in double figures, led by tournament MVP Ivey's 19. Riley also tallied 19.

"Georgia was a great game to play that early in the season because you really can't lose," Muffet said. "You get to see where you are, you get to see what you've got against a really good team.

"We made a couple of critical turnovers near the end and basically looked like a team playing in November at the time. However, that game was the one that got us thinking, 'Dang! We are pretty good.' That was as important a win as any for us during the season."

Fordham was Notre Dame's next victim on November 27 at the JACC, and it finally was the bench's time to shine. With her Riley cheering her on from the bench, Meaghan Leahy had a career night, scoring 16 points, most of them on a 12-for-14 effort from the free-throw line in 24 minutes of play.

"It's just a matter of getting the playing time," said the highly recruited Leahy.

The defense was working. But then again so was the offense. This was a team on a roll, and their next game against North Carolina resulted in a 77-55 win in the Elite 4 Holiday Classic in Orlando, Florida. It was another shellacking of a better-than-average team. Again, a quick first half gave them a huge lead (42-19 at half-time) and for the sixth time in seven games, the opponents shot at less that 40 percent. Meanwhile the offense was shooting at around 50 percent from the field consistently.

The Big East opener on December 6 was in the JACC in front of 3,168 people. The Irish, now ranked No. 4, almost doubled up on Villanova. The Wildcats could only manage 20 percent shooting as Notre Dame set its record at 7-0, their fastest start in history.

Purdue and its No. 6 ranking came calling on December 9 and Notre Dame treated the large crowd of 7,330 to its 27th consecutive home win, beating the Boilers 72-61. It was the third-largest crowd in team history and was accomplished without the usual barrage of free tickets. Ericka Haney scored 16 points, including her first 3-pointer ever, while Ratay scored 19 on a 5-for-8 performance from beyond the stripe. Purdue, however, proved to be the first team to shoot with Notre Dame, connecting at a 46 percent clip. The Irish also had to overcome Ivey's leg cramps, which forced her out of the action with just under 10 minutes to go.

A 3-point dagger by Ratay ignited the crowd and was the turning point of the game, according to Kristy Curry, the Purdue head coach. "Ratay's quick release, and the way she shoots off the dribble is even better than it was last year," she said. "You can't give her an open look. But Notre Dame isn't all Ruth and Alicia."

What was becoming apparent was that this team had good chemistry. There were no fragments. The practice sessions saw fewer storms, as the seniors took the "I" out of team. Seniors Leahy and Dunbar subjugated their egos and took over the second unit and took, as their source of pride, their ability to beat the first unit in practice.

The team attitude began there. Teammates who are not playing very much can become a cancer to a team. Instead, Leahy and Dunbar drove the second unit in a manner similar to the way Ivey and Riley ran the first unit.

The Irish express, now at full steam with four impressive wins under its belt, whacked Western Michigan, with Assistant Coach Sheila McMillen, 84-54, on December 18, before 3,108 fans and the students heading out for winter break.

Leahy started due to a death in Siemon's family, but Siemon came off the bench with an 8-for-11 shooting performance and won her job back quickly. Ratay was her usual impressive self, scoring 21 points on nine straight shots. Western Michigan was held to 29 percent shooting.

December 21 saw Muffet's crew in Milwaukee, and it was Ericka Haney's turn. The 6-foot-1 junior was 10-of-12 from the field and Riley and Ivey added 18 apiece. Again the 2-3 zone held the Marquette Golden Eagles to 32 percent shooting. The final result was a 75-56 win and suddenly Notre Dame was 10-0.

Ruth Riley took control of Notre Dame's 11th win, a 70-61 win in Los Angeles over Southern Cal. Ruth scored a season-high 23. USC was held to 32 percent shooting while Notre Dame was in control the whole way, shooting 53 percent. Ratay and Haney added 12 apiece.

Notre Dame returned home for a New Year's Eve matchup with Rice. The 80-40 lambasting that the Irish handed out to the Owls marked McGraw's 300th career win at Notre Dame. The coach, now in her 14th season, was genuinely touched when son Murphy brought out a bouquet of flowers after the contest. Haney and Riley led the way for Notre Dame with 18 points and the whole team saw some floor time during their 12th win.

With the team now in the backstretch, they headed into Big East play. It was, in so many words, Riley time. The tinkering done, McGraw put her Ruth-first offense into full gear. The January 3rd game at Virginia Tech saw her score 27 while Ivey added 18, Haney 11, and Siemon 10.

Notre Dame, now ranked No. 3, hosted No. 9 Rutgers and served notice again that the undefeated record was no fluke. Stringer's team, again exhibiting one of the toughest defenses around, could not control Riley, who scored 22 points in a 67-46 win before 5,227 fans. The Irish shot 53 percent and held the Scarlet Knights to 36 percent.

It was a total domination job by McGraw's team, and the now more laid-back coach was having trouble in practice finding things to yell about.

Another blowout in New York saw the Irish wallop St. John's, 84-49. Riley now was playing like a Naismith Award winner should, blocking five shots, scoring 23 points and getting 11 rebounds. But she was playing under control and was whistled for only two fouls in 25 minutes of play.

To go inside against Riley now was to invite either a blocked or altered shot. The exterior of the zone defense was harassing outside shooters like so many mosquitoes on an early evening cookout.

The worst thing that could possibly happen did during the January 13th afternoon game against Virginia Tech, which Notre won, 75-55.

In that game, Siemon broke her hand and with just over 14 minutes to play, Riley twisted her ankle moments later and spent the rest of the game trying to walk on it and loosen it up. The Irish were now 16-0, and the biggest game in their history would be played in two days.

McGraw hovered somewhere between worry and panic that Saturday night. Going into the UConn game with one "what-if" was bad enough. Two "what-ifs" was unbearable.

After the fastest and brightest start in Notre Dame history, suddenly the immediate future was put in great doubt. As usual, Muffet paced and fretted, trying to figure out something she could do to give her team a better shot at the top-ranked Huskies.

But, realistically, there was no time to prepare anymore. The team had to do it itself. Sometime that Sunday afternoon, Muffet felt a sense of calm come over her. As any warrior before a big battle, she knew she was as prepared as she could possibly be.

Her time, and the team's time, was now at hand.

CHAPTER 13

THE UCONN GIANT *SLAIN,* OR AT LEA*ST* HOBBLED

The biggest day in Notre Dame women's basketball started very early.

At midnight, to be exact.

Kelley Siemon could not sleep.

Kelley had to know if she could shoot the basketball, if she could rebound the basketball, if she could even feel the basketball.

The doctors could give all the medical opinions they wanted to. Only Kelley would know if her broken left hand would allow her to play.

So she talked a male friend into accompanying her over to the JACC where, in the late-night solitude before the frenetic pace of the day that would dawn barely seven hours later, she passed and dribbled, and shot, and then passed some more.

There was, of course, some pain. But that pain would pale by comparison to the disappointment if she could not play in the biggest game in Notre Dame women's basketball.

It was a self-confidence session for Siemon. It was a determination session for Siemon. It was a session which would precede, by only 12 hours, the biggest basketball moment in her life.

Dozens of passes, dozens of shots, and dozens of dribbles later, Kelley left the JACC. The clock approached 1 AM as she crossed campus that night, but her heart was light, her concentration now could be focused. For the matter had been settled in the quiet confines of the basketball floor.

Kelley was going to play. And Notre Dame history was going to be written on the very cast that would protect her hand.

A certain M. McGraw tossed and turned that night. A house-full of guests from New Jersey had done little to detour the intense amount of pressure McGraw felt. At 2 PM the following afternoon, the women's team would play before the very first sellout in Irish basketball history, would be on ESPN, and if things went their way, would be in almost certain position to be the first basketball team in Irish history to be ranked No. 1.

An hour of fitful sleep would be followed by 15 minutes of checking the clock, an occasional water run or a bathroom break.

Then McGraw would lie down again, pulling covers off the sleeping spouse and doze for another 45 minutes or so, only to wake up, short of breath, and hope that the clock would run faster.

Would the night never end?

Yes, Matt McGraw admitted later he had trouble sleeping that night. "I slept like a real baby," he said, repeating an old joke. "I woke up every hour and cried."

And he wondered how Muffet, who usually would be pacing the floor at that time, could be as relaxed as she was and be so deep in peaceful slumber.

South Bend is a town that has a love-hate relationship with sports in general. Because of its diverse choice of things to do, the true fan base for any sport other than Notre Dame football or men's basketball in South Bend is small.

Around South Bend, media attention surrounding Notre Dame football is like media attention around an Elvis Presley rumor. There is so much interest that if a player important to the team sneezes during practice, reporters are sent to find out why.

In short, Notre Dame football sells papers and attracts viewers to sportscasts. Because of that, the attention given other sports is dealt out only after the required Notre Dame football story has been presented, gauged for importance, and sized.

So it had taken a while for the local media to figure out there was a sort of miracle happening just across the street from the football stadium. The early-season crowds at the women's games were presentable, but small by comparison to the crowds that men's basketball star Troy Murphy and his resurgent team were attracting.

Somehow, the word was spreading about Muffet, Ruth, Niele, Kelley, et al. Crowds were getting larger as the season progressed, but there was always the Connecticut disclaimer. It went something like, "Yeah, they are good, but wait until they play a real team like UConn."

That day had arrived.

And the crowd came out to see just how good this Irish team was. To local basketball media members, it was reminiscent of a high school game played 10 years earlier when the man-child Shawn Kemp, who later would become an NBA star, came to South Bend with his basketball team from nearby Concord High School to play against a highly ranked team from South Bend St. Joseph's High School.

That night, the people of South Bend literally jammed into the JACC, which had hastily been appropriated at the last minute when school officials realized that the large crowd would literally swamp the small high school gym originally scheduled to host the game.

Long lines and a carnival atmosphere delayed the start of the game for 30 minutes while officials tried to accommodate the crowd. It was a night that South Bend basketball fans remember as if it was yesterday, for it showed the power of a sporting event to take something quite ordinary and make it somehow larger than life.

The same thing was about to happen, only on a larger scale. The early morning broke cold and snowy. As Sean Stires headed his car through the early-morning blackness toward the radio station broadcast center on Cleveland Road, he had a feeling something big was going to happen.

He was not sure whether Siemon was going to play and mentally he made some notes on how to broach the topic with Muffet, who was scheduled to make her pre-game early morning radio appearance.

It was just about the time Siemon was being shepherded by trainer Mike Miller into Dr. Fred Ferlic's office. Siemon had already decided she was going to play, so for her it was more of a formality. The cast fit well, allowed for a reasonable amount of dexterity, and would allow for some contact without incurring permanent damage to the already tender hand.

Siemon heard exactly what she expected. A hand specialist, probed, prodded, examined X-rays, scratched his chin a while and then said. "You can play, but it's gonna hurt."

Apparently he didn't know this was a linebacker's daughter.

Kelley's father, Jeff, had made a living dealing pain to others for years in professional football. Pain was a way of life for him.

His daughter figured that broken hand was no reason to miss a shot at history.

Ironically and most fittingly, Kelley would be wearing a modified linebacker's cast to protect her hand. Her father would be in attendance and the life circle was again being made complete.

Siemon would play. In doing, she reminded Matt McGraw of the night New York Knicks star Willis Reed limped out of the dressing room and led his team to a big playoff win over the Los Angeles Lakers.

It was spring break, and the players who lived in the dorms had been moved to the Varsity Club hotel. Their dorms had been closed for maintenance. So, many of the players awoke in the sterile atmosphere of the high-quality surroundings. Still others roused in their own apartments, scratched around in familiar surroundings, watched cartoons, ESPN and CNN while waiting for their date with history.

Ellen Quinn had been to nearly every one of Kelley Siemon's games and had full plans to be at the JACC for this game of all games. However, she was back home in Indianapolis, a full three-hour drive away on a wintry day. So Ellen, with her heart torn between family and friend, chose family. She was hoping she would get good enough news that she could make a deadhead drive for South Bend in time to be part of the action.

By early morning, Muffet had fled the house.

"Everyone else in the house was so nervous, it was making me nuts," she said.

Her radio stint done, she went to the office to settle her thoughts and handle the obligatory ESPN interviews. "I was remarkably calm," she said. "We were prepared."

Matt wasn't. "I got up and hid under my desk all morning," he laughed. "I really think it was unfair for everyone to point to this one game as a measurement of our program.

"There are 31 games or so in every season, but clear back in the summer people were telling me that if we couldn't get past UConn, then the season will not have been a success."

The team, meanwhile was at Bibler's Pancake House, a small but team favorite eatery about a mile east of the JACC. Riley strode in and announced she was ready to go, sore ankles and all.

A few minutes later, the already-buoyed spirits were raised

even higher with the arrival of Siemon, who announced that she, too, would be in the starting lineup.

The 2:00 PM starting time just could not come soon enough. As the team vacated Bibler's and headed for the JACC, it had not quite hit them just how big of a show this was about to become.

As they pulled into the parking lot north of the JACC, they were all greeted by an unusual sight. Here, a good two hours before game time, a crowd of people was trying to snap up any last remaining tickets.

By now, even to the new fans, Siemon's hand was big news. As Kelley walked from her car on that cold windy morning toward the JACC, she was met by an excited woman, who upon recognizing Kelley, came running from the ticket line she was standing in.

She rushed up and said, "Kelley, are you going to play?" Kelley said yes and the lady turned around and yelled, "Hey Linda, Kelley's going to play." The entire crowd in the ticket line burst into applause.

"It was like they were going crazy," Siemon said. "It was a very exciting moment for me."

Matt McGraw had the responsibility to pick up Murphy. It was a makeup day at school. An unusual December series of snowstorms had played havoc with school schedules. As they pulled into the lot, Matt was in what he called a "tad of a panic," but he felt good about the Irish chances.

"We got there really early," Matt said. "The arena was empty, but you could feel the electricity. The hair was standing up on my arms. I have never felt anything like it."

If nothing else, Matt was training Murphy in the finer points of enjoying basketball from a distance.

"We always climb up to the top of the stadium, no matter where we are, before the place gets too crowded, and we just look down on the floor. It is quite a view sometimes."

It was Beach Day, and the crowd was either attired in some beachwear or wearing a shirt with the words Dead-Eye Ratay. Matt, never one to assume an air of pompousness, wore an Hawaiian shirt while Murphy wore the Ratay get-up.

His wife, meanwhile, was strangely confident. Two days ago she had seen Riley and Siemon spend the last 10 minutes of the sidelines of the Virginia Tech with what appeared to be serious injuries. This morning, she knew they would play and she knew that Niele was ready to be the floor leader.

If the moment had come to beat UConn, she would know by about 4:15 that afternoon.

As Sean Stires and his sister, Shanele, headed east on Cleveland Road toward Juniper for the southbound trip to the JACC, they were very aware that they were to be calling the biggest game of their lives.

"I was very excited going in," Sean said. "It was mainly because of the track record. For me, it was the first Notre Dame-UConn game.

"I had a history with women's basketball. Shanele plays for the Minnesota Lynx in the WNBA. I had talked to Mike Miller, the trainer, after the Tech game and I knew the extent of both players' injuries.

"Ruth's ankles were always a bit of a problem. After every game she would get them iced down and sometimes she would walk through airports with big bags of ice strapped around her ankles. So it was a fairly routine thing. Muffet had said on her radio program that she was pretty sure Siemon was going to play."

When the Stireses arrived at the JACC about 12:30, there already was a large crowd. The line of hopeful ticket purchasers now stretched out the southwest side of Gate 10 and reached over halfway to Juniper Road.

South Bend had another happening. A miracle in the making. This might be as sweet as the football game when Notre Dame had beaten top-ranked Florida State, or maybe when the Digger Phelps-led men's team had stopped the UCLA-Bill Walton winning streak with a final-minute rally.

South Bend loved those moments. And somehow, the people of the town hoped, they would be there for it.

At Between the Buns, Schneider was opening for business. Since it was Martin Luther King, Jr., Day, a national holiday, he knew the lunch crowd would be more slow-arriving and more relaxed.

He wasn't sure what effect the game would have — only that it probably would be good. The 2 PM start meant that the lunch crowd would be in and out and the normally dead time between 1 and 5 would be busier.

Good basketball is good for business, he decided. He didn't know it, but some of those disappointed late-arriving ticket seekers would spend the afternoon, eyes transfixed on the large TV screen, in his establishment.

Muffet had skipped the Bibler's breakfast, as is her custom. Actually, it is a team defense mechanism. The pacing she does before a game would get her to the shores of Lake Michigan and back if the steps were made in a straight line.

If the team saw her all wound up, they would get all wound up also. So she paces in private.

But she knew this was going to be something different. "For the first time, both the team and I felt we could really win against UConn," McGraw said. "In past years, we thought we could beat them but this year we knew we could.

"I arrived at the JACC about 9:30 and one of the ushers told me it was a sellout and that got me all pumped. After that, I did some interviews for the media and things, and there were people coming in, but I was still so relaxed…I was loose and excited to be playing in this game."

Siemon spent some extra time in the trainer's room while the rest of her team came out for the pre-game shoot-around about an hour before gametime. By now, the stands were edging toward being full and the ND players already out on the floor were commenting to themselves how big the crowd was going to be.

On the other end, the UConn players were oblivious. This, to them, was standard operating procedure. It isn't easy being the New York Yankees of the women's basketball world and always getting the other team's soldout houses and best efforts. This sellout, no matter how vociferous, was really nothing new for them.

What was about to happen, however, was new for them and for everyone else.

Siemon, her hand now wrapped, emerged from the locker room. It was, in Matt McGraw's words, a "Willis Reed moment."

As Siemon emerged from the dressing room, the crowd noticed her and suddenly the roof of the JACC was being raised by a thunderous ovation. Stires stood five feet from her, when the sudden ovation began.

"It was an incredible moment," he said. "Kelley looked around like she was wondering who they were cheering for. She really had no idea."

It was at that point that the role player would become a star.

"I could not believe the noise," Kelley said of that moment. "Everyone was just standing and cheering...for ME. The combination of everyone exploding when I walked on the floor and then contributing so much to the game changed the way I thought of myself on the team. That really changed my attitude."

Yes, this would be a different sort of game. When the cheering subsided, a new hue settled over the arena. Prior to that, only the team and the coaches really believed the Irish could upend the Huskies. Now, apparently, everyone believed.

South Bend Tribune columnist David Haugh ran into Matt in the tunnel just shortly before tip-off. It is standard procedure for print media reporters to arrive at a game about 45 minutes or so before a contest and he was dangerously late, always cause for anxiety among journalists.

And, according to McGraw, Haugh was flustered. "It took me almost an hour to get here," Haugh said to Matt. "You just can't believe the number of people out there."

Muffet did not alter her pre-game routine. Not being one for "Win one for the Gipper" speeches, she kept the pre-game schedule the same as it always had been. "I didn't want the players any higher than they already were," she said. "They were already way up there."

When the players went back out for the 20-minute pre-game warm-up routine, athletic director Dr. Kevin White made his usual stop-by in the dressing room.

"I think it's so that I can make him nervous, too," Muffet laughed.

McGraw now realized the impact of what was about to happen. "I told Kevin that I had been waiting for this moment all my life. This is why I'm in coaching, for moments like this and we are ready for it and I am going to enjoy it."

When she emerged as she usually does with barely 10 minutes remaining before tip-off, she also was greeted with a thunderous ovation. "The emotion was unbelievable," she said. "And I'm saying to myself to stay calm, because I had to coach. I talked briefly before the game with [UConn coach] Geno Auriemma, and he said that the atmosphere reminded him of going to Tennessee to play."

The atmosphere is what would keep Matt and Muffet up late talking that night when they were home, without the cameras, the team, or the reporters. "What a great environment," she would say.

There were 11,418 people inside the JACC that day.

One person who deserved to be there missed it. Ellen Quinn was frantically dialing her AM radio at 2 PM when the tip-off was just minutes away. She had gotten a late start from Indianapolis but figured that she could walk into the game late.

As she got closer to South Bend, the ever-improving reception of WHLY radio told her something was completely different.

It was a sold-out house. Her favorite yellow seat was full. She would not be at the biggest game in Notre Dame history. She would not see her friend Kelley ascend to stardom.

Instead, she spent the game like most other sports fans in South Bend did that cold afternoon, cheering out loud and shouting at the radio in her dashboard. She made it home in time to watch the second half on ESPN, wondering if Kelley would notice that she wasn't there.

Back in the JACC, however, the time had come, and even the unflappable Ratay was nervous.

Then the ball went up and Ruth Riley was on her way to winning the Naismith Award and Kelley Siemon was on her way to Notre Dame folklore and Niele Ivey was on her way to achieving yet another dream. It would be against the best Connecticut had to offer, for UConn was at full strength for this game.

"I was afraid the team would be so up that we wouldn't make a shot for the first five minutes," Muffet said. "Every time in the past that we had a big crowd, we were so thankful we just wanted to play well for them and we ended up being tight."

But this year, that also was different. "The seniors looked at it like this was the opportunity we have been waiting for," McGraw continued, "and they weren't going to let it go by without showing the people why they were cheering for us.

"Heck, it was Beach Day, it was fun. And the emotion was pouring out of the crowd was all positive. It wasn't like they were demanding us to show them what we could do. It was all good vibes and so electric. It was like the roof was about to come off the place."

On the radio, Stires was unable to contain his excitement. Ivey, showing the nerves of steel of a fifth-year senior, quelled Muffet's fear about being tight with an early layup after a steal for the first points.

"Welcome to the track meet," Shanele Stires chimed in.

The first three minutes would be an indicator of the rest of the game. Connecticut had an early opportunity to take a lead but wasn't able to take advantage. Three minutes into the game, two straight Riley layups would establish an 10-3 lead, and McGraw knew she could not have asked for more.

But UConn had substituted several times in the early going while McGraw played her few trump cards early. The bench strength decidedly stood in the visitors favor and the starters would have to stay in the game and still stay fresh if Notre Dame was to win.

When a layup and foul was converted by Siemon, Notre Dame had established a 16-7 lead. The offensive strategy was working. When Ruth was double-teamed, Siemon would break down the lane and Riley would find her.

On the other end, the 2-3 zone and Riley's demanding presence inside took away the inside game of the defending national champs without putting Riley into a foul problem.

Janeka Joyce electrified the crowd with a 3-pointer to give her team a 19-10 lead with about 13 minutes to go in the first half. "That nylon splashed all over the place," Stires commented. A Joyce layin off a Riley assist gave Notre Dame a 23-12 lead before UConn mounted its first challenge midway through the first half.

The Huskies closed to within four before McGraw called a timeout to settle her crew down. The Irish changed to a man-to-man defense, but UConn later ran off nine straight points to close to 23-21. Then UConn blew a chance to tie the game. A Siemon rebound using her broken left hand thwarted that challenge and then Ivey dropped a 3-pointer to establish command again.

That pattern would be repeated three times during the game. Each time UConn got seriously close, the Huskies would miss an opportunity to get it closer and Notre Dame would counter-attack. Ivey nailed her third 3-pointer with two minutes to go and Notre Dame led by 13. At halftime, Notre Dame led, 40-31.

"My buddy said it would be UConn by 20," Shanele Stires said as the half closed. Her brother didn't reply.

The stage was set for Riley time, and Ruth didn't disappoint. Early in the second half, UConn closed to within three. Riley countered with a shot and then rebounded off the defensive board to set up a huge 3 for Joyce. The lead was back to eight.

Back came UConn. The Huskies were hungry. They wanted to be the only undefeated team in the NCAA Division 1. They wanted to grab first place in the Big East. They wanted to add to their 11-game winning streak over the Irish. And they wanted to end Notre Dame's 31-game home-winning streak.

The Huskies closed to within six. Siemon stepped forward for four straight points, the last two on a layup evoking an ecstatic, "Give it to her baby" from Stires, whose voice was barely audible amid the deafening crowd noise.

That shot said a lot to McGraw. "That play when Kelley ran the break and made a nearly impossible shot with her right hand indicated to me that it was going to be our day," McGraw said.

At Between the Buns, the crowd was ecstatic. The usual bar banter was replaced by cheering and stomping by the patrons. It was, as sophisticated people are wont to remark, a most unusual spectacle.

By now, Auriemma was changing his game plan. With the clock beginning to become a factor, his usually patient team began shooting from beyond the 3-point arc. While the first half had been relatively foul-free, the experienced and highly successful coach was forced to tell his charges to foul to extend the game.

The obvious person to foul was Siemon, and everyone in the JACC knew it.

Another Irish flurry extended the lead to 18 with just under nine minutes to go. UConn began its "foul Siemon" strategy.

The strategy worked, as Siemon responded by missing free throws. It was, as Stires said to his listeners, time to put the nail in the coffin. Kelley had the hammer, but she kept missing the nails.

Riley stepped in to the rescue. She rebounded two of Siemon's missed free throws and then put a fake move on Christine Rigby that had Stires screaming, "Hey, where are your shorts," again barely audible above the crowd noise.

It was Riley who carried the team the last 10 minutes. UConn never got seriously close again and with 29 seconds left, McGraw pulled Riley off the floor.

"Twenty-nine seconds remaining! Can you feel it?" screamed an almost-hoarse Stires as Riley exited.

"Connecticut looks like a flat tire out there," yelled his sister.

A 3-pointer by senior Imani Dunbar as time expired added a fitting exclamation point to an incredible effort.

Notre Dame 92, Connecticut 76.

Riley ended up with 29 points (8-for-11 from the field and 13-of-13 from the free-throw line), 12 rebounds, four assists, and five blocked shots).

Dunbar's shot wasn't even allowed to hit the floor. Longtime Irish announcer and longtime Notre Dame friend Bob Nagle had conspired with Matt McGraw to rush the floor and hug Muffet. Nagle, purely by accident, was under the net as the ball swished through and the game-ending horn went off.

He swiped up the ball as the officials, normally responsible for such things, raced to the safety of the dressing room as the Irish faithful rushed the floor.

In a day of firsts, this was possibly the most publicly sweet. No crowd had ever rushed the floor at Notre Dame for a women's game. Now, no evidence of hardwood could be seen from above the floor as a mass of joyful humanity surrounded the players.

Strangers hugged strangers, parents hugged children, husbands hugged wives. McGraw finally ushered her team into the dressing room for a couple of minutes before changing her mind.

"Heck, let's get back out there," she said. "That was fun."

Finally, with all the celebrating done, McGraw was entering the interview room when she ran into Auriemma.

"Geno was absolutely gracious," McGraw said. "He complimented our team, and how good it was for the Big East to have this rivalry and how good it was for women's basketball. He never ever said that his team did not play well, just that we had an answer for everything they tried and that Ruth was outstanding."

Riley, of course, had her own admirers, as autograph seekers and well-wishers crowded around the friendly girl from Macy who had just been elevated to Superstar status.

Things the rest of the season would be different, and Riley knew it as she patiently signed caps and T-shirts and programs.

But it was to be the same old Ruth, with or without the Super-woman cape.

And Muffet and her crew wandered over to Between the Buns that evening for their usual fare. And maybe it wasn't so surprising that the whole place stood up and applauded.

Over an hour later, Matt McGraw strolled into the basketball arena for one final look around. By now, the fans were gone, the media was gone, the ushers were gone and the vanquished UConn team was on a plane headed for Storrs.

Out of the corner of his eye, he noticed two people, sitting in the lower arena. Even in the semi-darkness of the now-empty arena, McGraw had no problem recognizing the pair.

For it was Ruth Riley, Superstar, sitting alone talking to her mom...most likely about guys, and school and other things that only moms and daughters can talk about.

THE LINESCORE

CONNECTICUT (76) Svetlana Abrosimova 7-17 1-3 20, Swin Cash 2-7 3-4 7, Kelly Schumacher 1-4 0-0 2, Sue Bird 7-20 0-2 17, Shea Ralph 1-4 0-0 2, Diana Taurisi 2-7 0-0 6, Asjha Jones 4-11 1-1 9, Morgan Valley 0-1 0-0 0, Kennitra Johnson 1-4 0-0 3, Tamika Williams 4-4 2-3 10, Christina Rigby 0-0 0-0 0. Totals: 29-79 7-13 76.

NOTRE DAME (92) Ericka Haney 4-11 5-7 13, Kelley Siemon 6-9 3-16 15, Ruth Riley 8-11 13-13 29, Alicia Ratay 3-6 2-4 10, Niele Ivey 4-6 3-6 14, Jeneka Joyce 3-7 0-0 8, Amanda Barksdale 0-0 0-0 0, Imani Dunbar 1-1 0-0 3. Totals: 29-51, 26-46 92.

Halftime score: Notre Dame 40, Connecticut 31. 3-point shooting: Connecticut 11-33 (Abrosimova 5-11, Bird 3-11, Taurasi 2-6, Johnson 1-3 , Ralph 0-1, Morgan 0-1), Notre Dame 8-12 (Ivey 3-3, Ratay 2-4, Joyce 2-4, Dunbar 1-1). Shooting: Connecticut 29 of 70 for 37 percent, Notre Dame 29 of 51 for 57 percent. Total fouls (fouled out): Notre Dame 14, Connecticut 32 (Taurisi, Jones, Valley). Notre Dame 41 (Riley 12), Connecticut 44 (Abrosimova 14), Assists: Notre Dame 23 (Ivey 10), Connecticut 18 (Bird 6), Turnovers: Notre Dame 16 (Ivey 5, Ratay 5), Connecticut 15 (Abrosimova 4, Bird 4).

CHAPTER 14

VIEW FROM THE TOP

Well, they were going to be No. 1.

Now it was a question of playing basketball again.

The instant fame that arose after the UConn game threatened to overwhelm McGraw's squad in the week they would have to wait for the polls to proclaim that the Irish had claim to the top spot.

In their way lay a visit to South Orange, New Jersey, where a better-than-average Seton Hall team could ruin the party before it began.

Fortunately, or unfortunately, the party had already begun. The players were now celebrities — in particular Riley, Ivey, and Siemon — whose faces were prominently plastered on the pages of the local newspapers and on TV broadcasts.

Students, who had virtually ignored the players in classes, were now asking for autographs for little brothers, little sisters, and nieces. Trips to the local Martin's Super Market were becoming nearly impossible for the starters as well as some of the subs. Strangers were coming up and offering congratulations.

The media pressure also increased. The possibility that Riley would be named the Naismith Award winner was making her a moving target for every magazine writer and TV station, in South Bend and on the road.

Riley, no longer shy and retiring — "I think she got over that in college," Sharon Riley said — withstood the pressure and showed an ability to treat every interview request and each repetitive question as if it were a brand-new one.

Riley had, in fact, assumed the media image as sort of a "Mother Teresa in tennis shoes." She was the kind of person every parent wanted their kids to be like. And it wasn't an act. This was the real Ruth.

McGraw knew, however, the most dangerous game of the year might be Seton Hall. After a day off on Tuesday, she called the seniors together and told them the first practice would be one of the toughest of the year.

"We [the coaches] are going to be on you all day," she told them. "We are going to be looking for things to blow the whistle to make you run."

McGraw had a method to her madness. "We were going to make sure that we kept our focus," she said. "At that point, we were playing so well that it was hard to find things to whistle them for, but we got our point across. We were going to be No. 1 and we had to work hard to stay there."

As it was, the Sunday afternoon game at Seton Hall was the last game the Irish would play well offensively for a month. With Siemon sitting out while her hand healed, Leahy started and split time with sophomore guard Monique Hernandez and Amanda Barksdale.

The Irish shot at a 55 percent pace and held Seton Hall to less than 31 percent. It was no contest. Notre Dame jumped out to a 40-20 halftime lead. Four players scored in double figures, led by Haney's 20.

Now it was just a wait-and-see situation. While everyone following the team was certain the No.1 ranking was in the bag, Muffet recalled the many times that the pollsters and the selection committees had decided against what Muffet saw as a clear choice.

So she waited...and waited..."It was like we were all watching the phone waiting for Whitey [Notre Dame assistant sports information director Eric Wachter] to call," McGraw said. "But he never called. I knew when the polls would be announced, but he didn't call then either. Finally I called him and he said, 'Yeah, didn't you hear? We knew 30 minutes ago.' I was beside myself with happiness.

"It was a huge thrill for me," she continued. "I couldn't wait to drive home and see the No. 1 sign on Grace Hall lit up.

"We didn't have practice that day, but I remember Ruth came in for some media things and I said, 'Ruth, we are No. 1!' and she looked at me like, 'And?'

"Later, one of the reporters asked Kelley Siemon how she felt and she started playing with her fingers saying, 'Well, there is some pain here and there and I'll miss some games, but...'

"No," he interrupted her, "how does it feel being number one?" She said, "Ummm, well, I didn't know we were No. 1, so I guess it feels OK."

McGraw suddenly realized that if the team wasn't getting over-hyped by the ranking, then neither should she.

"For me, it had a been a 14-year project," she said. "But for them, I think it was more or less expected. So I was definitely way up there and they were so grounded. The next day, we sat in a circle before practice and I asked them how they felt and they all kind of looked at each other like, why is she [McGraw] making such a big deal about this?

"Finally, someone said, 'Well, it kind of feels the same way it did last week,' so I said, 'yeah, I feel the same way!'" she laughed.

After the Seton Hall game, the Irish offense slowly began to deteriorate. The comfortable winning margins got progressively smaller in the days leading up to the trip to Rutgers as the shooting percentages began to decline. Tough defense was keeping the squad undefeated, and McGraw could only hope that the offense would eventually return.

The January 24th contest against West Virginia at Morgantown saw Notre Dame's shooting percentage dip below 50 percent for the first time in six games. Riley scored 28 points and Ratay added 24, however, as the Siemon-less Irish whacked the Mountaineers, 87-64. The Irish were now 19-0 and appeared to still be hitting on all cylinders.

The offensive numbers hit a season-low 36.7 percent in a 64-44 home win over Providence before 6,131 on January 31. Notre Dame, in fact trailed, 18-11, with 5:43 remaining in the first half before rallying. Riley led all scorers with 19 and Haney added 17.

Siemon returned the next game, an 81-65 win at Boston College, but could only contribute four points. Riley again dominated, scoring 24 points and getting 13 rebounds, as the Irish shot a respectable 47 percent from the field. Ivey scored 16 points to go with five steals and seven assists.

The winning margin declined another point in Notre Dame's 72-58 win over Pittsburgh on February 7 in front of 7,025 at the JACC. Ruth was playing like a woman possessed now, scoring 29 points and pulling down 12 rebounds while blocking seven shots.

With the Irish still undefeated at 22-0 and ranked No. 1, the lines in South Bend were much larger as fans waited to meet her and have her sign things.

"It was really very different now," McGraw said. "The crowds were bigger and so were the lines waiting for autographs. It got to be rather overwhelming. And reporters were calling from everywhere.

"Finally, in a joking manner, I said, 'Hey, OK. Enough. Maybe we should lose one.'

"A lot of the attention was focused on Ruth, of course. Kelley and Niele were a little more outgoing and enjoyed it more because they had never really had this much attention. Ruth was experienced with it and she was fine not getting any at all, but she is hard to disguise in public so everyone wanted to talk to her.

"There really wasn't a whole lot we could do. I empathized with her because I was getting a lot of attention too, but she is so nice that if she gets 200 letters a week she wants to send 200 notes back."

The coaches watched the declining offensive numbers with worry. "The difference between being No. 3 and No. 1 is incredible," McGraw said. "Every team is giving you their best shot and are devising ways to beat you. We were not getting as much in transition anymore and Ruth was getting triple-teamed so she wasn't shooting quite as well.

"Ericka Haney really stepped forward during that time and our defense was outstanding. When we would go into the locker room, we would tell the team that we were playing great defense. Here we are, not shooting well, and we are still beating people by 10-12 points. So we are fine, don't worry."

But worry they did.

The game at Syracuse on Valentine's Day saw Orangeman Beth Record score 25 points for game-high honors. That was the first time an opposing player had been the game's leading scorer since Katie Douglas had scored 20 in the Purdue game.

However, four Irish players scored in double figures and Notre Dame won 75-61. Riley earned her fourth consecutive double-double with 24 points and 11 rebounds while Haney added 16.

It was now time for the Rutgers game, and the *big worry* was about to become real.

Being No. 1 had taken away from the focus of the team, or so Assistant Coach Kevin McGuff thought. "Everyone on the team was getting called by reporters, including me," he said. "If you watched the UConn game, you saw that we treated the game as if every play was important. After that game, the plays were still important, but we were starting to lose that extra edge we had against UConn."

Mind games are part of sports, and the Rutgers people are as good at it as anyone. Traditionally, the day of the game, both teams are allotted time on the court hours before the tip-off for a pre-game walk-through. However, that same day, the Rutgers men were scheduled to play in the afternoon on the floor and Scarlet Knight coach Vivian Stringer used all of her allotted two hours for her team to practice before it was handed over to the men to get ready for their game.

That left Notre Dame with no option other than to practice at a local high school.

"We were given the option of coming in at 7:30 AM for the 7:00 PM game, but that is rather ridiculous. When we pressed the issue, the sports information people said that Vivian always takes two hours on the day of a game," McGraw said.

So off to a local high school they went for their practice.

Not only did Notre Dame have to battle a very good defensive team on the court, but Rutgers crowds are well-known for being hostile toward visiting teams. And, they were out for revenge. Not only was Notre Dame ranked first, but the year before, Alicia Ratay had spoiled a certain victory in their minds with her Rutgers Miracle.

So as the Irish filed onto the floor, the catcalls began. "Usually, when you are getting yelled at like that, it just bands you closer as a team," McGraw said. "I can't say that we were particularly affected by it, but that crowd was getting very personal with their comments."

It was one of two games that Riley was to foul out off all year. Notre Dame led by two, 53-51, when Riley fouled out of the game on a short shot by Tammy Sutton-Brown with 28 seconds to go. Sutton-Brown converted the free throw to put her team ahead. Seconds later, she would block a shot by Niele Ivey as time expired to ensure the win.

No more No. 1.

"We were all disappointed," McGraw said. "Some of them

were crying. I took the blame for it, though. We had the ball with 20 seconds remaining and even without Ruth I'm thinking we can break their press by throwing two passes and get a layup. Instead we dribbled the ball up.

"I should have called timeout but we still had a plan, which was to get the ball to Ericka or Kelley or drive the ball and attack the basket. We ended up not even getting a good shot. I should have called timeout, I think. But there are others who think I did the right thing."

Muffet sighed.

"I hate to lose...but I really hate to lose to Rutgers. We just don't seem play well there. I was really upset with myself. Then we fly all the way back to South Bend and find out that my manager didn't tape the game and just didn't tell anyone.

"I always watch the tapes of losses, figure out what we did wrong and how to fix it. For me not to have tape was really upsetting. If I don't get the tape, I'm not able to function.

"So we ended up calling a friend in New Jersey who happened to tape the game off his TV and he put it on the next plane to South Bend. I ended up watching it at 10:30 the day after the game. It was definitely not a good loss for us."

It did, however, re-energize the team. The Irish exploded on Miami three days later in front of 6,533 in South Bend. Riley scored 20, in a game where all 12 players scored. They held Miami to 28 percent shooting while defeating the Hurricanes, 81-43.

"Kevin McGuff leaned back toward the end of the game and asked me if I thought we would have played as well against Miami if we had beaten Rutgers," McGraw said. "So, maybe in hindsight it was a good thing. But my goal was to go undefeated during the regular season and then lose to UConn in the Big East tournament if we were going to lose one at all.

"We always play well after a loss, so even if UConn would beat us then, we would have a good week of practice before the tournament."

The February 24th game against Georgetown was significant for several reasons. It began the awakening of Siemon as a consistent part of the scoring offense. From this game forward, Siemon would score in double figures in every game except one and would become, according to McGraw, the final piece of the champion-ship puzzle.

"Kelley stepped up and began more aggressively looking at the basket," Muffet said. "That was the key for her. Getting her the ball for an open look at the free throw line just wasn't working. So, this year the offense was designed so she was cutting down the lane a lot more...When we figured that out, like a light sud-denly went on in the coaches' heads.

"Kelley is really smart," McGraw continued. "Her thought pro-cess was I need to get the ball to Ruth if I can, but if I can't, it's my job to score. So she went from thinking that she had to throw the ball to Ruth to thinking that Ruth was Option No. 1, and she was No. 2, and both were good options.

"Mentally she made the adjustment in her own head. She knew she could score, she didn't have to be selfish about it, but she could score. This let Ruth become a better passer, and Kelley and Ruth played so well together in the second half, especially when Ruth was getting double and triple-teamed."

Siemon scored 13 points on Senior Night, as the Irish played to their second sellout and outlasted Pittsburgh, 65-53. The emo-tional start foreshadowed an even more emotional ending, during which streamers and confetti floated down from the roof for the first time ever. The crowd roared its appreciation for what had become an almost miraculous season.

In between, the Hoyas put up quite a fight and were down by only seven points with four minutes to go. That, however, was before Ivey, who had picked up her fourth foul with over 16 min-utes to go, scored off a nifty pass from Siemon and then returned the compliment a moment later. Suddenly, Notre Dame was ahead by 11 and the contest was over.

Riley led all scorers with 21 points, Siemon added 13, and Ratay 12 as the Irish went to 25-1.

Siemon scored 17 and pulled down eight rebounds, despite being sick the day before, in Notre Dame's regular-season finale, an 82-63 victory over Pittsburgh. Ivey tallied 15 and added nine assists to the cause as Notre Dame burst out to a 36-18 halftime edge and shot at an incredible 63 percent rate while holding the Lady Panthers to 36 percent. Notre Dame finished its best regular season ever at 26-1.

On to the Big East tournament in Storrs, Connecticut, and the Gampel Pavilion, where the Huskies had reigned supreme in the six years that Notre Dame had been in the Big East.

Notre Dame, which drew Georgetown in the first round, was now playing with a purpose. The game wasn't even close and Notre Dame won 89-33. Every player for Notre Dame played more than seven minutes and every one of them scored. The Irish blew out to a 44-10 halftime edge. Riley played only 15 minutes. The 56-point margin was the largest since a 78-point victory over Liberty in 1989.

Amanda Barksdale gave opponents a view of the Irish future as she blocked six shots and pulled down nine rebounds. Ivey scored 16 points and added eight assists while Siemon continued her consistent scoring with 14 points and six rebounds.

Virginia Tech was next, and the Irish defense allowed the Hokies only 17 field goals in 64 tries for a measly 26.6 percent in a 67-49 win. Siemon and Ratay scored 14 each while Riley was held to a mere two for the first time all year.

"I think Ruth scored her first point in the second half of that game from the free-throw line," McGraw said, "and she kind of laughed about it. She was keeping her sense of humor about it, but it solidified our thinking that the rest of the team could pick up the slack.

"By that time," McGraw continued, "Ruth had been named the Big East Player of the year and now she was the target both on and off the floor. Everyone was coming out to see just how good she was and I was afraid she would feel a lot of pressure to play great all the time.

"We talked about it a little, but to be honest I didn't want to put a lot of that kind of thinking into her brain. But this year's team was different than ones in the past. Niele would cover, or Kelley would cover. Whether Ruth was scoring a lot didn't matter as much and it allowed her to play her game more."

That set the stage for Round Two of what had now become a nationally known rivalry. The UConn press and fan base were primed for the rematch and despite a huge snowstorm the night before, Gampel Arena was sold out and rocking long before the opening tip.

"We knew they [the fans] thought they were going to beat us

by 30," Muffet said. "In their minds, the whole buildup had been one like, 'Just wait until Notre Dame has to play here.'"

"I was just hoping that with all the snow that no one would show up for the game," Muffet laughed. "I said after the semifinal game the night before that it would be great if no one came back tomorrow to see us play UConn. I mean, after all, there were safety considerations."

But the crowd showed up in Klondike boots and mufflers, all 10,027 of them. And an Irish supporter was as rare as a bikini at the South Pole. "Connecticut has a great crowd there," McGraw said. "They are like our crowds, intelligent, good sports, not a lot of name-calling."

UConn was the undisputed king of the Big East tournament. The Huskies had won every Big East tournament game they had played since 1997. The hometown crowd would be a distinct advantage. But this was not your mother's Notre Dame team. This would be a battle royale.

The game was better than advertised. "This was a great game for us to play going into the NCAAs," McGraw said. "We knew we had beaten them good at our place, and we knew we were good enough to give them a real battle at their place. But our first-half defense was abysmal. They scored 52 points. Just horrible."

UConn coach Geno Auriemma had been confident going into the game.

"The second time we played Notre Dame," Auriemma said. "we were playing a lot better than we were before the first game. We were more focused and we knew that without Svetlana Abrosimova [first-team Big East forward] that it would be hard to beat them.

"When we lost Shea Ralph [who had made second-team all Big East as senior point guard] 14 minutes into the game [with a season-ending ACL injury], I was really happy with the way the team responded. Her loss took a lot out of us, but we knew after the game that we had the talent to go somewhere in the tournament. The trick was, we had to either take away their inside game or their outside game, so we decided to take away their 3s."

The game was televised on ESPN2, and again Stires would man the radio microphone for WHLY. This time he would call the game alone. With the crowd decidedly pro-Huskie, Stiles kept his delivery much calmer than the January 15th encounter.

It was a classic battle of two extremely talented and determined teams and was the best contest of the three the teams would play that season.

UConn took a 52-46 lead into the locker room on the strength of a wonderful but controversial shot by Big East first-team guard Sue Bird. The Huskies had the ball with 1.9 seconds to go before halftime. The inbounds pass went to Bird, who dribbled a couple of times to get past Siemon and then launched one of those "what the heck" shots as time expired.

The shot barely moved the net, and the Huskies had a six-point lead and a major headstart on momentum. There was some discussion on press row about just how Bird could do everything she did in the 1.9 seconds.

"I counted over three seconds when I went back and analyzed the tape," Stires said.

Such is the advantage of the home court.

Bird's shot, of course counted. And 20 minutes later, Bird would add insult to injury. It would also be a form of retribution for the courageous Bird.

The two teams battled tooth and nail throughout the second half. Notre Dame tied the score at 73 with just over three minutes to go.

Siemon stood at the free-throw line with two shots and a chance to put the Irish ahead after freshman Diana Taurisi fouled out with 1:15 to go. She missed both, the second one an air ball.

Bird then nailed a 3-pointer with 50 seconds to go for a 76-73 edge. Riley went around Kelly Schumacher to get ND back within one. Ivey then forced Bird to bounce the ball out of bounds on the dribble with 16.3 seconds remaining and Connecticut ahead 76-75.

The turnover gave Notre Dame an opportunity to pull a major upset for the second time this year, and the Notre Dame strategy was obvious.

Of course the ball would go into Riley. A 30-second timeout set up the play where Ivey got the ball to Riley, who was fouled by Schumacher. Riley stood at the line with a chance to put Notre Dame into the lead.

Stiles was by now screaming into the microphone but still barely heard above the thousands of UConn fans. The respect now fully granted, Huskie fans were screaming out their prayers for victory.

"The first one up and it's off the back iron," yelled Stires into his microphone.

"So now, the best that Ruth can do is tie the game. Looking for her 23rd point. The UConn fans not wanting Riley to have a good shot...This one up and good...It's tied...Tie ballgame at 76.

"Two seconds, one second...Bird fade away left side, rolling around and THROUGH!!!..." Stires voice was tinged with unbelief. "Sue Bird...a la Tyrus Edney...a la Danny Ainge driving all the way down with 5.1 seconds to go...The fadeaway and the University of Connecticut wins its eighth straight Big East Women's basketball championship game."

Bedlam. UConn 78, Notre Dame 76.

Ironically, it was Riley who had the best angle to watch the UConn winner. "I was a centimeter too short," said Riley said of her effort to block Bird's final shot. "I turned around just in time to see it go in. I was devastated."

"It looked from my angle like Ruth was going to block it," McGraw said.

McGraw will admit that she learns more from a loss than she does from a win, and this was no exception. As the UConn fans stormed the court, McGraw was already contemplating what she could have done to avoid the loss.

THE LINESCORE

NOTRE DAME (76) Ratay 5-8 1-2 14, Siemon 7-13 2-4 16, Riley 8-13 7-10 23, Haney 2-5 0-2 4, Ivey 3-10 5-6 11, Severe 0-0 0-0 0, Joyce 3-6 0-0 8, Swanson 1-1 0-0 2, Barksdale 0-0 0-0 0. Totals: 28-55, 15-24 76.

CONNECTICUT (78) Jones 6-15, 1-2 13, Cash 3-14 1-1 7, Taurisi 5-14 0-0 14, Bird 6-12 0-0 15, Ralph 4-5 2-2 11, Conlon 0-2 0-0 0, Schumacher 4-7 2-2 10, Johnson 1-6 0-0 3, Williams 2-4 1-5 5. Totals 31-79 7-12 78.

Halftime score: Connecticut 52, Notre Dame 46. 3-point shooting: Notre Dame 5-10 (Ratay 3-3, Joyce 2-5, Ivey 0-2), Connecticut 9-25 (Taurisi 4-12, Bird 3-5, Ralph 1-1, Johnson 1-5, Conlon 1-2). Shooting: Notre Dame 28 of 55 for 51 percent, Connecticut 31 of 79 for 39 percent. Total fouls (fouled out): Notre Dame 11, Connecticut 19 (Taurisi). Rebounds: Notre Dame 42 (Riley 9), Connecticut 39 (Jones, Cash, Schumacher 6), Assists: Notre Dame 19 (Ivey 9), Connecticut 21 (Ralph 5). Turnovers: Notre Dame 17 (Riley 5), Connecticut 10 (Bird 5).

"It was really a horrible way to lose a game," McGraw said. "I was kind of mad because the same thing had happened at half-time and when the last play was going down at the end of the game, I wanted to run out on the floor and tell my team what to do.

"But the coaching point was that we had always practiced game special situations with the ball. It was always our ball with four seconds to go, or our ball, down by two with 10 seconds to go."

Another light had gone on in McGraw's head. For the next week, they would practice for the NCAA's "special" situations from a defensive standpoint. Such practice, of course, would come in handy in the last 5.8 seconds of the season.

Notre Dame could have used a U-Haul to cart back the hardware from the Big East Conference awards. Riley was named Player of the Year, McGraw Coach of the Year, Riley was Defensive Player of the Year, Siemon was Most Improved Player, and Riley completed the hat trick by being named Big East Scholar-Athlete.

In all, Notre Dame swept five of the six major awards. Ivey and Riley were named to the All-Big East first team, Ratay made the third team, and Siemon won honorable mention.

It had been an incredible year for the Irish in the Big East and, if the UConn monster had not been slain, it was at least tamed. The Huskies, despite the best Irish efforts, still won the tournament and also a share of the conference regular-season crown.

The rivalry was real, finally.

"To be a rivalry, one team cannot always be beating the other," Auriemma said. "It became a rivalry this year. There are good rivalries and there are bad rivalries. The UConn-Notre Dame rivalry is built on respect and competition. The games are challenging, hard-fought, joyful, and heart-breaking...everything that makes coaching such a great profession...everything that makes the game of college basketball so great. I think, because it is a conference rivalry, that the Notre Dame-UConn series could get as big or bigger than UConn-Tennessee."

Rivalry or not, it was time for the second season, the NCAA tournament. The two teams almost certainly would meet again.

It was time for the Big Dance.

CHAPTER 15

THE BIG DANCE —
PART*S* 1 AND 2

Going to the NCAA Tournament is a lot like what going to the senior prom used to be like if you were a girl.

First, you have to get asked.

Then, you see who else gets asked.

Then, you might scheme about who you really want to get to dance with.

And finally, you get to see who gets to be King and Queen of the Prom.

Maybe that's why they call the NCAA Tournament the Big Dance.

And, just like the prom, sometimes you don't get asked even though you think you should. There are other times you might find yourself going, but with the wrong date.

Notre Dame had suffered both fates in the past. While in the MCC, they had been snubbed for not hanging around with the right crowd and therefore were left home while all their popular friends played.

Then, barely two years ago, they had not received a opportunity to host the tournament. In short, they were going to the prom, but with the ugly guy with glasses who continually sneezed into his sleeve.

So, that Sunday night, the whole team awaited their fate at the McGraw house. The whole team except Ivey, that is. Niele had flown home to St. Louis after the UConn game for a couple of days of rest and relaxation.

This year the only question was whether Notre Dame would be seeded No. 1 or not. With a record of 28-2 and the losses being by a total of three points to ranked teams, it would appear Notre Dame should get that top spot.

Still the doubt lingered.

"The weird thing about the tournament is that it is truly a whole new season," Matt McGraw said. "You are in a little bit of a panic from the word go from the day the pairings come out and you are not only finding out who you are playing first but then also who is in your bracket. And then you look deeper and you try to estimate who you may end up playing if you are lucky enough to get to the Final Four.

"Once that happens," he continued, "you realize you are one of 16 teams in the country that gets to host a tournament game. And you have all that anxiety."

"We really wanted to focus on our first NCAA games," Muffet said. "There is a lot of pressure hosting because you are expected to win. It is easier to win at home for sure, but the pressure is enormous because, after all, it is No. 1 versus No. 16 and you are expected to win.

"People told us that we couldn't possibly lose the first game and all of the sudden we went from being free and loose to a little tight. And if you look, the first half of most of the first-round games tend to be close. It was hardest on me because my stress can sometimes get to the players."

McGraw's stress was unnecessary. The March 17th Saturday afternoon opener against Alcorn State was played at the JACC. After a slow opening sequence, the much-more-talented Irish doubled up on the Braves, 98-49.

Five players scored in double figures, including sophomore center Amanda Barksdale who recorded her first-ever double-double with 10 points and 11 rebounds as well as five blocked shots.

Alcorn's tallest player was shorter than four of Notre Dame's five starters and so the Braves threw up an amazing 41 3-point shots, connecting on only nine. For the game, the Braves shot a paltry 21 percent from the field. Notre Dame shot at a 54.5 percent clip.

"It was actually a game for a while," Muffet said. "They hit some early threes and then we went man-to-man and shut that down."

THE LINESCORE

March 17, 2001   NCAA Championship First Round
NOTRE DAME (98)
Haney 7-13 0-2 14, Siemon 6-10 1-2 13, Riley 6-6 4-4 16, Ratay 4-6 2-2 13, Ivey 2-8 4-4 9, Severe 2-3 0-1 4, Joyce 2-7 0-0 5, Swanson 1-1 2-2 4, Hernandez 2-4 0-1 4, Barksdale 3-6 4-6 10,

Dunbar 1-1 2-4 4, Leahy 0-1 2-2 2. Totals:36-66 21-30 98,
ALCORN STATE (49)

Haynes 0-6 4-6 4, Wellington 2-5 0-0 4, Wood 4-24 1-3 9,
Reed 3-10, 0-0 9, Turk 0-1 2-2 2, Levy 0-1 0-0 0, Coleman 5-12 0-0 15, Fadeyi 0-3 2-2 2, McGee 1-9 1-2 4, Honeysucker 0-0 0-0 0.
Totals:15-71, 10-15 49.

Halftme score: Notre Dame 47, Alcorn State 43. 3-point goals:
Notre Dame 5-11 (Ratay 3-4, Ivey 1-4, Joyce 1-3), Alcorn State 9-41 (Haynes 0-4, Wellington 0-1, Wood 0-6, Reed 3-10, Turk 0-1, Levy 0-1, Coleman 5-11, Fadeyi 0-1, McGee 1-6) Rebounds: Notre Dame 62 (Barksdale 11), Alcorn State 34 (Wood 7). Turnovers: Notre Dame 12, Alcorn State 13. Assists: Notre Dame 22 (Ivey 8), Alcorn State 12 (Haynes 4).Total fouls (fouled out): Notre Dame 11 (none), Alcorn State 24 (Wood). Blocks: Notre Dame 8 (Barksdale 5), Alcorn State 0. Steals: Notre Dame 5, Alcorn State 6. A: 8,553.

Second-round action the following Monday night brought Michigan. The Wolverines, too, were outmatched by an Irish team that appeared to be reaching an operating peak.

Riley scored 21 points on an 8-for-11 effort from the field while Jeneka Joyce came off the bench to add 14 points. Again, the defense was special, as Michigan shot at only a 33 percent clip, including 2-of-16 from the 3-point area.

Almost 9,600 people watched the last game this group of seniors would ever play at the JACC. The final score was Notre Dame 88, Michigan 54.

THE LINESCORE
March 19 2001 NCAA Championship Second Round.
NOTRE DAME (88)

Haney 1-5 0-0 2, Siemon 8-15 0-1 16, Riley 8-11 5-5 21, Ratay 3-7 2-2 11, Ivey 3-8 1-1 8, Severe 0-1 2-2 2, Joyce 5-9 0-0 14, Swanson 1-2 0-0 2, Hernandez 1-1 1-2 3, Barksdale 2-3 1-1 5, Dunbar 1-20-0 2, Leahy 1-2 0-1 2. Totals: 34-66 12-15 88
MICHIGAN (54)

Goodlow 8-15 0-0 16, Gandy 5-8 0-0 10, Bies 0-6 1-2 1, Thorius 2-9 0-0 5, Ingram 3-18 3-4 9, Jara 0-0 0-0 0, Leary 1-2 0-0 3,

Robinson 0-3 0-0 0, Dykhouse 0-1 0-0 0, Smith 4-8 2-4 10. Totals: 23-70, 6-10 54.

Halftime score: Notre Dame 44, Michigan 28. 3-point goals:
Notre Dame 8-18 (Ratay 3-6, Ivey 1-3, Joyce 4-8, Swanson 0-1),
Michigan 2-16 (Gandy 0-1,Thorius 1-6, Ingram 0-4, Leary 1-2,
Robinson 0-3). Rebounds: Notre Dame 46 (Ratay 8), Michigan
38 (Smith 12). Turnovers: Notre Dame 14, Michigan 11. Assists:
Notre Dame 21 (Ivey 8), Michigan 12 (Thorius 6). Total fouls
(fouled out): Notre Dame 10 (none), Michigan 15 (Goodlow).
Blocks: Notre Dame 5, Michigan 3. Steals: Notre Dame 5 (Ivey
3), Michigan 8 (Thorius 3). A: 9,597.

Not only had Muffet-Mania hit South Bend in the middle of
January, but it had stuck around until the day before spring. That
was, perhaps, one of the most telling signs that a fundamental
change had occurred in South Bend. There would, of course, be
more to come.

Another fundamental change was that the women's team was
getting as much or more attention in the local media than the
men's team, which had been knocked out in the first round of the
tournament after an inspiring season of its own.

It was another first for a Notre Dame women's team, any
women's team, to sustain public interest. Even the opening of spring
football practice, a meaningless non-news exercise made mean-
ingful only by the media attention it receives, took second spot to
this team.

Now for the third time in four seasons, the Irish had made it to
the Sweet 16, a feat in itself, but the expectations for this team
were higher.

Notre Dame's route to St. Louis went through Denver, where
McGraw's squad would face a relatively unknown but highly tal-
ented and 17th-ranked Utah team which, according to Matt
McGraw, no one in the free world had seen play.

"We didn't know anything about them at first," Muffet said.
"All we had was a tape of the conference final at first. We knew
the statistics, however. We were ranked No. 3 in team defense,
they were ranked No. 1, so we knew it would be a lot like playing
against Villanova.

"That really is the best part about playing in the Big East," Muffet continued. "I told them we would be playing against a Rutgers-like defense and a Villanova-like offense. Villanova is always a struggle for us."

"They were an underrated team," Muffet concluded. "Everyone here was talking like they had never heard of Utah, so again you go into the game with these expectations, which puts the pressure on you."

But as the college basketball world was well aware by now, this Notre Dame team thrived under pressure. And perhaps the best at it was Riley.

She would need to thrive against the Utes' outstanding defense. Utah had a defensive specialist in Amy Ewart. Ewart was impressed with Riley's unselfish play as well as her court vision. "She's an awesome passer," she said of Riley.

Notre Dame led only by one, 24-23, late in the first half when Ruth led an 8-2 charge to close the half with Notre Dame up, 32-25. Then she scored every Notre Dame basket in the first nine minutes of the second half.

In the end, she would score 24 points to go with 14 rebounds, six assists and no fouls. It was as complete a performance as the UConn game on January 15 had been for the now-official Naismith Award winner.

Ivey, named the best player in the nation under 5-foot-6, also had six assists to go with 15 points.

"We knew Ruth was in there working," Ivey told the assembled media after the game. "Coach McGraw told us at halftime to make sure we were looking for her because Ruth dominates the game. It is easy to get the ball inside to her, so we just made sure we kept pounding the ball the first five minutes of the second half."

"Outlined against a gray March roof, the Notre Dame horsewoman rode again," wrote *Denver Post* sports columnist Woody Paige the following day, parodying Grantland Rice's famous Four Horseman story.

"She took the Utes for a ride...Ruth was a mile high and rising, though. She has a nice short jumper, a calm demeanor, and an effective defensive presence. The psych major also psyched out Utah. And the Irish are enjoying Denver."

THE LINESCORE
March 24, 2001 NCAA Regional Semifinals, Denver
NOTRE DAME (69)
Haney 5-7 0-2 10, Siemon 3-6 0-1 6, Riley 8-12 8-9 24, Ratay
4-9 0-0 11, Ivey 5-13 2-2 15, Severe 0-0 0-0 0, Joyce 0-4 0-0 0,
Swanson 0-0 0-0 0, Hernandez 1-2 1-4 3, Barksdale 0-1 0-0 0,
Dunbar 0-1 0-0 0, Leahy 0-0 0-0 0. Totals: 26-55 11-18 69
UTAH (54)
Anderson 4-10 0-0 9, Ewart 2-2 4-4 8, Beckman 2-9 0-0 4,
Stireman 1-2 0-1 2, Herbert 2-9 0-0 4, Gibbons 3-10 6-6 14,
McColl 2-3 2-2 6, Sutak 0-1 0-0 0, Red-Castagnetto 3-7 0-0 7,
Totals: 19-53, 12-12 54.

Halftme score: Notre Dame 32, Utah 25. 3-point goals: Notre
Dame 6-15 (Ratay 3-6, Ivey 3-6, Joyce 0-3), Utah 4-19 (Aderson
1-3, Stireman 0-1, Herbert 0-5, Gibbons 2-7, Red-Castagnetto 1-
2) .Rebounds: Notre Dame 41 (Riley 14), Utah 28 (Anderson 8).
Turnovers: Notre Dame 12, Utah 9. Assists: Notre Dame 18 (Ivey
6, Riley 6), Utah   11. Total fouls (fouled out): Notre Dame 13
(none), Utah (McColl). Blocks: Notre Dame 3, Utah 2 . Steals:
Notre Dame 4, Utah 6. A:10,559.

Denver provided a family reunion of sorts for radio announcer
Stires.
Earlier in the season, he had brought his young children out to
South Bend, where they had the opportunity to play with Meaghan
Leahy and Imani Dunbar after one of the games. It was, of course,
things that little kids' dreams are made of.
Now it was a cross-country trip the opposite way as the Stires
family drove to Denver for the three days of the NCAA tourna-
ment.
"I am considered part of the official traveling party," Stires said,
"So I ride with the team everywhere they go. Same plane, same
hotels. It gets a little different during the tournament because the
NCAA treats me as media, which reduces access. But during the
season, it is like I am part of the team."
Having the family stay with him during the regionals was a
blessing for Stires.
"During that time, my kids got to know all the players pretty

well," Stires said. "And they found out that Ruth Riley's favorite cartoon is Scooby-Doo. Well, my son made me go get some of those Scooby-Doo fruit gelatin things and the afternoon before one of the games, he marches up to her while we were waiting for something and handed her this bag of Scooby-Doo candy."

That win brought McGraw face to face with her most dreaded opponent. She would have to get past her mentor, Jim Foster, and the Vanderbilt Commodores, to get to the Final Four.

Coaches understand friendship and coaches understand competition.

But coaching against one of your best friends is never easy, and certainly not when there are such huge stakes involved. Foster had assembled a team based on an excellent 6-foot-6-inch sophomore center, Chantelle Anderson, who was named second-team All-American behind Riley in nearly every vote.

Due to a mix-up at the hotel, the two coaching staffs ended up rooming directly across from each other.

It would be similar to having parents of the defendant and the victim stay across from each other the night before the big trial. Yes, there was understanding and polite friendship. And, yes, there was a certain amount of competitive tension and conflicting goals.

Matt, ever the free spirit, accidentally walked into a Vanderbilt tape session that Sunday and recognized the team on the screen. "Hey, that's us!" he said, before beating a hasty retreat.

Foster would repeat Matt's error later in the day.

Still, the friendship held strong. "Why would anything change?" Foster wondered aloud later. "We choose not to schedule each other during the regular season, but if the NCAA tells us we are going to be in the same bracket, so be it."

Foster knew the Irish were stacked with talent.

"The bottom line is if you get players on your team that want to be coached," he said. "Ones that want to be in the gym and practice hard, it becomes an easy year. This year Notre Dame had a very good mix of seniors. Kelley won her job back, Niele battled through all those injuries, and Ruth is a player the public relations people didn't have to create. Muffet understood what she had and coached accordingly."

Irony is a strange thing. For it was truly ironic that Muffet would be coaching against the guy who gave her a start in college basketball, against the guy who called up Notre Dame and told them to go after her, against the guy who sent Imani Dunbar and Carol Owens to South Bend, and against the guy with whom Muffet had discussed all her bad coaching habits.

McGraw knows she owes Foster a lot.

But Monday, March 26, was not payback time.

She gave him a pre-game hug and then crossed the line separating the two benches. The line would not be re-crossed until two hours later, when she would be headed for St. Louis and he would be headed back to Tennessee.

Instead, it was again Riley time. One thing that can be said for the Big East Conference is that if your team survives the Big East wars, your team can handle whatever the NCAA tournament sends your way.

It was billed as a possible Chantelle Anderson coming-out party, and the sophomore was impressive while she was on the floor. The problem was, Riley by this time, knew all the tricks that would get Anderson off the floor.

As Kyle Ringo wrote for *Rocky Mountain News.com*, "Anderson...is the player Riley used to be."

Anderson was, as Foster had noted in a pre-game press conference, a work in progress. Riley, on the other hand, was the finished product. Not only finished, but polished as well.

Riley had a field day over her slightly taller and more athletic opponent, scoring 32 points, including 10 of 12 from the free-throw line. More impressively, Riley accrued only two fouls.

By contrast, her younger counterpart played only 24 minutes and finally fouled out with just over six minutes remaining in the game after scoring 14 points.

Riley played most of the first half lightheaded and slightly sick to her stomach. The Commodores' Zuzi Klimesova tried to step into the breach of Anderson's absence, scoring 27 points. And the first half ended with a 40-40 tie.

Again, it was Riley time. And again, she didn't disappoint. She started the second half with four straight points and ended it with 11 straight. When the die was cast, Muffet looked at her mentor, coaching a losing cause barely 10 yards away and felt a twinge of sadness.

McGraw knew that Foster's time may come the next year or maybe the year after, if Anderson continued to improve. Foster attributed his team's loss to the maturity of the Irish squad.

"I'm happy that Muffet gets a chance to compete for the national championship," he told the media. "She deserves it and her team deserves it. Riley was terrific, she played like the best player in the country.

"She never loses her composure. She's really been good for college basketball. Her maturity as a player and her basketball IQ was significant tonight."

Anderson knew she had been taken to the woodshed by the more experienced Riley. "For the first time in a long time, I acted young and immature," the 19-year-old Anderson said in a voice barely above a whisper, "and Ruth definitely took advantage of that. Hopefully, I can be that tough and that strong as I get older."

THE LINESCORE
March 26, 2001 NCAA Regional Final, Denver
NOTRE DAME (72)
Haney 2-4 0-0 4, Siemon 8-11 0-1 16, Riley 11-21 10-12 32, Ratay 7-11 0-0 17, Ivey 1-3 0-3 3, Joyce 0-1 0-0 0, Hernandez 0-1 0-0 0, Barksdale 0-0 0. Totals: 29-52 10-16 72.
VANDERBILT (64)
Klimesova 12-19 3-4 27, Benningfield 1-5 0-0 3, Anderson 6-11 2-3 14, McElhiney 3-11 4-4 12, Danker 3-10 0-0 8, Colli 0-0 0-0 0, Hager 0-4 0-0 0. Totals:25-60 9-11 64.

Halftme score: Notre Dame 40, Vanderbilt 40. 3-point goals: Notre Dame 4-6 (Ratay 3-4, Ivey 1-1, Joyce 0-1), Vanderbilt 5-19 (Klimesova 0-1, Benningfield 1-1, McElhiney 2-8, Danker 2-5). .Rebounds: Notre Dame 29 (Siemon 7), Vanderbilt 35 (Klimesova 12). Turnovers: Notre Dame 10, Vanderbilt 13. Assists: Notre Dame 15 (Ivey 9), Vanderbilt 20 (McElhiney 7). Total fouls (fouled out): Notre Dame 15 (none), Vanderbilt 13 (Anderson). Blocks: Notre Dame 4, Vanderbilt 1. Steals: Notre Dame 5, Vanderbilt 5. A:8,422.

"We wanted to get this one," said Muffet after the game. "Riley was amazing. This is definitely an emotional time right now. We are all elated, it has been a storybook season. This is my proudest moment as a coach."

How appropriate it was that Foster was part of it. In a sport of full ironies, this was probably the most ironic.

"The thing is, nothing has changed between us. Now, maybe if we had lost, things might have changed," Muffet laughed. "We have that good of a relationship and it wasn't going to affect us. We both knew that one of us was going to be happy, but not that happy because the other one lost."

Minutes after the game, Matt McGraw ran into Foster's wife as she waited for her husband to gather his stuff and head back home. Donna Foster, a very affable sort, saw Matt coming toward her and deflected him, saying simply, "Not now, Matt. Let's talk later."

There are times when coaches understand even when their spouses don't.

And, as both teams flew out that night for their respective homes, one flight seemed to only take an instant. The other probably seemed like an all-night affair.

"You were hoping you could get some sleep on the flight on the way back," Matt McGraw said. "But it was a short flight and here you are landing at 3 AM. You have been working off caffeine and adrenaline for two weeks and you know that there is another week to go.

"And it is the greatest ride of your life."

CHAPTER 16

UCONN — ROUND 3

The ride Matt McGraw alluded to arrived at 3 AM at the South Bend airport.

"The interesting thing about the tournament is that you don't ever really celebrate. We had just made the Final Four and we get up the next morning and it is business as usual," Muffet said. "You are on the course you want to get on, but you never stop. We got out of the arena, got on a plane and got home. The next day it was back to film.

"Fortunately, playing Connecticut was easier because we had just played them," McGraw continued. "Kevin McGuff had all his stuff ready for us, but having played them, we knew what they were going to do and they knew what we were going to do, so it was easier.

"In the middle of all this, Ruth had to leave Wednesday for the ESPN award and we thought Niele was going to also, but we found out at the last minute that she didn't win. It was a new award this year. They pick the best player at each position and then the best player in the nation. This year they picked Jackie Stiles.

"So we had just gotten back from the game Tuesday at 3 AM and then I barely remember practice that day," Muffet continued. "And then I left Wednesday on a separate plane because there was a dinner I had to go to with some of the staff. So we practiced early Wednesday and then I left about noon and Carol and the team came later while Ruth flew in from Minnesota."

Meanwhile, the Ivey house on Sacramento Street was a madhouse. As soon as the last basket went through the net against Vanderbilt, the phone was ringing at Tom and Theresa's house.

The calls were from friends. The calls were from family. The calls were from reporters. Flowers were showing up. Gifts were showing up. TV crews were showing up.

All this, and Tom and Theresa still had to work. "Never, in a million years, did I ever think anything like this would happen," Theresa said.

Tom even had to ask for time off so he could be at the UConn game on Friday night.

It, of course, was more than happily granted.

It was the Iveys' chance to see what the Big Time was really all about. Two simple down-home folks were rubbing shoulders with people whom Theresa would call "elite."

They were invited to the Thursday night Salute Dinner, but Tom had to work, so Theresa took a friend with her. "Somebody had to make some money," Tom agreed, smiling.

"That whole thing, with all the people and all the activity, was something to see," Theresa said. "It was something to be a part of."

"That Thursday was a long, long, day for us," McGraw continued. "We had media meeting at 9 AM, then signed autographs, then we had practice in the center from 12-1:30 and then we had a real practice at St. Louis University and then Ruth had a meeting for her Kodak All-American thing, so we did not get back until 4:30.

"We were trying to rest Ruth, of course, and here she is running all over everywhere. Then we had the Salute Dinner that night. It was a long day."

The game was played that Friday night. "We felt, still, that teams did not respect us," Muffet said. "All the papers talked about was Tennessee and Connecticut, then Tennessee loses and everyone thinks UConn will win. We were thinking, 'Well, what do we have to do?'"

The whole team knew what they had to do, of course. They had to beat the Huskies again.

"We had a lot of incentive going into the UConn game because despite how we had played them before, all the papers said they were going to win," Muffet said. "Obviously we were glad to be in St. Louis and now my worry was if we would all show up and be motivated to win or were we happy just to be in the Final Four.

"That is what had happened in Cincinnati and I was part of it. We were having a great time just being there. We were walking around, meeting people, the whole thing.

"This time it was so completely different," Muffet said. "We didn't do any of that. We focused as much as we could on the game. The team was focused in practice and the walk-through on Friday and then for the pre-game meal. I really have trouble with the pre-game meal because I'm too nervous to eat. Five minutes and I'm done."

The team was loose, but silent, according to Muffet. "There is an unwritten rule that you never talk on the bus on the way over," she said. "I'm not sure when it started. But once they get on the bus, no one says anything.

"They all have their headphones on. Everyone gets ready in their own way. No one speaks. Then once they get to the locker room, they loosen up again."

Stires was joined by his sister, Shanele, again for the NCAA Final Four. It was easily the biggest game he had ever broadcast and he took a bit of time to take in some of the atmosphere. "This is what you go into broadcasting for," he said.

"This is the Mecca," his sister added.

Sue Bird's 3-pointer 90 seconds into the game started what would be an excellent first half for UConn. As well as UConn played, Notre Dame played just as poorly. Kelly Schumacher took advantage of Riley's attempt to stay out of foul trouble and UConn owned the boards the entire first half.

Still, Notre Dame managed to stay close. UConn got up, 23-13, at the 12-minute timeout mark, but a jump shot by Siemon started a 9-5 run that got Notre Dame within six at 28-22.

"The Irish are being worked over on the boards tonight," Stires told his audience with about nine minutes to go. "Schumacher may get a double-double in the first half!"

The score was 28-22 when Riley picked up her second personal foul with 6:35 to go in the first half. She was called for backing in, a foul not often called at the collegiate level but one that sent the Irish superstar to the bench.

At that point, she had been less than expected, scoring only three points.

"We said at the top of this game that the Irish ability to work the inside-out game would be a big factor," Sean Stires commented into the microphone.

"It would be one of the keys to the game and Ruth Riley has been a non-factor. She has taken only three shots, has three points and two fouls. That foul was a tough one to call, she was just backing in using her posterior."

"I think it came at a critical time when Notre Dame was beginning to get their legs offensively," Shanele agreed during that timeout. "They are playing more aggressively. But that time the aggressive play landed their All-American center on the bench. Notre Dame is definitely hurt by that foul."

At that point, Notre Dame was down by six and UConn's inside-out game, which was already dominating, suddenly had nothing to fear going inside.

If anyone was having a worse night than Riley, it was UConn's outstanding freshman, Diana Taurasi, who sat down with her third foul with just under six minutes left in the half. But Notre Dame, without aircraft carrier Riley in the middle, was dead in the water.

Ivey picked up her second foul with 2:32 to go in the half, and the two stars sat within a few feet of each other as UConn rallied and took advantage. The Huskies pulled out to a 47-31 lead when Maria Conlon converted an old fashioned 3-point play with just over two minutes remaining.

"This is what Connecticut has done in the past years before this year," a troubled Stires remarked to his equally troubled radio audience.

A huge 3-pointer by Joyce with just over a minute to go before halftime would be the ignition that got the Irish going ("I can't tell you how important that shot was for us," McGraw would say later). A Schumacher layin set the lead back to 15.

That was when the crack in the UConn armor began to widen. Swen Cash was fouled by Siemon in the last minute before halftime but missed both free throws. That gave Notre Dame an opportunity to score, and Dead-Eye Ratay let fly from the top of the key.

Her first 3-pointer brought Notre Dame back to within 12. Dead-Eye, it seemed, had found her holster.

"A timely 3-pointer by Ratay," said Shanele.

The halftime edge was to UConn, at 49-37.

"We played a horrible first half, and Niele and I both got into foul trouble," Riley said later. "It was just one of those halves. I remember that Niele and I both looked at each other while we sat on the bench and talked about how rough it was to sit there and watch. We knew the way the game was being played was not the way we could play."

The game was dominated by Huskie post player Kelly Schumacher through most of the first half, notching 10 points and nine rebounds.

UConn head coach Geno Auriemma said the 3-point weapons Ratay and Ivey put the hex on his team.

"In the first half, we were much more aggressive and really played as well as we are capable of playing," he said. "In particular, there were a couple of key plays toward the end of the first half, a couple of 3-pointers by Ratay and Ivey [actually Joyce] which combined with a couple of missed free throws and suddenly the momentum swings their way.

"If we hit the free throws at that time and Notre Dame misses the threes, the game takes on a whole new perspective. But you have to give Notre Dame credit for taking control of the game. They really kept the pressure on and that was it."

McGraw was held up from following her team into the locker room by the ESPN sideline reporter. Normally, Muffet's halftime routine is as scripted as a high school production of *Our Town*. This was no exception.

"I never go right into the team locker room," she said. "I will gather with the assistant coaches and I will vent. It is a great time for me because if I feel like screaming I will, and the assistants just sit there and let me do it. I let it all out.

"If there is room, I will walk and vent," Muffet laughed. "If there is a lot of room, I will sprint and scream at the same time. I've got to let it out before I talk to the players.

"We do the same thing during a timeout. It gives me time to get down to what we need to do to win. But always, at somewhere between the 10 minute and eight minutes left of the 15-minute halftime, we will go in to the players."

The size of the room this night didn't allow Muffet to pace, so instead the coaches discussed just how poorly the team had performed in the first half.

"We were looking at each other wondering, 'Who are those guys on our team?'" Muffet said. "I mean, we hadn't played that badly all year long. We had gotten out of the gate in every game and played well, every... single... game. We had never been down 12 before, let alone at halftime.

"So we had the feeling that it could not get any worse. Ruth had two fouls, Niele had two fouls, so we would be getting our team back on the floor in the second half. It wasn't like a venting when several individuals aren't playing well. All we had to do was play our game.

"Our problem had been shot selection," McGraw stated. "Kelley and Ericka had taken a lot of shots, which we didn't mind but they were taking shots they weren't very good at making and they weren't making any of them. We didn't have the wrong people shooting, they were just taking the wrong shots.

"Alicia wasn't getting threes, Niele wasn't getting shots and Kelley was taking 10-12 footers. So we decided that what we had to do was rebound better, we have to get out and guard the 3-point shooter, and we have to get the ball to our shooters."

But McGraw really didn't need to say anything when she went to the locker room where her team waited.

Something highly unusual had happened. The usually quiet and reserved Ratay, who until that time never said anything at halftime, spoke up and implored her team to get going.

"Twelve points," she said. "We can come back from 12 points."

Riley spoke up.

Siemon spoke up.

Ivey spoke up. "I'm not planning on coming back to this locker room crying," she said.

The words of the teammates would mean more than the words of the coach. "When I got there, they were ready to go," Muffet said. "All they wanted to know was what I wanted them to do. We talked quickly about what we wanted to do and we knew rebounding was the key. So we worked on that."

Muffet knew that UConn didn't blow a lead very often as a rule. This game would have to be the exception.

"We didn't panic at halftime," Ruth said. "In fact, Coach said that we just should go out and play our game in the second half, because we sure couldn't play any worse than we did in the first half."

"They didn't hang their heads at halftime," Muffet said. "None of them are quitters. And that's leadership. They didn't want to end their careers on this note. The feeling was that they wanted to go out and play, give it their best shot and if they lost, at least they knew they had done their best."

The second half was perhaps Notre Dame's finest hour as a team.

"We got aggressive and we started running our offense and getting the rebounds," Riley said. "Our 3-point shooters lit up. If you would have told me we would have won by 15 after going in down by 12 at halftime, I would not have believed you. Doing something like that really shows our character."

Ratay's second 3-pointer, this one from the corner, opened another wound in the Huskie confidence and brought the Irish to 54-44.

Haney converted a three-pointer from the free-throw line and the lead was nine with 17 minutes to go. Siemon then tallied a left-hand runner and suddenly the lead was seven.

"The Irish are able to get out on some breaks for some easy layups," Shanele said.

It already was a different half...and it would get better.

Riley hit a turnaround to get it to 57-51 with 15 minutes to go. Ivey nailed a 15-footer and suddenly it was four. Riley scored another turnaround and it was two.

"Notre Dame is attacking from every angle," Shanele told her audience. "Don't look now, but somebody woke up the Irish."

Schumacher's layin gave the severely wounded Huskies a four-point cushion, but Niele Ivey's three just seconds later made it a one-point deficit for the now-confident Irish.

Dead-Eye dropped a thunderous 3-pointer at the 12:34 mark to give the Irish their first lead, 61-59. She was the only Irish supporter in the nation who didn't break a grin. There was, of course, still a game to be played.

"Bring it, Baby! Bring it!" screamed the now-jubilant Sean Stires. "Alicia Ratay knocking it down! Thirteen for Alicia and the Irish lead for the first time!"

That mysterious and fickle visitor, Momentum, was now parked on the Savvis Center floor right next to McGraw. It took a seat on the Irish bench for the rest of the game.

Taurasi put the Huskies back up by two, converting a free throw after a foul and the score was 63-61. Riley tied the score, but Tamika Williams returned the favor and Notre Dame was down two again. Ratay scored a two-pointer to even it up. Ivey hit two free throws with just under 10 minutes to go. The score was 67-65, Notre Dame. Something had to break.

It was either Ruth time or Ratay time.

Dead-Eye stepped forward first, unholstering yet another killer three. It was such a momentous shot that if you looked closely enough you could probably see the souls of the Huskies fly right out the door. Ratay simply ran back downcourt to defend.

The game was decidedly in Notre Dame's favor, with the score 70-65.

Sean Stires was now calling it a "completely different second half for Notre Dame." And it was. While Auriemma called timeout after timeout to quell the Irish charge, it wasn't going to happen.

The Irish suffered a scary moment with just under six minutes to go when Ivey went down after being fouled by Taurasi. The first thought everyone had was that it was another knee injury, but it became clear pretty quickly that it was simply an ankle turn.

The point guard responsibility would be handed to freshman Janeka Joyce but only for a moment. Ivey wasn't about to let anyone else run her team in her hometown.

But at that point, it didn't matter. Old-time comedian George Burns could have played point guard those last five minutes, as pumped up as the Irish were.

Auriemma called off the dogs with about 45 seconds to go and Stires' voice rose as the reality of the victory began to hit home. "The Notre Dame crowd is coming to its feet. 90-75, the Irish by 15," he screamed. "Notre Dame fans! You listen! And you listen closely! Once again, the Fighting Irish women's basketball team is gonna play for its first-ever national championship Monday night. Riley took the rebound...3 seconds...2 seconds Conlon from the top of the key...Forget about it!

"Notre Dame-Purdue coming up Sunday night," Stires triumphantly announced. "Notre Dame was out of this game in the first half. They come storming back in the second half. Notre Dame will play Purdue Sunday night in the Savvis Center! Welcome home, Niele Ivey."

"I'm stunned," Shanele said. "After what we saw in the first half...unbelievable!"

Believable. And now real. The team continued to make history. They were the first Irish team ever to play in the national championship game.

Things had broken Notre Dame's way that Friday night at the Savvis Center. The terrible-horrible night suffered by Taurasi opened the door for Notre Dame to walk through. Taurasi could only manage one shot in 15 attempts, including a horrid 0-for-11 from beyond the arc.

Great athletes understand bad nights. There would be other nights for Taurasi. Tonight belonged to the Irish.

The rivalry had added another chapter. When the dust settled, Notre Dame had won the most important match this year.

Purdue's second-year coach, Kristy Curry, had devised a defense to shut down the NCAA all-time leading scorer Jackie Stiles earlier that evening as Purdue defeated Southwest Missouri State, 81-64. Now she would have another All-American problem to defend.

Make that two All-American problems.

And one gunslinger, who, if you looked real close, may have even cracked a smile.

LINESCORE

NOTRE DAME (90)

Haney 4-12 7-9 15, Siemon 5-12 1-2 11, Riley 6-13 6-10 18, Ratay 6-10 4-4 20, Ivey 5-9 8-8 21, Joyce 1-1 2-3 5, Hernandez 0-0 0-0 0, Barksdale 0-1 0-0 0. Totals: 27-58 28-36 90.

CONNECTICUT (75)

Taurasi 1-15 2-3 4, Cash 2-4 4-8 8, Schumacher 5-13 2-3 12, Bird 7-21 0-0 18, Jones 1-2 5-8 7, Conlon 3-6 1-1 8, Valley 0-0 0-0 0, Johnson 2-9 3-3 8, Williams 5-7 0-0 10, Totals 26-77, 17-26 75.

Halftime score: Connecticut 49, Notre Dame 37. 3-point goals: Notre Dame 8-11 (Ratay 4-5, Ivey 3-5 Joyce 1-1), Connecticut 6-30 (Bird 4-11, Conlon 1-3, Johnson 1-4, Schumacher 0-1, Taurasi 0-11). Total Fouls (Fouled out): Notre Dame 17 (none), Connecticut 28 (Jones Taurasi). Rebounds: Notre Dame 43 (Haney 10), Connecticut 51 (Schumacher 17). Assists: Notre Dame 16 (Siemon 6), Connecticut 18 (Taurasi 5). A: 20,551.

"We certainly thought we had the players to win the NCAA tournament," Auriemma said later. "It would be a question of how well Taurasi responded under pressure. It was unfortunate that we played Notre Dame in the semifinals and not the finals, but by the time you get to the Final Four, with the injury problem we had, you cross your fingers and hope for the best."

"If you make the threes, you are going to win," Muffet agreed. "If you don't, you won't. And that was the difference between the two halves."

An exhausted but happy Muffet returned to the hotel that night, imposed the curfew on her players, and strolled down to the hotel lobby where it seemed to her that every Notre Dame graduate of the last 15 years was there to greet her. But she was on an adrenaline rush, and spent the evening greeting old players, friends, and families.

"The lobby was packed, it was a huge night," she said. "You had all these Notre Dame people there. We were down there for I don't know how long. It was already late when we got back to the lobby anyway."

Muffet's late-night schedule would not be tested too severely. There were tapes waiting.

Ellen Quinn had watched the UConn game on campus, surrounded by friends. Alternating between jumping for joy, screaming at the TV set, and pacing nervously, Quinn was desperately trying to figure out a way to get to St. Louis to be with her buddy Siemon.

But cash was short, as it is for most college seniors just before graduation. Two friends had offered to pay her way for her, but they were just as cash short as she was, so she declined.

Her brother came to the rescue, however, and offered to pay her way right after the game was over. Another friend had secured a hotel room in the same hotel that the team was staying, and had gotten tickets.

Incredibly, the tickets were in an eerily similar location to where she had sat at the JACC, when seats were cheap and much more plentiful. She made the seven-hour drive to St. Louis on Saturday.

It seemed that everything was now in place.

Now the dance was down to only two. Purdue was the only obstacle between Notre Dame and its dream's end.

The critics were stilled for Notre Dame had beaten UConn fair and square, two out of three, by combined scores of 258-229.

But the Irish were thinking about other things. More pressing things.

Early the next morning, Matt McGraw climbed out of bed and wandered into the hotel lobby for his first Saturday cup of coffee. At the little bar sat a disheveled man silently sipping his own eye-opener.

Matt stopped for a second, examined the guy, and noticed the man was wearing a T-shirt that said, "Linebacker Lounge."

Matt stuck out his hand and said, "Hey, we have one of those in South Bend!"

The guy smiled, "That's where I was last night," he replied. "The place was packed and really crazy, and after the game three of us decided to hop in a car and drive all night here for the final game. We decided that we weren't going to miss this for the world."

CHAPTER 17

CHAMPIONSHIP ACQUIRED

A true championship game is a thing of beauty.

It is not the trumped-up Super Bowl blowouts, the drawn-out seven-game series between highly paid professionals, nor the decision of pollsters.

A true championship game is decided on the court in a single winner-take-all game.

And that, perhaps, is the beauty of the NCAA basketball tournament. In the end, just put two deserving teams on the same floor for a 40 minutes, play the game, and see what happens.

In the women's NCAAs, the championship game is played by two teams that have won five consecutive games over three weekends against ever-increasing opposition. On the floor, the two teams have usually outlasted a tough conference year, an even-tougher conference tournament, and then forced their way in the tournament past teams that have done essentially the same thing.

Off the floor, by the time the team reaches the championship game, the team has been dissected by every supposed expert in America, many of whom have never see the team play in person. Every time they turn around, there is another photo session, another group interview, another TV camera with a reporter standing behind it, hoping for the unique angle for that day's story.

The star players have been asked all kinds of strange questions, usually more than once. They have lost their privacy, have blocks put on their phones and emails, are hounded at the local malls, and are still expected to finish term papers and assignments along with their fellow students.

The coaches have had their management questioned, their clothing choice questioned, their coaching methods questioned, and at the same time, they are expected to always be "on" when they attend the formal dinners, open practices, and post-game functions.

No, it ain't easy getting to — or being in — a championship game.

Yet, two teams in the year 2001 had made it there. Notre Dame, at 33-2, had lost its two games by only three total points. Both losses depended on last-second heroics by the opposition.

Purdue, at 31-6, had overcome three coaches in four years and the death of one of the players on the 1999 national championship team. Katie Douglas, who would try on the hero's mantle this night, had lost both of her parents in the last five years.

If Notre Dame's story was inspirational, Purdue's was just as emotionally draining.

If Notre Dame was a team of destiny, Purdue wasn't far behind.

Senior forward Douglas was the heart and soul of the Boilermaker team. If the average human life is considered tough, Douglas' last five years were nearly impossible. Her father, Ken, had died after a long illness in 1997, when she was a high school senior. In fact, he died the night before she was to play in the annual Kentucky-Indiana All-Star game. Her family waited until after the game to tell her.

Just over two years later, Douglas and her team had celebrated their first national championship and were getting ready for their next season when they were called to an urgent meeting during the summer. Their teammate, Tiffany Young, had been killed by a drunken driver.

Then, in the spring of 2000, Douglas' mother Karen passed away from breast cancer.

For a girl who had her heart ripped out three times in five years, Douglas somehow kept coming back. On top of the personal tragedy, Douglas had played for three Purdue coaches in her four years and twice gotten to the Final Four. She had been named Purdue's first two-time Kodak All-American.

To say she had overcome obstacles would be like saying snow is white. Her history would make most grown men cry.

In fact, Douglas was to the Boilers exactly what Riley was to Notre Dame.

"Katie was always willing to go the extra mile for the team," Purdue coach Kristy Curry said, "Whether it was signing autographs or making appearances, she was really the heart of the team."

It was Douglas' late shot that gave the Boilers a 74-72 win over Texas Tech in the Sweet Sixteen, and she led her team past

Xavier, 88-78, to get to the Final Four. The win over Texas Tech cost Purdue their freshman starting point guard, Erika Valek, with a torn ACL.

Purdue then disposed of Southwest Missouri State and NCAA all-time leading scorer Jackie Stiles in the opening game of the Final Four. The Irish win over UConn later that evening set the stage for the Sunday night finale.

The Irish officially were given the moniker of favorite. They had defeated UConn, usual tournament favorite Tennessee wasn't there, and they had defeated Purdue once already. They were clearly the team to beat.

ESPN was to broadcast the game in prime time on Sunday night. The money men behind the camera hoped that the ever-present remote control channel changers would not be used by their predominantly male audience looking for something interesting to watch.

They needn't have worried.

This was a game that exceeded the hype.

A championship game, between two championship teams, with a last-instant showdown by two champion players, Riley and Douglas.

This was what a championship game is all about.

Muffet didn't sleep much the night after the UConn game. Between the usual adrenaline rush that usually keeps her going well into the next day, now she had all the outside activities as well as the championship game to think about.

"Basically, I stayed up all night," Muffet said. "Although I probably got two-three hours somewhere in there. Fortunately, we had a late practice time for the next day.

"We didn't really want to keep the team on their feet too long anyway. Niele had turned her ankle in the UConn game, so we were worried about that anyway. She didn't even walk through things."

The day of the game dragged by for the Irish players. They, of course, had a regular routine for night games, but this was not your regular-season night game. Time in the hotel was spent either studying, if concentration allowed, or hanging around in other player's rooms, at least as long as the other player was willing.

As game time got closer, the bags were packed and prepared

for post-game departure to South Bend. There would be no return to the hotel for the night. Win or lose, the team would be back in South Bend for the night.

Purdue's Curry was equally all business. "We made sure the team got a good breakfast," she said. "Then we did our walk-through. We went to pre-game chapel. Our real goal was to keep the players off their feet."

Purdue had thoroughly scouted the Irish. "We were really prepared," she said. "We had been very thorough with our scouting reports and our first goal was to defend their 3-point shooters and then hope we could get Riley off the floor with foul problems or at least contain her."

By now, even the most chauvinistic of men in the bars in South Bend were watching in wonder at the abilities of Riley and her crew. Few, if any, of the men age 25 and older in the bar, would openly brag that he could take Riley one-on-one.

The respect that McGraw had so earnestly desired had been earned. The crowd at Between the Buns that evening arrived early, ate a lot, and focused on the game when it was on. It was a crazy night, and it was about to get crazier. Schreiber loved it.

It would be Ericka Haney's night to step forward. The junior forward was the only starter not to be recognized in any way by the Big East, and she was also the most overlooked talent on the Irish team.

The three seniors had all had their share of publicity and awards, and Ratay's ability to come up with the big bombs at key times hadn't gone unnoticed.

Haney's style was more slash and burn. Not a flashy player, she had a tendency to play a steady, even-handed game, allowing her teammates to get open for her passes and take the big shots.

Tonight, Ratay would sink into the background, due to heavy-duty foul difficulties. It was a coaching victory for Curry. Shutting down Ratay meant someone else would have to step forward. Ratay, in fact, would make only one 3-pointer. It would, however, be a big one.

If Notre Dame thought it was going to be an easy game, that idea was dispelled immediately. Purdue shot out to a 10-2 lead before the first TV timeout.

Stires was once again at the WHLY radio microphone along

with sister, Shanele. It was the biggest game of his young life. It was the biggest game of a lot of young lives.

Douglas buried a 3-pointer with 13 minutes to go in the first half to put the Boilermakers up 16-5, forcing McGraw to spend a timeout.

"Purdue looks really prepared for the zone," Sean Stires said during the break.

"Credit Kristy Curry for that," Shanele said. "They are being very patient."

After a Riley layup, Douglas nailed another 3-pointer and the lead was a game-high 12.

"All of the sudden, it's nothing new for Notre Dame to be down double-digits," Sean noted to his listeners. It was only the second time all year they had sunk that low, the other being just two nights before against UConn.

But the Irish had learned against UConn how to come back. They would just have to be patient and stay with the superstar who got them there.

That, of course, was Riley. She got Notre Dame back to within six at 21-15 with a turnaround jumper with just over eight minutes to go. A minute later, Riley got Cooper on her hip and scored her 12th point on the free throw after the layin. Notre Dame was within three at 21-18 with 7:53 remaining.

"Purdue is playing their best ball of the year right now," Shanele Stires told her radio listeners. "I'm sure Kristy Curry is very excited about that."

The third foul on Ratay put her on the bench with just under seven minutes to play.

Curry's plan was working. She knew Purdue could play with the Ratay-less Irish. This night would have to belong to someone else. Notre Dame's balance would have to come into play.

Riley picked up her second foul at the 4:19 mark, as Purdue freshman Shalicia Hurns was fouled attempting a shot. The resemblance to the UConn game two nights earlier was almost nightmarish at this point, the difference being that Ratay had taken the place of Ivey as the one strapped with fouls.

Purdue was dominating in rebounds at 24-13 when Riley exited. The 3-point attack of Notre Dame was non-existent.

A 15-footer by Ivey with 20 seconds left in the first half sent the teams to the locker room with Purdue ahead, 32-26.

Stires called it lucky that Notre Dame wasn't down by a lot more. Riley had scored 14 points in the first half. Purdue had been denying the entry pass as well as extending its defense to shut off the perimeter shots.

"Purdue just shot the heck out of our zone," McGraw said. "So it looked like another night of wondering what had happened to us? I don't know if it was the energy things, nerves, I don't know. We didn't play well. As a matter of fact, I don't think we played well the whole game.

"So we go into halftime down six, figuring it is better than being down 12 and now we are used to playing from behind," Muffet laughed. "In the second half, I really thought that we would pull away. I thought we would get up six or eight and then it would be 10 and that's how it would go."

The eerie similarities between the UConn game and the Purdue game did not extend into the second half.

Yes, the Irish made a run and, in fact, went ahead in the second half. Siemon made a runner to tie the game at 32-32 at 17:40 remaining. Riley put the Irish ahead with a pair of free throws less than a minute later and the Irish fans were hoping that Purdue would fall apart the way UConn had.

After a Purdue basket, an old-fashioned 3-point play by Ivey gave Notre Dame a 37-34 edge, their largest lead so far on the night.

But the blowout wasn't going to happen. In fact, Douglas tried on the Superwoman cape and nailed her third three of the night almost immediately, starting another Purdue rally.

"How about Katie Douglas just calmly scoring that 3-pointer just as it looked like Notre Dame was going to go on a big spurt?" Shanele wondered aloud to her audience.

It was one of many All-American plays the Purdue All-American would make that night.

Meanwhile, Riley was doing her part. Early in the second half, she grabbed her sixth rebound of the night and her 1,000 of her career. She became the first player in Irish history to score 2,000 points and get 1,000 rebounds for a career.

Purdue's other All -American was having a rough night. Camille

NICE GIRLS FINISH FIRST

Cooper picked up her fourth personal foul with just under 16 minutes to play, but a momentary letdown by the Irish defense allowed Purdue to burst out to a 42-37 lead.

McGraw spent her second timeout. Ratay picked up her fourth foul with just over 14 minutes to go, and the Boilers went up 45-39 after Hurns converted a layup plus foul.

"Boy, Ruth is just about the only one who can score inside tonight," a concerned Sean Stires said into the microphone at that point.

The Boilers built the lead to eight at 49-41 with just under 13 minutes to go. That was as far ahead as they would get. Ratay returned with 8:01 to go, but saddled with four fouls, would only have one bullet in her holster. At the eight-minute media timeout, the score was 55-55.

"Again, if you are Notre Dame and the game has been as sloppy as it has been and you have had Ratay on the bench for most of the game, you have to be pretty pleased to be as close as you are," Shanele Stires commented.

Purdue, however would not go away, and the teams traded baskets for the next two minutes. "This one looks like it's going down to the wire," Stires laughed to no one in particular. His words would be prophetic.

The Irish still had not knocked down a 3-pointer as the game approached the final five-minute mark. Purdue led, 62-59, when Ratay ("a shooter shoots," she would say later) nailed the only 3-pointer of the night for Notre Dame to tie the game with just under four minutes to go.

The final media timeout came with 3:25 to go. The Irish regrouped for the last stand. All the starters were on the floor, though some were hampered with fouls. The game would be decided by the best players either team had to offer, the way great championship games are decided.

Riley blocked a shot by Purdue at the 2:50 mark and Muffet called a 30-second timeout. Each possession was now taking on a tug-of-war mentality. A score one way or the other could prove the difference. But Siemon turned the ball over right out of the timeout and Haney had to foul Purdue freshman Shereka Wright to stop a layup.

Wright hit one-of-two for a 63-62 Boiler lead. Ivey converted a layup with 2:01 to go and the Irish led 64-63.

It was becoming hero time, and Douglas struck first.

Haney rebounded the next Boilermaker missed shot, but Siemon had the ball stolen by Douglas on a spectacular play with 1:20 to go. Katie went the length of the floor and laid it in for a 65-64 lead. She converted the foul shot for a 66-64 lead.

"I thought we were going to win the game after that steal," Curry said.

Back came Ruth. Ratay gave her a pass down on the blocks and, in a move perfected on the gym floors of North Miami High School just four years earlier, she turned and laid it off the glass to tie the game with 52.5 seconds to go.

Now, if you are an Irish fan and believe in such things, in stepped the ghost of George Gipp.

Gipp is the Notre Dame halfback who had the unfortunate destiny of dying after a stellar career at Notre Dame. His fame came when Notre Dame's legendary football coach, Knute Rockne, repeated his dying words before a crucial football game against Army.

The words so inspired the Notre Dame team that they went out and won a game they were supposed to lose. It also inspired a movie, with none other than future President Ronald Reagan playing "The Gipper."

There are those who believe his ghost still walks at Notre Dame's Washington Hall. The Gipper too has been credited with pushing a field goal along a couple of extra feet over the crossbar, or quieting the wind in the face of the Irish offense at key moments.

There are others, of course, who don't believe that at all.

But the last four shots of the championship game, if not guided by some mystical hand, were at least very fortunate in the eyes of the Irish.

Curry, who had coached toe-to-toe with McGraw all night, designed a play in the huddle that would break down the Irish defense and get Douglas the ball for an open three. Siemon was closely guarding Douglas, however, so the Boilers reversed the ball to the other side to Wright.

The improvised play worked perfectly, and Wright drove the

baseline, putting the ball off the glass and nearly through the net.

The key word, of course, is nearly. Instead of falling through, the ball hit both sides of the iron and popped out. Riley grabbed the last rebound of her career and suddenly it was advantage Notre Dame, with 29 seconds to go.

Muffet told the story from there.

"We had a 30-second timeout and I wanted everybody on the same page. Because it was a tie game and I kept telling them to look at the clock…We are going to get one shot, but it will be the last shot of the game. Because we had worked on it before, and sometimes we would shoot it with 12 seconds left. And Kelley is in my ear saying, 'What are we running. What are we running?' And I'm thinking, 'I'll get to that, I'll get to that.'

"I want to make sure that we get the last shot," Muffet continued. "In my head, I had two offenses, and they both went to Ruth, but I was trying to decide which one I wanted to go with and it had happened so quick that I hadn't decided yet.

"And then I think Niele asks, 'What are we running?' Finally, I looked at her and I said, 'OK, OK, I'm ready.' Then we decided to run High, which is a play that Kelley is in, but it was funny because they didn't want to know anything else. Kind of like, 'We know, we know, we know all about the clock, now get to the good stuff.'

" I was just afraid that we would shoot it too quickly and miss, and then they would get the ball with 10 seconds left, which is a lot of time. And even after the timeout, five seconds seemed like a long time. So we were trying to get the timing down.

"Now they go back out to run it," McGraw continued.

Purdue defended it very well.

"Ericka is on the wing and they don't even defend her. So Ruth has basically a triple-team down there. And so Kelley just puts the ball up there, up in the air, which was something we had worked on all year. One thing that we said all year long, on their passing, was, 'Just throw it up. Ruth will go get it. Just get it in the air."

"Kelley did a great job getting it to Ruth, and Ruth did a great job going and getting it. Because that ball was up there for grabs in between three people and she was like, 'It's mine,' and she went and got it and I thought clearly that there was a foul, but one of the ESPN announcers thought it was all ball.

"The ESPN announcer said something to me after the game after the foul and I came back and watched the tape about 3:45 that morning after the celebration, just the end of it and I'm wondering what is she talking about? They did call the foul, though, and I thought it was the right call."

At that point, the game was out of Muffet's hands, other than calling the defense.

"The game is tied, so the game will go on if you miss them both, so it's not like we are going to lose. We would have to stop the break if we miss. So we talked about what we were going to do defensively to make them miss.

"We said, 'After we make these shots, here is what we are going to do. Ruth looked calm and I didn't want to say anything because I didn't want anything to be in her head. I didn't say a word to her.

"I actually said, 'After Ruth makes these shots...I didn't know until afterwards that the coach [played by Gene Hackman] said almost those exact same words in the movie [*Hoosiers* in a similar scene].

"I did not say, 'You will make these shots,' like Hackman said. If I had said that, forget it. It would have been too weird. I think Ruth was already thinking about Ollie [the player who made the crucial free throws in the movie].

"Then Purdue comes down the floor," Muffet continued, "and the defense we worked on for two weeks we blew. Kelley was supposed to double-team Douglas, but she ran toward the person who was taking the ball out. Then she realized her mistake and went, 'Oh shoot' and tried to recover.

"But the pass went to Kelly Komara. Ruth was all the way down the floor. Ericka was on Douglas, she was supposed to shut her down. Komara wasn't supposed to throw it, but because Cooper was so open, she threw it to her. I think that if Cooper would have thrown it to the basket it might have gone in...but she traveled badly as she passed to Douglas.

"Ericka then kind of let up," Muffet said. "Expecting the whistle to blow for the travel and where she had been denying Douglas the ball, Haney thought, 'Oh-oh, she walked.'

"However, Douglas kept on going. That gave Douglas enough

of a chance to get an open look and I thought she got a pretty good shot. I'm glad it didn't go in, because I would have hated to see that travel non-call decide a game like that.

"It was a pretty obvious travel. It was kind of like 'Hooo,' and then all the sudden the exhilaration...We had finally done it...ended the season with a win.

"My initial reaction was pure joy."

The ending to the game was as perfect as it could possibly be from Notre Dame's perspective. The entry pass that began the victorious Irish sequence went from St. Louis' sweetheart, Niele Ivey, to Kelley Siemon, who was looking for a way to make up for two crucial late-game turnovers.

Her pass was to America's new role model and superstar, Ruth Riley. Riley was triple-teamed and had to tip the pass from one hand to the other before getting fouled by Wright.

The exquisite beauty of that final, game-determining sequence was that Wright's foul was obvious, if you were looking through Irish spectacles, and not so obvious, if your spectacles were Purdue black and gold.

There were no spectacles, however, worn by the official who whistled the foul. Such fouls, called or uncalled, will keep this game alive for years after the official scorebook is closed.

Now, however, it was Riley time for one last magnificent moment.

Ruth is an avowed fanatic of *Hoosiers*. She used to watch the movie every February on the night before her high school sectionals were to begin. She knows every scene, and nearly every line from it.

Many Indiana high school basketball aficionados do the same. In that movie, a bench player named Ollie somehow gets to the free throw line with the chance to go to the state final game on the line.

Ollie is not a good player, but he sinks both of them using underhanded tosses. The other team barely misses a game-winning shot at the other end as time expires.

Ruth now found herself at the free-throw line, life imitating art in a most profound and very real manner. The small-town girl from Indiana was now front and center in the big time. Somehow, she had made it from Macy to St. Louis with her heart and soul and her Superwoman/Mother Teresa reputation intact.

There was no worry in her eyes as she stood at the free throw line. She took the ball from the official after the Purdue timeout, dribbled thrice, bent her knees, and let fly.

Whether the hand of Gipp was somewhere in that stadium or not is fodder for conjecture. But Riley's first free throw, hit the very front of the rim, bounced straight up, and somehow made it over the rim and into the net.

"She had it all the way," Siemon would say later.

Purdue called another timeout.

"At that time, we decided what we would do once we got the ball back," Curry said. "We designed the play that we would run once the second free throw was taken. We didn't run it exactly as planned, but we still got a reasonably good shot. The other thing we wanted to do was 'ice' Riley. Give her credit, she made the free throws."

The only ice Riley had was in her veins. Pumping her fist as the last bit of adrenaline surged through her body, she was not the be dissuaded. Her second shot, equally as important as the first, was only a little less dramatic, bouncing off the front edge of the rim and off the backboard before falling through.

Had it all the way? Siemon didn't comment on the second shot.

Instead, Riley's moment on center stage was over, and she had been triumphant. Two points ahead, staring the national championship in the face, the Irish allowed the excitement of the moment to overcome them.

Siemon guarded the wrong person, Haney was too far off Douglas, and Riley was standing in the free-throw lane, guarding no one in particular.

Purdue's Komara made the smart play, firing the ball to Cooper, who appeared about to take the 3-point shot before passing the ball off to Douglas.

Now it was Douglas' time.

Heroes are made for moments like these. It matters not whether her shot goes in or not, in the long run. True heroes want the ball in instances like these. She found she was open behind the 3-

point arc, from about 18 feet out, aimed quickly, and fired with her left hand.

"It looked good when it left my hand," she said later. "It just didn't go in."

That's the funny thing about last-second shots. Some go in, some don't.

Wright's layup with 30 seconds left should have gone in, but it didn't. Riley's first free throw with 5.8 seconds to go should not have gone in. It did. As did the second.

As a nation watched, Douglas's ball could have gone in. It hit the rim at the exact same angle as Riley's second free throw, bounced off the backboard as Riley's shot did and bounced...out.

Notre Dame was the national champion in women's basketball.

Ratay gathered the rebound as the horn blew and then bounced the ball away as if it were no longer useful, which of course, it wasn't. Then, she chased her teammates down the floor for a wild celebration.

Ivey leapt into the arms of McGuff, Leahy pounded on Riley's back. No one noticed, no one cared.

There was only joy.

Siemon said she felt oddly stunned and emotionless and almost out of habit, looked over to where Quinn and her friends were jumping up and down in their seats. Siemon's eyes caught Quinn's and, as only friends can do, mouthed the words, "I played so bad."

Quinn yelled back, "That's OK, Kelley."

And it was OK. The game was won.

Pandemonium reigned on South Bend Avenue inside Between the Buns.

Schreiber watched as strangers hugged strangers, beers spilled on tables, and the place literally jumped with joy. This was as good as anything this new location had ever seen, and the people of South Bend were part of it.

Such are the things of a perfect championship. Such are the results of hard work and determination.

Such are the things of dreams come true.

Notre Dame. National Champions.

THE LINESCORE

PURDUE (66)

Hums 7-13 3-5 17, Wright 6-15 3-5 17, Cooper 3-9 0-0 6, Douglas 6-15 3-3 18, Hicks 0-0 0-0 0, Parks 0-3 0-0 0, Crawford 0-2 0-2 0, Noon 0-1 0-0 0. Totals: 25-67 9-15 66.

NOTRE DAME (68)

Haney 6-11 1-2 13, Siemon 5-11 0-0 10, Riley 9-13 10-14 28. Ratay 1-6 0-0 3, Ivey 5-13 2-3 12, Joyce 0-2, 2-2 2, Barksdale 0-0 0-0 0. Totals: 26-56 15-21 68.

Halftime score: Purdue 32, Notre Dame 26.

3-point goals: Purdue 7-17 (Douglas 3-6, Wright 2-4, Komara 2-5, Parks 0-2), Notre Dame 1-10 (Ratay 1-4, Joyce 0-2, Ivey 0-4). Fouled out: None. Rebounds: Purdue 41 (Douglas, Hums 7), Notre Dame 38 (Riley 13). Assists: Purdue 12 (Douglas 5), Notre Dame 16 (Siemon 6). Total Fouls: Purdue 16, Notre Dame 14. A:20,551.

CHAPTER 18

A CHAMPION'S WELCOME

Champions.

The Irish were excited and giddy as they loaded onto the plane for the flight back home. With most of the TV-viewing America snuggling safe into bed, McGraw's squad was trying on the new phrase that would precede their official title.

This year they had been called the "top-ranked Irish" or the "undefeated Irish," but now, at least for the next 12 months, they would be called the "NCAA champion" Irish, or the "defending champion" Irish.

The new monikers carry an enduring notation. Only one team each year can go to a recruit's house and say the words NCAA champion.

Only one will get the high level of notoriety that the ESPN crew will use when describing women's basketball, the term "defending champion."

They had already been to their first post-game presentation, the Sears Trophy award. That ceremony complete, Muffet turned to more pressing matters. Murphy now sat in the seat next to her, occupying a space many times held by an assistant coach.

But now, Murphy was the object of Muffet's attention, for he had school the next day. So, at 1:00 AM, airborne somewhere over Illinois, Muffet, coach of the newly crowned NCAA champion Notre Dame women's basketball team, quietly helped her 10-year-old son solve the intricacies of long division.

The Irish wondered what kind of reception, if any, awaited them back home. Surely, it was too late for much to be going on. Maybe a few stragglers here and there would wait in the cold of that April morning.

They were wrong.

A throng of community well-wishers met them at the airport and then the bus carrying the team was given a police escort through the town.

As they turned north on Notre Dame Avenue, they saw some

people carrying signs and waving. As they got closer to the end of the avenue, in an area known simply as the Circle, the team saw a crowd of about 3,000 people waiting for them in 20-degree temperatures.

"The police escort was unexpected to us," Assistant Coach McGuff said. "But when we saw the students waiting there for us, it was really a neat moment. It really brought home to me just how important sports are to a place like Notre Dame.

"It was a great moment for me, but these kids have friends they go to school with and to have many of them come out there was really a highlight for our kids."

The rally had been a grassroots idea.

"From what I understand," McGuff said, "someone circulated an email either just after the game was over or phrased it that if we won, there would be this thing on the Circle and it kind of went around from there.

One of the guys had a sign that said, "Marry me, Kelley." Riley had a marriage invitation as well waved by another admirer.

Muffet answered the crowd's request and made a speech through a megaphone loudspeaker, thanking the crowd for coming and comparing the moment to how she felt when she walked out onto the floor of the January 15th UConn game.

Ruth then made a short speech about how great it was and how excited it was to come back to such a reception.

Niele added her thoughts. The team then formed a circle and danced its pre-game ritual circle dance as the crowd cheered.

Then, in the finest of Irish tradition, the band played the Notre Dame Alma Mater and 3,000 chilly fans and one brand-new championship team raised their No. 1 fingers in unison as the song rose as one voice to its finale.

If you were there, and Irish, it was a night you'll never forget.

Kelley Siemon finally returned to Farley Hall about 3 AM after dropping Karen Swanson off. But her day wasn't over. As she reached the hall, there was a huge sign that said, "Congratulations, Kelley,"

She smiled, then walked upstairs only to find three of her dorm mates sprawled out in front of her door, waiting for her.

"It was hilarious," Kelley said. "I didn't even know these girls very well and there they were. One of them played for the soccer team, which had made it to the Final Four in the fall, and she said, 'We are so proud of your guys.'

"People had decorated my door with downloaded pictures from the Internet. They had all kinds of neat stuff there. It was absolutely amazing and so neat to come home to that. I didn't even get to bed until 6 AM because the dorm rector had recorded the game off TV and we sat there and watched it.

"What a great night that was."

Murphy McGraw would put the final exclamation point onto the season. The 10-year old, the biggest little fan of the team, was sound asleep in his dad's car as Matt headed home. Muffet would, as usual, spend a few minutes watching the tape. She had been troubled by an ESPN announcer saying that the final foul that sent Riley to the free-throw line for the storybook finish was actually a clean block.

While she was satisfying herself that it was, indeed, the correct call, Matt decided he had had enough and poured Murphy into the car and headed back home.

"Suddenly, Murph sits straight up in the seat and says, 'Dad, we need to drive past Grace Hall to see the No. 1 sign,' Matt said. "I thought the kid was sound asleep, but we found an area where we could see the sign clearly, and Murph looks at it for a minute, looks at me, and gave me a high-five."

He was back sleeping moments later, leaving his father to wonder at the moment.

A scheduled annual team post-season banquet, which normally draws about 150 people during a good year, was moved from the smallish Monogram Room to the floor of the JACC, an honor reserved normally only for the football team.

The dinner served 750 people and then about 3,000 more filled in the stadium seats to watch the team being honored by local politicians and media types.

Through it all, McGraw kept her composure and focus. When Riley, Ivey, and Siemon were selected in the WNBA draft, the coach flew to New York for the obligatory proceedings.

The next day she would fly to Iowa for a basketball clinic she had committed to earlier and then Sunday the flight was to Washington, DC, for a visit to the White House.

She worked through a scheduled vacation the second week

after St. Louis, reasoning that it isn't very often that a team wins its first-ever national championship and that, as head coach of the team that did, her previous plans could be put on hold.

McGuff said the meeting at the White House was one of the highlights of his life. "That was really neat," McGuff said. "It is something that you don't ever really dream that you are going to do.

"I was amazed at how immaculate it was," McGuff continued. "But we were out there taking pictures and suddenly President Bush says, 'Hey, would you like to see the Oval office?' And you could tell the Secret Service guys were a little surprised at it. So we all say, 'Yeah!' and we all paraded into the room.

"His desk is the same one John Kennedy used and the same one they took that famous picture of JFK Jr. when he was sitting under the desk.

"The president was very personable and was having a great time," McGuff continued. "In fact, twice his chief of staff came in and told him he needed to get to another meeting, but he was having such a good time, he didn't want to go.

"The other thing that was neat was when we were watching TV in the airport waiting for our plane, they had a news program talking about him coming out with his stance on Taiwan [a major policy statement].

"We had been there right in the middle of all that, of some major world politics. Later, we were on the floor of the House of Representatives. Congressman Tim Roemer gave us a tour and showed us how they vote. The whole trip was pretty high on my list of great things I've done in my life."

The seniors, without Riley who was on her way to Miami, also appeared on the Regis Philbin show the day after McGraw had been honored as coach of the national championship team by the New York Athletic Club.

It's called the Wingfoot Award. "All the seniors and coaching staff were invited," McGuff said. "They picked us up at the airport in limousines and dropped us off in Manhattan in this very prestigious building.

"It's really nice and you have to wear a coat and tie just to walk in the lobby. The first night we had a banquet, which was really nice and the next day we went to Broadway to see *The Lion King.* Everywhere we went it was a limo."

The Regis Philbin show was next, and Kelley, Niele, Meaghan, and Imani played 3-on-3 with the two co-hosts. "Regis was really great off the air," McGuff said.

The last official time the team would be together was at the celebration put on by the city of South Bend on April 25.

"We were all picked up by a trolley and given a police escort downtown," McGuff said. "And all up and down the streets there were people with signs and everything. It was kind of neat because you saw how excited the town was. A lot of people wanted autographs."

The crowd was treated to a speech from McGraw and Dunbar before closing the ceremony by singing "Happy Birthday" to Murphy.

The ride, which had begun with a frank and stormy meeting in the bowels of the JACC a year ago, was now ended on a sunny bright April afternoon, in front of a crowd of new believers.

The realization that things would never be the same again had not yet dawned on anyone.

There would be time for that, later.

CHAPTER 19

KEEPING IT ALL TOGETHER

Ascending to the top of the basketball world was accomplished in part because Muffet McGraw has been able to balance her professional life with a strong family life.

Doing so requires some extra work on everyone's part. Fortunately for Muffet, her husband, Matt, is an ideal balance.

Muffet and Matt McGraw have a modern American marriage, if such a thing exists. Both parents have a career, and both are concerned with raising their son, Murphy, to be a responsible adult.

It is a relationship with a slight twist. Traditional marriages had the man as the one with the higher-profile job, the one who is gone nights and weekends, the one who works overtime.

But this isn't a traditional marriage. It is, however, a model for the new age of equality. Matt and Muffet have worked out a relationship that allows her to pursue the highest level of achievement as coach while Matt pursues his own interests.

Whether they knew that their relationship was unique, or if it has just been a series of adjustments, doesn't really matter. Matt has set aside some of himself to become part of a truly inspirational duo.

In some cases, the pressure of having a high-profile coach in the house would be enough to crack the marriage relationship wide open, especially when the coach was a woman.

But this isn't most cases. Matt is Muffet's biggest fan. And vice versa.

In this case, their relationship is built around a mutual trust and admiration for each other.

They took the championship ride together. Muffet will tell you this. Matt will tell you this. Their friends and people who know them will tell you this.

Matt has been in sales for several different companies. After Murphy was born, Matt made a decision to work his job around his family and not vice versa. With Muffet in such a visible, time-consuming position, it has been Matt who fills in the cracks.

"The beauty behind our relationship is that what I know about basketball you can write on a bottlecap," Matt cracked. "We very rarely talk basketball when we are home because I know so little about it.

"A couple of times that we have, I'll say, 'Hey why don't you try this,' and it will be something so absolutely off-the-wall that she will give me a weird look and that will be the end of that.

"We will talk occasionally about the players and what is happening," Matt continued, "because she really does like the kids. But as far as anything else, I'm pretty much lost. And that is really good, because if I really knew anything about it, it might hurt the relationship. I've figured out that my first job is to NEVER second-guess the coach."

Matt does all the cooking, too.

"Occasionally Muffet will get the wild notion that she's going to try to boil something but very rarely. I also pick up Murphy from school and whatever else it takes to make life easier for her. I try to make it as simple for her to do what she has to do. That's what I do, I take everything else away."

The national spotlight has been cast on Matt as well, though he tries to avoid it. "I'm perfectly happy to stay out of the spotlight," Matt said. "Although during the NCAA run, it was hard to when Murphy was painting his face and getting on camera all the time. My thing is, I'm not the story, I've never been the story, and I know nothing about it. I'm just a fan, watching the game, and that's all there is to it.

"The neat thing about this year's team is that among the five seniors and especially the three seniors, no one cared who scored the points," Matt continued. "As a matter of fact, Ruth Riley's biggest concern was if she was scoring too much.

"I very rarely have serious discussions with the players, too, even though I see them quite a bit. I'm not on the same wavelength as the coaches and staff are. Besides, they are 18 and I'm 47. Niele Ivey still calls me Mr. McGraw, and I kind of like the fact that I am perceived as someone different."

Matt also thinks that there is a fine line that coaches must tread.

"As a coach, you have to be intense, there is no question about it. And Muffet is, but she is not overboard intense, and I have seen coaches who are and sometimes I think it hurts their success. In my opinion, as a coach, you cannot become the show on the sidelines."

Muffet has been able to keep the whole thing in perspective.

"For me, professionally, winning the national championship has been one of the best things that has happened to me," she said. "But as far as my life goes, it doesn't compare to Murph and Matt and my family.

"Someone said, if you are not happy before you win the national championship, you won't be happy after you win one," Muffet continued. "I really love my life. With Matt and Murph and my family, I have so much that I can put the championship in a different place. And because of that, I really think that lets me be calm on the sidelines. It doesn't feel like basketball is my whole life. Win or lose, it's not my whole life."

That lesson took a long time to learn.

"I learned to balance my life just recently," she laughed. "Having Murph has helped me a lot. Having him really keeps my perspective. The 1997 Final Four we went to, we were on a bus in Texas and I was thinking that I have so much. It makes the game seem not as stressful. But on game day, it is the most important. Afterwards is the part I don't take as seriously anymore."

Matt has always filled in the holes, according to Muffet.

"When we were at Lehigh, he was helping with the shot clock and the scorebook and he also did some of the taping. Now he is more of the PR guy. He shakes hands with people and talks to them so when I have my game face on I don't get interrupted. He does so many things. At home, he has to do everything. Homework, cooking, everything.

"There are not that many married college women basketball coaches," Muffet said. "I think there are like 10 of them in the whole country. It's harder on Matt than it is on me because of all the things that he has to do.

"His willingness to change jobs and work out of the home is what really makes us work, because raising Murphy is as important to him as it is to me. I think a man has to be really confident in himself to do that because most men are just not willing to do it."

The solid marriage has affected Muffet's team management style too. Her relationship with Matt secure, the next step to the championship was to develop a management technique to take advantage of the team's strengths.

McGraw is an emotional sort and minces few words and individual's feelings in practices and games. However, in the championship season, her demeanor quieted.

"It was a maturing process, both for them and for me," Muffet said. "I feel like I've been on this track for a couple of years. Trying to change my demeanor and working on it. And this year, it went both ways. This year I was very much more conscious of pulling someone. That was the biggest thing I had to work on, I think."

The perfect example of the more laid-back style was epitomized in the last five minutes of the national championship game.

Siemon, who had played a great game, suddenly began making errors as the game clock wore down. McGraw kept her in the game and in fact called the final play in which it would be Kelley's responsibility to place a perfect pass to Riley.

"Maybe I should have rethought that," Muffet laughed. "If she had turned it over, I would have blamed myself for eternity."

With the championship leaders gone, Muffet looks forward to future teams.

"I am so anxious for next year to start," she said. "I want to see if I've finally changed or if it was just because of the team I had. This team this year made it so easy for me.

"I know I have to be more patient. I haven't had this many freshmen expected to contribute right away in a long time, since this last group. And I remember I had to reorient my thinking and I know I had some trouble with that.

"I think I have matured since then," she continued. "But I also think they are going to test me. My real worry is that the freshmen will come in hungry and the older players will sit around and admire their rings.

"Having Murphy has affected my management style dramatically," Muffet said. "Murph is now playing organized basketball and now I'm a basketball parent.

"When I go to his games, I look at the whole thing differently. Now I want to see him on the floor, and I don't want him to be yelled at, even though I think I yell at him more than the coaches do. I'm seeing things from a different way.

"I am changing the way I approach players now," she said,

thoughtfully. "When I was younger, I used to tell them straight up that they weren't working hard enough or that they weren't any good or things like that.

"Now I listen a lot more. Karen Swanson would come into my office last year and talk about how she wanted to contribute more, and by now I would listen and try to figure out a way to get her more involved. When I was younger, I might have said, 'Yeah, you are right, we don't need you because we've got Ruth.'"

Muffet also acknowledges the contribution of Leahy and Dunbar.

"Those two were responsible for keeping morale up on the bench. If they had complained all the time, it would have been a horrible season. That was what had happened the year before and there was no chemistry. I think those two learned from that experience and decided they were not going to be like that.

"When you looked at this team," she said, "you saw a group of people who loved what they were doing and had a passion for it. They worked hard, but they were the embodiment of what a real team is. And there was such a feeling in the way they played that when you watched it, you go caught up in it.

"It was definitely a feeling that there was something special about this group and everybody wanted to be a part of that. They were great role models."

CHAPTER 20

NICE GIRLS FINISH FIRST

To a school used to champions, this was just a little more special.

At Notre Dame, the men's football team is expected to win the national championship every year, and the long list of ex-head coaches who have been run through the system trying to do so is long and impressive. However, the demands of the so-called subway alumni are heavy. The people who drive, fly, or are chauffeured in on weekends to experience Notre Dame football do not tolerate a non-championship coach very long. Even the coaches who have won championships in relatively recent history have been run out of town by the "what-have-you-done-for-me-lately" crowd.

But that is peculiar to the football program. The other money making program, the men's basketball program, faces greatly reduced expectations. The pressure on the players and coaching staff in the program, while very real, is strikingly less.

No one expected this women's basketball team to win a championship outside of the relatively few people who went to the games regularly and had watched the development of the team. To them, McGraw and the players were a godsend in the year 2000-01. Muffet's team was always glad to support local causes, always hung out after games for autographs, and were always appreciative of the small media band which grew as the season went on.

But the triumph of the Irish had more far reaching implications.

Sports in the late 20th century had become a sort of high stakes carnival. Before the advent of television and the continual over-hype and over-kill of modern day sports, people had gone to carnivals to be sold the get-rich quick and cure-all balms. Now, with a beer companies telling us that their beer makes us somehow more attractive or a tennis shoe manufacturer telling us that their shoes help us jump higher, the high profile sports have become carnival-like in atmosphere. And just as back in the carnival days, the main attractions tended to center either around the freak shows or the barker with the biggest megaphone.

Big time sports had become, at the end of the 20th century, a me-first, in-your-face, get-rich-quick scheme designed to line the pockets of the insiders at the expense of the fan. The more tattoos the better, it seemed.

But every once in a while, the true meaning of sports sticks its head above the barkers and colored balloons. Once in a while a surprise team comes out of nowhere and for a brief moment, the fan is reminded that sports is about teamwork, and hard work, and practice.

Notre Dame's athletic image has always been about winning the right way. It is an image the university has fought long and hard to establish and maintain. There are those who have feared the luster on the Golden Dome has been tarnished by the football team's lack of success in recent years or by the men's basketball travails in the 1990s.

However, those who fear that, need to have listened to the feisty little coach as she addressed the huge crowd at the post-season banquet. McGraw, again showing her knack for timing and for having just the right thing to say, spoke very briefly to the crowd.

In an emotional moment during that short speech, McGraw hushed the crowd, saying that the "joy of winning a national championship pales in comparison to the joy of spending time with Matt and Murphy."

McGraw and her team had done it. They had won a national championship in the ideal Notre Dame way. With class, with composure, and with humility. The very idea flies in the face of Leo Durocher's "Nice Guys" comment.

But, along came Muffet. And Ruth. And Niele. And Kelley. And Meaghan. And Imani. And the rest of the team. Their actions spoke louder than words and those actions let the legions of teen-age girls, soccer moms, and grade school boys know, that maybe Leo wasn't right after all. Maybe hard work, enthusiasm, and team spirit can win.

So, the question needs to be asked of this team the same way it was asked of Mr. Durocher back in the 1950s. Was this just a short-term aberration in sports? Was this just a unique group of nice girls who happened to finish first? Or was this team a new statement that Americans need to pay some heed to.

After years and years of watching the movies and TV shows tear down all the nice things that Americans are so used to, is this the sweeping statement that can change our attitudes?

Nice girls. Finish first.

or

Nice girls finish first.

Now, put the punctuation where you wish.

The following is the complete text of the speech given by President George W. Bush at the White House reception for the team on Monday, April 23, 2001:

You can sit down, this might be a long speech.

First of all, I want to welcome two great teams from two great universities. It is an honor to greet you all here at the White House. I want to say congratulations to Coach K — the reason I call him Coach K is sometimes I have trouble pronouncing the long words — Coach McGraw and the players and representatives from Duke and Notre Dame. I want to welcome two fine United State Senators, Senator Helms from North Carolina and Senator Lugar from Indiana. Members of the United States Congress who are here, thank you all for coming.

In reviewing the rosters and the success of these clubs, it is clear that Duke and Notre Dame are recruited for athletic talent, but they are also recruited for character as well. These championships go to prove that good people do finish first.

It is such an honor to welcome Duke back here. Turns out that there was another president named Bush that welcomed the Duke team and they dedicated the basketball court here on the South Lawn during their visit. The weather's been such that I haven't been practicing my sky hook lately. Looking at the size of some of these guys, I'm not sure I want to do that.

I know it took a lot of hard work to get here, and it took a lot of very close games and tough contests, particularly the Fighting Irish in their final game, winning in the last second. I'm reminded about what Coach McGraw's son, Murphy, said as he watched as he watched the game. He said, "That was scary!" Murphy, I know what you are talking about. It reminds me of election night.

There is no question that teams are born of good leadership. I was struck by one of the star's here who said about Coach K — just to prove to the press Coach Krzyzewski — "To me, he's been a friend, a mentor and a brother. I'm a better person for having had him a part of my life." That's what leadership is all about. That's what it means to be somebody who can set an example and somebody who understands the responsibilities of the assignment. It's not just to win championships; it's to shape lives in a positive way.

And I love what Coach McGraw said. She said, "Usually there are negative things that occur during the season, but this year I didn't call one team meeting. I've got no complaints from the professors. I can't even yell at the players because they do everything we ask,"…I need your help in Congress.

Championships bring awesome responsibilities. Now that you've won a trophy, I think you've got an obligation of understanding that you have an enormous influence on people's lives-people you don't even know. People look at champs and say, "How does the champ behave? What are the champs supposed to do?"

Champions not only cut down nets, but they can influence people's lives by sending positive signals about how they behave, not only on but off the court. It's a big responsibility. It's a huge responsibility. That's why these two teams are so fortunate to have great teamwork and great players.

I know this is a team effort, and I know that the two players I'm going to mention, Battier and Riley, are going to be somewhat concerned that the President has singled them out. But I want to remind people who may not know their histories that not only are they great players, they are great people.

Not only did they set goals about being the best on the basketball court, they set goals about becoming all-academic stars and they were. They set goals of understanding the golden rule and living by it. These are good people, and I'm sure your teammates are as well. But they set the kind of example America needs, and all of us are in positions of responsibility. All of us, whether we're President, or coach, or player, or president of a university.

We must understand that with that responsibility comes the necessity to send the right signal throughout America. That there is a difference between right and wrong. That we can be compassionate. So, it's my huge honor to welcome good teams and good people to the White House.

1997-98 RECORD AND STATISTICS

Date	Opponent	ND	Result	ND	Att.
11/18/01	BUTLER	W	71-65	1-0	1011
11/22/01	at Duke	L	62-80	1-1	2362
11/28/01	at UC Santa Barbara	W	86-75	2-1	1811
11/30/01	at UCLA	W	93-91	3-1	350
12/3/01	at Rutgers	L	67-80	3-2	1268
12/6/01	CONNECTICUT	L	59-78	3-3	2253
12/8/01	at Wisconsin	L	77-89	3-4	6225
12/10/01	PURDUE	W		4-4	1570
12/13/01	SOUTH FLORIDA	W	73-50	5-4	412
12/28/01	SAN FRANCISCO	W	62-47	6-4	1176
12/31/01	at Pittsburgh	W	66-46	7-4	324
1/6/01	at Georgetown	W	69-44	8-4	579
1/8/01	MIAMI	W	75-47	9-4	842
1/10/01	at St. John's	W	77-57	10-4	3102
1/14/01	WEST VIRGINIA	W	86-78	11-4	1125
1/17/01	at Boston College	L	76-78	11-5	3100
1/21/01	at Syracuse	W	87-69	12-5	754
1/24/01	PROVIDENCE	W	109-60	13-5	5056
1/28/01	at Villanova	L	54-70	13-6	843
1/31/01	SETON HALL	W	91-35	14-6	2623
2/3/01	at Miami	L	76-77	14-7	727
2/12/01	ST. JOHN'S	W	76-44	15-7	1512
2/15/01	PITTSBURGH	W	75-60	16-7	3424
2/18/01	GEORGETOWN	W	80-54	17-7	1287
2/21/01	at Connecticut	L	61-73	17-8	10027
2/24/01	RUTGERS	W	71-64	18-8	2594
	BIG EAST TOURNAMENT				
2/28/01	vs St. John's	W	94-57	19-8	2723
3/1/01	vs Villanova	W	56-48	20-8	3133
3/2/01	vs Connecticut	L	53-73	20-9	3816
	NCAA TOURNAMENT MIDWEST SUB-REGIONAL (LUBBOCK, TEXAS)				
3/13/01	vs Southwest Missouri State		78-64	21-9	8174
3/15/01	vs Texas Tech		88-83	22-9	8174
	NCAA MIDWEST REGIONAL (LUBBOCK TEXAS)				
3/21/01	vs Purdue	L	65-70	22-10	7823

Overall Season Record   Won 22 Lost 10
Big East Conference Won 12 Lost 6 (Tied for second in the Big East 6)
Unranked at End of the Year

	Games	Min/Gm	FG-A	3FG-A	FT-A	Reb	Fouls/D	Ast	Turn	Blk	Stls	Points	PPG
Sheila McMillen	31	29.1	129-330	68-172	97-121	85	53-1	45	65	4	33	423	13.6
Ruth Riley	32	21.1	141-235	0-0	86-115	233	109-8	21	64	71	27	368	11.5
Molly Peirick	32	31.6	111-316	57-163	67-80	157	76-1	199	137	22	50	346	10.8
Danielle Green	30	25.1	116-259	2-8	72-111	143	64-1	38	60	2	45	306	10.2
Niele Ivey	31	26.1	83-185	25-67	63-80	106	55-0	90	97	6	77	254	8.2
Kelley Siemon	32	23.5	96-186	0-0	65-110	165	90-3	42	90	5	28	257	8.0
Julie Henderson	30	13.4	51-91	0-0	22-43	89	64-2	19	40	4	13	124	4.1
Diana Braendly	31	12.1	48-103	2-7	17-25	71	56-0	28	35	26	19	115	3.7
Kari Hutchinson	32	15.2	31-68	15-25	25-46	85	46-0	46	58	10	22	102	3.2
Meaghan Leahy	22	6.5	9-22	0-0	23-35	40	27-1	5	9	2	6	41	1.9
Mary Leffers	13	3.2	7-15	0-0	6-10	10	11-0	0	9	3	2	20	1.5
Imani Dunbar	21	4.9	4-11	0-1	12-30	6	15-0	5	17	0	6	20	1.0
Team Rebounds						142			10				
Totals	32		826-1821	169-443	555-806	1332	666-17	538	691	155	328	2376	74.2
	32		684-1855	141-422	544-793	1128	650-13	426	664	91	317	2053	64.2

1998-99 RECORD AND STATISTICS

Date	Opponent	ND	Result	ND	Att.
11/14/01	UCLA	W	99-82	1-0	1813
11/18/01	at Butler	W	71-60	2-0	1221
11/21/01	DUKE	W	84-57	3-0	2716
11/24/01	ILLINOIS	W	101-92	4-0	1320
11/28/01	at San Francisco	W	74-43	5-0	1247
12/2/01	TOLEDO	W	82-64	6-0	1825
12/8/01	CONNECTICUT	L	81-106	6-1	5102
12/12/01	VILLANOVA	W	63-62	7-1	1886
12/19/01	at South Florida	W	83-63	8-1	925
12/21/01	at Michigan State	W	75-64	9-1	1386
12/30/01	at Boston College	L	65-78	9-2	4133
1/2/01	at Georgetown	W	93-61	10-2	1102
1/7/01	WEST VIRGINIA	W	111-90	11-2	2560
1/10/01	PROVIDENCE	W	79-56	12-2	2048
1/16/01	at Pittsburgh	W	81-72	13-2	639
1/20/01	at Seton Hall	W	87-47	14-2	407
1/23/01	ST. JOHN'S	W	99-60	15-2	6384
1/26/01	at Syracuse	W	94-61	16-2	688
1/30/01	at Providence	W	97-59	17-2	1012
2/3/01	BOSTON COLLEGE	W	74-59	18-2	2617
2/6/01	SETON HALL	W	77-49	19-2	5231
2/10/01	at Villanova	W	74-52	20-2	2209
2/13/01	at Rutgers	L	57-77	20-3	5414
2/17/01	SYRACUSE	W	82-60	21-3	2201
2/20/01	at West Virginia	W	89-54	22-3	1220
2/23/01	MIAMI	W	89-62	23-3	3146
BIG EAST TOURNAMENT					
2/28/01	vs Villanova	W	83-53	24-3	3413
3/1/01	vs Rutgers	W	68-61	25-3	4716
3/2/01	vs Connecticut	L	75-96	25-4	4304
NCAA TOURNAMENT					
3/13/01	vs St. Mary's	W	61-57	26-4	2746
3/15/01	at Lousiana State	W	64-74	26-5	2890

Overall Season Record   Won 26 Lost 5
Big East Conference Won 15 Lost 3 (Third Place, UCONN and Rutgers co-winners)
Finished the Year ranked 9th in the Associated Press

	Games	Min/Gm	FG-A	3FG-A	FT-A	Reb	Fouls/D	Ast	Turn	Blk	Stls	Points	PPG
Ruth Riley	31	25.5	198-290	0-0	118-171	260	106-3	40	81	101	25	514	16.6
Sheila McMillen	31	33.8	145-352	98-247	88-101	134	65-0	68	76	13	34	476	15.4
Danielle Green	30	29.7	157-369	2-9	116-151	216	69-0	52	93	3	38	432	14.4
Niele Ivey	28	31.4	121-241	47-105	80-92	106	56-2	181	85	1	74	369	13.2
Sherisha Hills	29	21.9	65-189	31-114	41-53	76	37-0	59	55	4	32	202	7.0
Ericka Haney	31	16.7	71-171	0-1	44-68	132	70-2	15	51	11	25	186	6.0
Kelley Siemon	31	20.7	66-141	0-0	47-74	154	94-6	63	85	7	15	179	5.8
Julie Henderson	30	12.8	17-37	0-0	24-36	82	48-0	30	36	6	12	58	1.9
Diana Braendly	26	6.6	19-43	0-3	10-14	35	25-1	13	14	13	4	48	1.8
Meaghan Leahy	24	4.4	10-21	0-0	10-16	30	13-0	6	9	2	5	30	1.2
Imani Dunbar	25	5.4	6-23	0-0	6-16	24	15-0	10	24	0	4	18	0.7
Team Rebounds						111			3				
Totals	31		875-1877	178-479	584-792	1360		537	612	161	268	2512	81.0
Opponents	31		718-1903	144-448	451-663	1054		485	582	69	272	2031	65.5

1999-2000 RECORD AND STATISTICS

Date	Opponent	ND	Result	ND	Att.
11/20/01	at Toledo	W	68-52	1-0	4207
11/27/01	at Illinois	L	67-77	1-1	5312
12/1/01	BUTLER	W	77-57	2-1	2324
12/4/01	vs North Carolina	W	99-86	3-1	4207
12/5/01	vs Liberty	W	85-68	4-1	3861
12/8/01	at Purdue	L	61-71	4-2	9094
12/11/01	MICHIGAN STATE	W	84-54	5-2	2219
12/19/01	at Florida Intl	W	68-62	6-2	1100
12/27/01	SOUTHERN CAL	W	74-59	7-2	2387
12/29/01	VALPARAISO	W	88-63	8-2	2215
1/2/01	MARQUETTE	W	75-60	9-2	2291
1/5/01	WEST VIRGINIA	W	75-54	10-2	1541
1/8/01	at Georgetown	W	82-60	11-2	917
1/11/01	SETON HALL	W	80-52	12-2	1704
1/15/01	SYRACUSE	W	71-56	13-2	2814
1/18/01	at Pittsburgh	W	67-53	14-2	1103
1/22/01	at Miami	W	76-54	15-2	440
1/26/01	at St. John's	W	69-49	16-2	285
1/29/01	GEORGETOWN	W	87-56	17-2	4324
2/1/01	at Providence	W	90-60	18-1	313
2/5/01	BOSTON COLLEGE	W	72-59	19-2	4413
2/9/01	PITTSBURGH	W	67-53	20-2	2750
2/12/01	ST. JOHN'S	W	94-51	21-2	7530
2/16/01	at Villanova	W	70-52	22-2	2617
2/19/01	at Rutgers	W	78-74	23-2	5397
2/22/01	MIAMI	W	83-68	24-2	3656
2/26/01	at Connecticut	L	59-77	24-3	16294
BIG EAST TOURNAMENT					
3/5/01	vs Miami	W	67-52	25-3	10027
3/6/01	vs Rutgers	L	72-81	25-4	10027
NCAA TOURNAMENT					
3/17/01	vs San Diego	W	87-61	26-4	5195
3/19/01	vs Geo Washington	W	95-60	27-4	5521
3/25/01	Texas Tech	L	65-69	27-5	8090

Overall Season Record   Won 27 Lost 5
Big East Conference Won 15 Lost 1   (2nd Place, UCONN won league)
Finished the Year ranked 5th in the Associated Press

	Games	Min/Gm	FG-A	3FG-A	FT-A	Reb	Fouls/D	Ast	Turn	Blk	Stls	Points	PPG
Ruth Riley	32	24.7	193-314	0-0	132-164	233	109-5	41	88	85	17	518	16.2
Alicia Ratay	32	31.2	145-294	73-152	84-101	159	46-0	75	75	7	49	447	14.0
Danielle Green	29	25.9	124-257	1-11	89-113	117	65-0	79	83	0	35	338	11.7
Niele Ivey	32	32.1	118-272	61-167	61-81	111	53-0	194	101	3	95	358	11.2
Ericka Haney	32	19.2	96-208	0-1	24-44	119	55-2	24	66	18	24	216	6.8
Kelley Siemon	32	19.2	81-154	0-0	47-84	160	74-2	47	67	9	25	209	6.5
Julie Henderson	32	21.6	71-137	0-0	26-41	147	73-1	61	58	4	33	168	5.2
Monique Hernandez	27	9.6	27-57	1-1	10-21	26	39-1	16	35	6	12	65	2.4
Meaghan Leahy	27	9.0	24-47	0-1	18-31	64	25-0	17	30	3	9	66	2.4
Amanda Barksdale	28	5.2	11-27	0-0	9-16	33	26-0	4	12	34	5	31	1.1
Imani Dunbar	26	9.6	5-14	0-1	19-31	36	32-1	49	55	0	14	29	1.1
Karen Swanson	23	2.7	8-22	1-7	4-5	9	2-0	0	9	0	5	21	0.9
Team Rebounds						109			10				
Totals	32		903-1803	137-341	523-732	1323	599-12	607	689	169	323	2466	81.0
Opponents	32		701-1976	125-420	454-652	1066	602-21	408	601	68	343	1981	61.9

2OOO-2OOI RECORD AND STATISTICS

Date	Opponent	ND	Result	ND	Att.
11/17/01	at Valparaiso	W	71-46	1-0	2018
11/20/01	ARIZONA	W	95-65	2-0	3087
11/22/01	at Wisconsin	W	83-56	3-0	6943
11/24/01	vs Georgia	W	75-73	4-0	6851
11/27/01	FORDHAM	W	89-44	5-0	3107
12/3/01	vs North Carolina	W	78-55	6-0	1972
12/6/01	VILLANOVA	W	64-33	7-0	3168
12/9/01	PURDUE	W	72-61	8-0	7330
12/18/01	W MICHIGAN	W	84-54	9-0	3108
12/21/01	at MARQUETTE	W	76-56	10-0	2412
12/28/01	At USC	W	70-61	11-0	2178
12/31/01	RICE	W	80-40	12-0	4060
1/3/01	at Virginia Tech	W	75-64	13-0	3418
1/6/01	RUTGERS	W	67-46	14-0	5227
1/9/01	at St. John's	W	84-49	15-0	385
1/13/01	VIRGINIA TECH	W	75-55	16-0	5873
1/15/01	CONNECTICUT	W	92-75	17-0	11418
1/21/01	at Seton Hall	W	72-47	18-0	1273
1/24/01	at West Virginia	W	87-64	19-0	364
1/31/01	PROVIDENCE	W	64-44	20-0	6131
2/3/01	at Boston College	W	81-65	21-0	5429
2/7/01	PITTSBURGH	W	72-58	22-0	7025
2/14/01	at Syracuse	W	75-61	23-0	1627
2/17/01	at Rutgers	L	54-53	23-1	8587
2/20/01	MIAMI	W	81-43	24-1	6533
2/24/01	GEORGETOWN	W	65-53	25-1	11418
2/27/01	at Pittsburgh	W	82-63	26-1	2050
	BIG EAST TOURNAMENT				
3/4/01	vs Georgetown	W	89-33	27-1	10027
3/5/01	vs Virginia Tech	W	67-49	28-1	10027
3/6/01	vs Connecticut	L	78-76	28-2	10027
	NCAA TOURNAMENT				
3/17/01	ALCORN STATE	W	98-49	29-2	8553
3/19/01	MICHIGAN	W	88-54	30-2	9597
3/24/01	vs Utah	W	69-54	31-2	10559
3/26/01	vs Vanderbilt	W	72-64	32-2	8422
3/30/01	vs Connecticut	W	90-75	33-2	20551
4/1/01	vs Purdue	W	68-66	34-2	20551

Overall Season Record   Won 34 Lost 2
Big East Conference Won 15 Lost 1   (1st Place Tie with Connecticut)
Won the National Championship

	Games	Min/Gm	FG-A	3FG-A	FT-A	Reb	Ast	Turn	Blk	Stls	Points	PPG
Ruth Riley	36	28.4	245-390	0-0	182-237	281	70	83	113	20	672	18.7
Alicia Ratay	36	31.9	160-318	81-148	65-73	185	79	68	14	48	466	12.9
Niele Ivey	36	32.0	149-322	57-129	79-111	147	247	109	8	94	434	12.1
Kelley Siemon	32	30.6	155-282	0-0	51-115	228	99	83	4	48	361	11.3
Ericka Haney	36	29.1	159-338	2-5	75-117	204	57	67	17	30	395	11.0
Jeneka Joyce	25	16.1	45-115	30-79	10-12	30	29	14	2	10	130	5.2
Meaghan Leahy	30	11.4	25-58	0-0	38-51	85	10	34	7	15	94	3.1
Monique Hernandez	25	11.0	24-65	0-1	18-35	28	17	28	1	11	66	2.6
Le'Tania Severe	22	10.3	10-35	0-0	21-32	40	13	18	4	11	41	1.9
Amanda Barksdale	35	8.2	16-54	0-0	17-33	77	5	17	58	6	49	1.4
Imani Dunbar	31	7.2	12-32	1-1	17-32	22	22	32	0	7	42	1.4
Karen Swanson	23	4.2	8-27	2-10	10-11	11	2	6	0	3	28	1.2
Team Rebounds						152			8			
Totals	32		1011-2036	173-373	583-859	1490	650	567	228	303	2778	77.2
Opponents	32		748-2228	157-625	355-560	1263	440	605	95	276	2008	55.8

ABOUT THE AUTHOR

Mark Bradford has been writing sports for both local and national publications since 1977. He is a lifelong resident of the South Bend area and grew up almost in the shadows of the Golden Dome. He attended Purdue University, graduating with a business degree in 1975 and later received an MSBA from Indiana University (South Bend campus) in the early '80s.

Although he has been successful in business, his real love has always been sportswriting. Beginning in 1977, Mark has covered a variety of sports at the high school, collegiate, and international level, all on a part time basis. His credits include the Women's World Cup in soccer, the NCAA finals in women's soccer, and the 2001 Rose Bowl as well as Notre Dame football and both men's and women's basketball over the last six years.

Mark lives in Mishawaka with his wife, Wendy, and three children — Glen, Julie, and Madeline. He spends most of his Saturday afternoons either at some sporting event or trying to figure out how to start the lawnmower.